THE CUBIST EPOCH

DOUGLAS COOPER

Publisher's note: This book was first published in 1970 to accompany a now legendary exhibition of Cubist art. A classic text, written by the foremost historian and collector of Cubist art, it has now been reprinted in its original form.

Phaidon Press Ltd
2 Kensington Square
London W8 5EZ

First published 1970
Third impression 1976
Reprinted 1994
© Phaidon Press Ltd 1970

A CIP catalogue record for this book is available from
the British Library

ISBN 0 7148 3242 1

Printed in Dubai

Front cover: Pablo Picasso, *Still Life with Compote and Glass* (detail), 1914-15. Oil, 25 × 31 in. Columbus Museum of Art, Columbus, OH

Frontispiece: Pablo Picasso, *Les Demoiselles d'Avignon* (detail), 1907. Oil, 96 × 92 in. Museum of Modern Art, New York, NY (Plate 2)

Contents

Foreword

More than thirty years have passed since Alfred Barr presented the broad panorama of Cubism and abstract art to the American public. Since that time there have been innumerable exhibitions of individual Cubist artists and of special aspects of Cubism. There has, however, been no exhibition which presented Cubism as an historic style, defining its aesthetic goals, its genesis and development, and its diffusion as far afield as Russia and the United States. The time is appropriate for such an exhibition. It is now possible to look upon Cubism with the historic perspective of a half century, and yet many of the artists, dealers, writers and collectors who created and furthered the development of Cubism are still alive to act as primary documentary sources. Douglas Cooper is one of these—an apologist for Cubism for some decades, a distinguished collector, a close personal friend of Picasso, Braque and Léger. He has published monographs on each of these artists, in which he often records his personal experiences with them and his immediate reaction to their works as they were being created. During the past twenty years he has prepared exhibitions of Picasso, Braque and Gris for museums in England, France, Germany, Switzerland and the United States. Douglas Cooper was therefore chosen as Guest Director to bring together from the collections of Europe and America Cubist paintings, sculpture, drawings and prints to present a vivid compendium of Cubism as an historic and aesthetic achievement — an achievement which transformed the visual world of the twentieth century.

Mr. Cooper was able to organize this exhibition only with the extraordinary help provided by those whose names are listed below.

Both he and we would like to express our special gratitude to: The late Lester Avnet, New York; Heinz Berggruen, Paris; Leigh and Mary Block, Chicago, Ill.; Mrs. Sidney Brody, Los Angeles, Cal.; Charles Buckley, Director, City Art Museum of St. Louis, St. Louis, Mo.; Dott. Giovanni Carandente, Rome; Mrs. Riva Castleman, Asst. Curator, Dept. of Drawings and Prints, The Museum of Modern Art, New York; George Cheston, President, Philadelphia Museum of Art, Philadelphia, Pa.; George Costakis, Moscow; Edward Fry, Chief Curator, The Solomon R. Guggenheim Museum, New York; Prof. Theodore Heinrich, Toronto, Canada; Dr. Jan Heyligers, Holland; Harold Joachim, Director, Dept. of Drawings and Prints, The Art Institute of Chicago, Chicago, Ill.; Miss Eila Kokkinen, Asst. Curator, Dept. of Paintings and Sculpture, The Museum of Modern Art, New York; Prof. Dr. Jiří Kotalík, Director, Národní Galerie, Prague; Claude Laurens, Paris; Jean Leymarie, Director, Musée National d'Art Moderne, Paris; William S. Lieberman, Director of Painting and Sculpture, The Museum of Modern Art, New York; Dr. Thomas M. Messer, Director, The Solomon R. Guggenheim Museum, New York; Dr. Franz Meyer, Director, Kunstmuseum Basel, Basel; Dr. R. W. D. Oxenaar, Director, Rijksmuseum Kröller-Müller, Otterlo; William S. Paley, President, The Museum of Modern Art, New York; Dr. Olga Pujmanova, Národní Galerie, Prague; Mrs. Barbara Roberts, Norton Simon, Inc. Museum of Art, Los Angeles, Cal.; Mrs. Bernice Rose, Asst. Curator, Dept. of Prints and Drawings, The Museum of Modern Art, New York; Prof. Dott. Franco Russoli, Chief Curator, Pinacoteca del Brera, Milan; Dr. Werner Schmalenbach, Director, Kunstsammlung Nordrhein-Westfalen, Düsseldorf; Mr. and Mrs. Taft Schreiber, Los Angeles, Cal.; Dr. Jiří Setlík, Director, Decorative Arts Museum, Prague; Norton Simon, Los Angeles, Cal.; Gordon M. Smith, Director, Albright-Knox Art Gallery, Buffalo, N.Y.; A. James Speyer, Curator of 20th Century Art, The Art Institute of Chicago, Chicago, Ill.; Dr. Evan

H. Turner, Director, Philadelphia Museum of Art, Philadelphia, Pa.; Dr. Herschel Carey Walker, New York; Mahonri Sharp Young, Director, The Columbus Gallery of Fine Arts, Columbus, O.

We should also like to express our appreciation to the following museum directors and curators, collectors and dealers whose loans of works of art and contributions of time have been indispensable:
Leon Arkus, Director, Carnegie Institute, Pittsburg, Pa.; Georges Bauquier, Director, Musée Fernand Léger, Biot; Jacob Bean, Curator of Drawings, The Metropolitan Museum of Art; Galerie Beyeler, Basel; J. Carter Brown, Director, National Gallery, Washington, D. C.; Dr. Richard F. Brown, Director, Kimbell Art Foundation, Fort Worth, Tex.; Robert T. Buck, Jr., Director, Washington University Gallery of Art, St. Louis, Mo.; Charles E. Buckley, Director, City Art Museum of St. Louis, St. Louis, Mo.; Bernard Ceysson, Director, Musée d'Art & d'Industrie, Ville de St. Étienne; Anthony M. Clark, Director, Minneapolis Institute of Art, Minneapolis, Minn.; Mlle. Bernadette Contensou, Assistant Curator, Musée d'Art Moderne de la Ville de Paris; Charles C. Cunningham, Director, The Art Institute of Chicago, Chicago, Ill.; Edward H. Dwight, Director, Munson-Williams-Proctor Institute, Utica, N. Y.; Eric Estorick, London; Miss Ebria Feinblatt, Curator of Prints and Drawings, Los Angeles County Museum of Art; H. J. Fischer, Marlborough Gallery, London; Martin L. Friedman, Director, Walker Art Center, Minneapolis, Minn.; Henry Geldzahler, Curator of Twentieth Century Art, The Metropolitan Museum of Art; Mrs. Dalzell Hatfield, Los Angeles; John Hightower, Director, The Museum of Modern Art, New York; Joseph Hirshhorn, New York; Henry T. Hopkins, Director, Fort Worth Art Center Museum, Fort Worth, Tex.; Dr. Pontus Hultén, Moderna Museet, Stockholm; Leonard Hutton, New York; Sidney Janis, New York; Dr. Beatrice Jansen, Director a.i., Haags Gemeentemuseum, The Hague; Dr. Ellen Joosten, Asst. Director, Rijksmuseum Kröller-Müller, Otterlo; Dr. Sherman E. Lee, Director, Cleveland Art Museum, Clevaland, O.; John Palmer Leeper, Director, Marion Koogler McNay Institute, San Antonio, Tex.; Louise Leiris, Paris; Galleria del Levante, Milan; Marlborough Gallery, Inc., New York; Klaus Perls, New York; Dott. Mercedes Precerutti-Garberi, Comune di Milano, Milan; Dr. Andrew C. Ritchie, Director, Yale University Art Gallery, New Haven, Conn.; Daniel Robbins, Director, Rhode Island School of Design, Providence, R. I.; Alexandre Rosenberg, New York; Daniel and Eleanore Saidenberg, New York; Thomas G. Terbell, Director, Pasadena Art Museum, Pasadena, Cal.; E. V. Thaw, New York; Jane Wade, New York; Dr. Hugo Wagner, Kunstmuseum, Berne; Dr. René Wehrli, Director, Kunsthaus, Zürich; Dr. James White, Director, National Gallery of Ireland, Dublin; Dr. E. L. L. de Wilde, Director, Stedelijk Museum, Amsterdam.

We should like to cite the members of our own staffs who have supported Mr. Cooper with the sustained enthusiasm and effort necessary to bring the exhibition into being: Theodore Rousseau, Curator in Chief, and Ashton Hawkins, Secretary of The Metropolitan Museum of Art, and Mrs. David Duque of the Los Angeles County Museum of Art, who has been, from its inception, head of the Cubist Secretariat.

KENNETH DONAHUE   THOMAS P. F. HOVING
Director, Los Angeles County Museum of Art   Director, The Metropolitan Museum of Art

THE CUBIST EPOCH

DOUGLAS COOPER

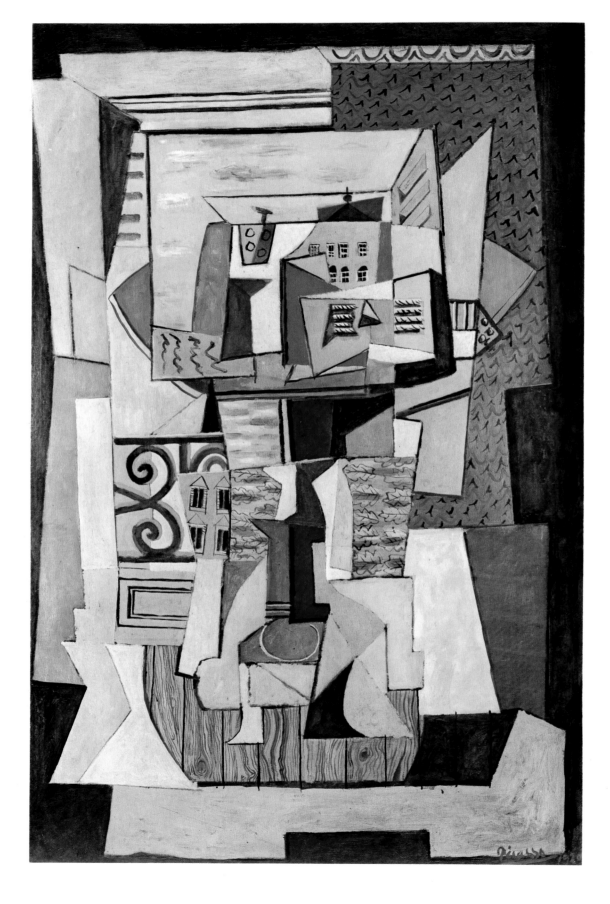

Introduction

Between 1425 and 1450 artists throughout Europe—Masaccio, Filippo Lippi and Donatello in Italy, Fouquet and the Aix Master in France, the van Eycks in Flanders, Konrad Witz in Switzerland, and Stefan Lochner in Germany—abandoned the medieval way of representing reality, by means of experiential conceptions, and began to rely instead on visual perception, one-point perspective and natural light. In other words, these Renaissance artists opted out of recording that fuller truth about reality which is known to the human mind in favour of recording only what the eye sees of things, incomplete and deceptive though this may often be. And for some four hundred and fifty years European artists followed this same principle until, coming to the end of its pictorial possibilities, Cubism was invented to replace it. Now Cubism involved a return to the earlier conceptual principle, insofar as the artist assumed the right to fill gaps in our seeing, and to make pictures whose reality would be independent of, but no less valid than, our visual impressions of reality, and was thus stylistically the antithesis of Renaissance art. Yet there is a parallel between them, for both styles were initiated by a few artists, spread quickly throughout the western world and became the starting-point of a new and more modern art.

Cubism originated in Paris between 1906 and 1908 and was the creation of Picasso and Braque, a Spaniard and a Frenchman. Within four years, however, the pictorial methods and technical innovations of these two young painters had been seized on by other artists—in France, Germany, Holland, Italy, Czechoslovakia, Russia, America and, to a much lesser degree, in England—who either imitated them or tried to transform them by imaginative efforts into new types of artistic expression. A knowledge

◀ Plate 1

Pablo Picasso
Still Life on a Table in Front of an Open Window, 1920
Oil, 64¹/₂ × 43 in.

No. 255

of Cubist methods and possibilities spread rapidly, and by this means Cubism played some part in the technical experiments and stylistic adventures which constitute virtually all the *avant-garde* developments in western art between 1909 and 1914. But there is more to it than that. For the influence of Cubism, though greatly diminished after 1925, certainly continued to affect the pictorial methods of most major artists until about 1940, when in turn it was supplanted by artistic conceptions of a wholly opposite order. As a result, Cubism has proved to be probably the most potent generative force in twentieth-century art and has transformed our western ideas concerning the purpose and possibilities of pictorial representation.

Any discussion of Cubist painting must begin by clearly establishing the distinction between 'true' Cubism, that is to say the work of Picasso and Braque, the creators, as well as of Gris who joined them later, and the derivatives of Cubism practiced by its many Parisian and foreign adherents. For Picasso, Braque and Gris are the only three artists of whom it can be said that they used the idiom in a pure, unsystematic way. Léger came near to being a 'true' Cubist for a while, but he does not finally qualify as such because his pictorial purposes were too different from those of the creators. The rest of the many dependents fall into three groups:

a.   those who 'cubified' as a mannerism,
b.   a few who tried to make a scientific method out of Cubism, and
c.   a greater number who used and transformed Cubism to achieve other (not always reconcilable) pictorial ends.

Next it is necessary to establish a terminology which will meaningfully cover not only the painting of the 'true' Cubists but also the many derivatives of Cubism produced during the Cubist Epoch (1907–21). It seems to me that, in this respect, the currently accepted division of Cubism into phases labeled 'analytic,' 'hermetic,' 'synthetic,' and 'rococo' is largely meaningless, since these words apply exclusively to stylistic methods—often found together in a single work—used by only certain artists and having no general application, and also because they cannot be properly defined. With today's hindsight, I see an extensive movement growing up around 'true' Cubism, developing and changing fast, and then falling apart. Therefore, to my mind, the divisions which count are historical rather than stylistic and may be said even to cut across the stylistic phases. For that reason I prefer to borrow the terminology which is generally used in discussing the evolution of Renaissance art, that is to say 'early,' 'high,' and 'late.' The 'early' phase of Cubism, as I see it, runs from the end of 1906 till the summer of 1910: it was a period of necessary experiment by Picasso and Braque alone and led to their first major achievements before any Cubist movement had started. The period of 'high' Cubism which followed was shorter, lasting only two years, from the summer of 1910 till the winter of 1912.

This was, however, a momentous and very active period, during which Picasso and Braque developed 'true' Cubism to its purest and fullest expression, Juan Gris painted his first Cubist pictures, and the new style attracted adherents on a widespread scale. A Cubist school, including Léger, made its first appearance in Paris at the Salon d'Automne of 1910, followed by further demonstrations with growing numbers of adherents at the Salons des Indépendants and

Salons d'Automne of 1911 and 1912. Paintings by Braque, Picasso, Gris and several other artists of the Cubist school were presented at exhibitions in Düsseldorf, Munich, Moscow, New York, Berlin, Brussels, Amsterdam, Budapest, Barcelona, Cologne and Prague, that is to say in major cities where Cubism was appreciated. The Futurist movement, which in 1911–12 drew on Cubist inventions, burst out of Milan and spread its influence widely through the capitals of Europe. The Neue Künstler-vereinigung and Blaue Reiter groups formed in Munich and included Cubist paintings in their exhibitions. The Section d'Or was organized as a comprehensive Cubist manifestation in Paris, where Orphism was also launched. Mondrian, Popova and Udaltsova came under Cubist influence in Paris, as did Malevich in Moscow, where Larionov and Gontcharova also borrowed from Cubism in the creation of Rayonnism. And lastly, in 1911, a group of painters in Czechoslovakia began to work under Cubist influence. In other words, this was the phase of Cubism's maturity and greatest expansion during which it dominated the contemporary artistic scene and appeared likely to develop into an international style.

No sooner had the movement begun to gather this momentum, however, than it started to disintegrate because of internal conflicts of personalities and funda-mental divergences of aim which the outbreak of war in August 1914 left no time to reconcile. Thus during the 'late' phase of Cubism, whose beginning can be situated at the end of 1912 when Picasso and Braque, having found the technique of *papiers collés* (pasted papers), developed out of it a 'synthetic' style, the attendant movements and groups progressively broke away, pursued other courses and eventually faded out. Léger, for example, began to pursue an independent line of development. Delaunay, Mondrian, Kupka and Malevitch passed beyond Cubism into various forms of abstract art. The Futurist movement became more concerned with politics than art and gradually petered out. Duchamp and Picabia put Cubism behind them and produced the first Dada works. Larionov and Gontcharova dropped Rayonnism to become stage-designers for Diaghilew. The Cubist movement gained no new adherents apart from sculptors such as Laurens and Lipchitz. And finally the Cubist groups in Paris were dispersed by the declaration of war, when most of the artists were mobilized, some left France, and the majority were to be prevented from working seriously for the next four years.

But this is not the end of the story. From 1914 to 1921 there was also an Aftermath of Cubism. For during the war years Picasso and Gris who, as Spaniards, were not subject to mobilization, were able to continue working without interruption and in their hands the language of 'true' Cubism was not only enriched but made suppler, increasingly personal and capable of more monumental achievements. Moreover, in 1917–18, when he was demobilized, Braque, unlike virtually all the pre-war adherents of the movement, returned to the Cubist idiom and proceeded to evolve for himself a freer, more poetic language. Thus the 'late' phase of Cubism is marked as well by triumphant developments on the part of the three major artists concerned, and not only is their work of these years a logical progression from, even a summation of, all that had gone before but was to be responsible for keeping the spirit of Cubism alive as an active force for several more years. As soon as the war ended, however, a reaction against the discipline and fragmentation of Cubism was proclaimed by the Purists, the Dadaists and the Surrealists, all of whom incidentally were able to take advantage of Cubist inventions to achieve quite opposite purposes of their own. Nor must we forget that from 1915 on Picasso had developed a collateral interest and by 1919 was actively testing the pictorial 'reality' achieved by Cubism against that of the naturalistic idiom, while by the end of 1920 both Braque and Gris had begun to develop 'classicizing' tendencies within their hitherto strictly Cubist idiom. It is therefore not unjustified to take Picasso's masterpiece *Three Musicians*, painted in the summer of 1921, in which both synthetic cubist and naturalistic currents meet, as marking the end of the Cubist Epoch, which had been initiated by that revolutionary painting now known as *Les Demoiselles d'Avignon*.

1 True Cubism: 1906–1912

Two short but striking statements will provide a good jumping-off point for this study of Cubism. The first is the opening sentence of the volume *Cubism* by Gleizes and Metzinger, written in the winter of 1911, which reads: 'To evaluate the significance of Cubism we must go back to Gustave Courbet.' The second, written about a year later by Guillaume Apollinaire, occurs in his book *The Cubist Painters* published in 1913: 'Cézanne's last paintings and his watercolors appertain to Cubism, but Courbet is the father of the new painters.' The link thus established between Realism and Cubism may seem surprising, but these two quotations signify that at the time the artists as well as the critics saw a chain of evolution which led directly from Courbet to Cézanne and on to Cubism. To find out what they meant we must look back over French painting since 1850 with the eyes of 1910.

What did the so-called Realism in Courbet's painting consist of? Essentially it is nothing more than his matter-of-fact approach, his refusal to make concessions to abstract ideals of beauty, subject or form, and his concentration on the solid tangible reality of things. However, this rational, down-to-earth aesthetic disappeared with Courbet, for although the Impressionists kept alive the spirit of naturalism, they were so fascinated by the sparkling tonal nuances which their eyes perceived in nature that they lost sight of the solider aspects of reality. With Impressionism, the Renaissance tradition reached its limit: illusionism could be carried no further and there remained no other possible subject for painting except light. But many artists could not accept that the image of man should be dissolved in a tissue of color and the post-Impressionist reaction reasserted the need for a picture to have both a supporting formal structure and a human content. Now these post-Impressionists had learned from the work of their predecessors that color was an ambivalent element, which contributed actively to producing an illusion of reality but could also function independently. So from 1880 on, artists like Seurat, Gauguin, Van Gogh and the Nabis had refused to recognize the eye as the sole instrument of understanding, had made it subservient to the imagination, reduced the descriptive role of color and begun to explore its structural as well as its innate expressive and symbolical possibilities. It is therefore fair to say that by 1890 painters were generally more concerned with expressing an Idea than with trying to represent the world around them. And this colorist school burst out into a glorious but final blaze when the Fauves appeared on the scene soon after 1900. Only Cézanne, working in solitude, had remained unaffected by these successive changes.

For almost forty years (1870–1907) French painters had allowed themselves to be so absorbed in considerations of a subjective nature that they had lost sight of that solid tangible reality with which Courbet had been concerned. A reaction against this over-indulgence in color and its concomitant cult of the immaterial was bound to follow, more especially since the hope was widespread that the new century would produce a vital new art. And so it did under the 'realistic impulse' which inspired the creation of Cubism.

But Cubism went further than a mere revulsion against color to achieve its revolutionary purpose, for Picasso and Braque also upset what Gleizes and Metzinger called 'the worst visual conventions,' from which Courbet had not attempted to free himself. By this they simply meant that

Courbet had subscribed to the Renaissance convention of naturalism and perpetuated the eye-fooling illusion of three-dimensional seeing. True, the artists who followed Courbet had greatly weakened the role of linear perspective and made the two-dimensional picture-surface more of a reality. But the pictorial devices they had used to achieve this flatness—tonal interplay, abrupt fore-shortening, shifting perspectives—without sacrificing a sense of volume in space were at best temporary expedients. And it was not long before artists discovered that abandoning the device of one-point linear perspective led to pictorial incoherence, because it amounted to removing the keystone of the structure which held the illusion together.

Gauguin had tried to find a way out through adopting a consciously primitive approach. For him, Naturalism in art was an 'abominable error' and he saw 'no salvation possible except through a reasoned and frank return to the beginning' of art. But meanwhile Cézanne had labored silently to find a more comprehensive solution. He wanted to give equal value to the mind and to the eye, to the permanent side of reality and to the transient effect, to volume and to flatness, to light effects and to the structure of space: all this without indulging in eye-fooling illusionism. Cézanne's painting thus represented for Gleizes and Metzinger what they called 'profound realism,' and it appeared to them as a bridge between Courbet and Cubism because they saw Cézanne too as having been concerned with the solid tangible aspect of things. Now because Cézanne had grown up among the Impressionists he envisaged his pictorial solution essentially through color, that is to say he built up forms and volumes and evoked space with color alone, avoiding linear definition. But in order to reconcile his awareness of

depth and roundness with his desire to preserve the
flatness of the picture-surface as a reality, Cézanne resorted
to changes of perspective within the picture itself. Already
the visible order of nature was being transformed by the
invented procedures of art.

Among the immediate fore-runners of Cubism, Gauguin
and Cézanne exerted the greatest influence on its formation.
Picasso can be absolved from having ever subscribed to
'the abominable error of naturalism.' Admittedly he
painted some scenes of Parisian life in a belated Impressionist idiom around 1900. But almost at once Picasso
had turned away from Impressionism and in his paintings
of the 'blue period' it is the influence of Gauguin which
emerges. These were years when the stylistic inventions
of the preceding generation were suddenly revealed in
their fullness to older artists like Matisse and Derain,
as well as to young artists like Picasso and Braque, through
exhibitions of Gauguin's work at the Salon d'Automne
in 1903 and again in 1906, and of Cézanne's work at
the same Salon in 1904 and again in 1907. Picasso profited
greatly by all he saw and modified his style of painting
accordingly. Here we are immediately concerned with
what occurred in the winter of 1906–7 when Picasso's
previously severely flattened but emotionally charged
human figures became more massive, sculptural, quasi-
archaic and impassive in appearance. The debt to Gauguin
still remains partly visible in Picasso's handling of space,
but these figures reveal above all that, through Gauguin's
leap backward 'to the beginning' of art, Picasso had been
led to discover and learn from the more primitive, less
naturalistically subservient art of ancient Mediterranean
civilizations, of early Greek art and of Egyptian art of the
fourth and fifth dynasties.

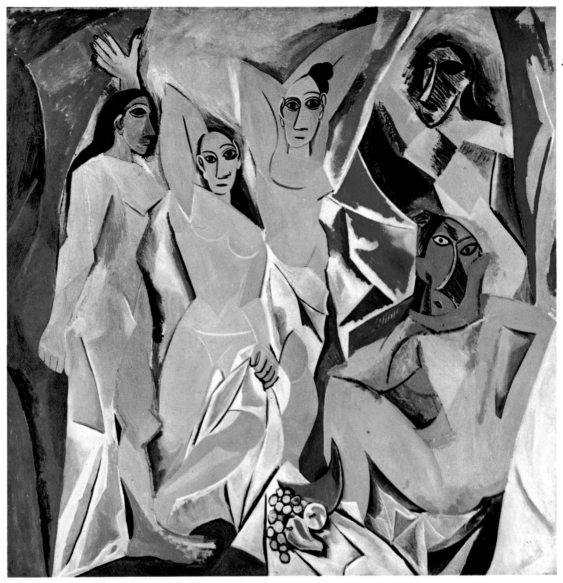

Plate 2

Pablo Picasso, *Les Demoiselles d'Avignon*, 1907   No. 226
Oil, 96 × 92 in.

Pl. 2
Picasso was to carry this 'primitivizing' tendency much further in *Les Demoiselles d'Avignon*, a composition on which he embarked at the end of 1906 and which began as a scene in a brothel with allegorical undertones, seemingly inspired by such paintings of Cézanne as *La Tentation de St. Antoine* or *Un Après-Midi à Naples*. But in the six months that elapsed between the first sketches and that moment in the spring of 1907 when Picasso eventually allowed a few friends to look at his large new painting, a violent transformation had occurred.

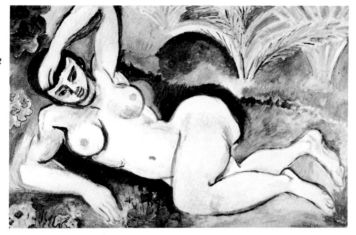

Plate 3

Henri Matisse
The Blue Nude, 1907
Oil, $36^{1}/_{4} \times 44^{1}/_{8}$ in.

The Baltimore Museum of Art,
Baltimore, Md.
Cone Collection.

There was no longer any trace of allegory, and though there were reminders of Cézanne in the poses of the figures, Picasso had flattened and simplified them aggressively, given them sharp contours, compressed them into a very shallow pictorial space and disregarded the consistent radiation of light.

The prime importance of the *Demoiselles* is the aggressive break that it represented with all other painting of the time. In his simplifications and wholly new treatment of space, which is suggested without either perspectival or coloristic logic, Picasso had gone far beyond Cézanne and Gauguin, not to speak of comparable works such as Derain's sub-Cézannesque *Bathers* of 1906 or Matisse's still largely naturalistic *Blue Nude* of early 1907. Here, for the first time, Picasso abandoned a perceptual for a conceptual way of representing things and de-personalized his figures by giving them mask-like faces and treating them in generalized terms. It is not easy to appreciate or judge the angular and aggressive *Demoiselles* as a work of art today because it was abandoned as a transitional and often re-worked canvas, with many stylistic contradictions unresolved. Indeed all that remains of the canvas in its first state would seem to be the two central figures, though even their faces were probably re-worked. For, André Salmon, writing in 1912, describes how when he first saw the picture 'there was neither tragedy nor passion expressed in the faces,' whereas soon after most of these had been given 'profile noses in the form of isosceles

Pl. 3

triangles on a full-face view,' while Picasso had added 'touches of blue and yellow . . . to give relief to some of the bodies.' Thus the *Demoiselles* is best regarded as a major event in the history of modern painting, where Picasso posed many of the problems and revealed many of the ideas which were to preoccupy him for the next three years. In short, it is an invaluable lexicon for the early phase of Cubism.

The Egyptian influence is quite marked in the *Demoiselles*, both in the pinch-waisted figures and in the low-relief treatment of the whole picture. Picasso himself has stated that another considerable 'primitivizing' influence was second-century Iberian art, an unrefined derivative of early Greek sculpture, of which he had seen several examples in the Louvre. But even these two forms of art do not account for all that was new in the *Demoiselles* because while he was still at work on the picture, in the spring of 1907, Picasso became acquainted with yet another primitive idiom*—Negro sculpture—and repainted the two heads on the right and a third on the left under that impact. This led him to inject an element of fierceness into an otherwise emotionally detached composition. These three heads are strongly modeled by contrast with the others; the body of the upper nude on the right is faceted as though it had been hacked with an axe; and Picasso has used heavy shadows to create relief. Moreover, he has activated the space around them with short planes tilted at angles to the surface of the canvas. But outside of these various contemporary and foreign influences, we are confronted above all in the *Demoiselles* with evidence of Picasso's own inventive genius, which has brought them together and wrung out of them the beginnings of a new, highly personal manner of representing reality.

* In the collections of the Trocadéro Museum, as well as through Matisse and Derain who owned many Negro pieces.

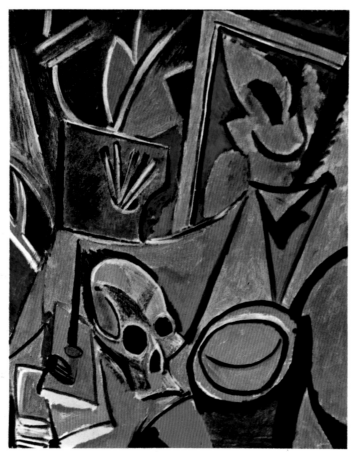

Plate 4

Pablo Picasso
Still Life with a Skull, 1907
Oil, 45¹/₄ × 34⁵/₈ in.

No. 227

The *Demoiselles* is generally referred to as the first Cubist picture. This is an exaggeration, for although it was a major first step towards Cubism it is not yet Cubist. The disruptive, expressionist element in it is even contrary to the spirit of Cubism, which looked at the world in a detached, realistic spirit. Nevertheless, the *Demoiselles* is the logical picture to take as a starting-point for Cubism, because it marks the birth of a new pictorial idiom, because in it Picasso violently overturned established conventions and because all that followed grew out of it.

Yet it was not the Cubist implications of the *Demoiselles* that Picasso was to pursue immediately after abandoning it in the fall of 1907. First he experimented, under the combined influences of Cézanne and Matisse (whom he had met in the winter of 1906), with bright color and an emphatic linear structure, as in the *Still Life with a Skull*. Here the composi-

Pl. 4

tion is based on broad planes of color—red, pink, blue and green; the highly simplified forms are sometimes outlined in black and cast black shadows, while in other parts they are outlined in blue or green and cast colored shadows; and there is some bold faceting as well as arbitrariness in the spatial organization. Again, this is not really a Cubist picture. But neither is it a Fauve work, most particularly because color does not function as a transposition of light and plays no decorative role. We may, however, justly claim that it represents a link in the development of Cubism, because everything happens on a single plane and objects are piled up in such a way that a few lines of direction enable us to read space into the composition.

Early Cubism in relation to Fauvism

It has been claimed that Cubism grew out of Fauvism and was for a while indistinguishable from it. The argument rests not only on a painting like the *Still Life with a Skull* but on the additional fact that Braque, and various painters who subsequently took up Cubism, had previously belonged to the Fauve group, while other adherents had painted in the divisionist manner. No reasoning could be more false, since the two movements—like their protagonists, Matisse and Picasso—were diametrically opposed, one being concerned with light and pleasurable sensations, the other with the solid tangible reality of things. Fauvism was the culmination of nineteenth-century painting, being a synthesis of elements drawn from Impressionism, post-Impressionism, Neo-Impressionism, Gauguin, and Van Gogh, whereas Cubism involved a new vision and a new pictorial language. Indeed the development of Cubism went hand in hand with a complete revision by Picasso and Braque of the accepted ways of handling each of the pictorial elements—color, form, space, and light—and finally led to their substituting new procedures of their own. Matisse's simplifications in the use of line and color were intended to increase the expressive and decorative effect of his picture. But when the first Cubists began simplifying forms and the color-structure, their aim was to represent things more literally and to recapture the direct, unsophisticated approach to reality of a primitive artist. Nor should one make the mistake of associating two other major Fauve artists, Derain and Vlaminck, with the beginnings of Cubism, for neither exerted himself between 1907 and 1914 to shake off an inherited tradition or to work towards the elaboration of a new pictorial language. Vlaminck, for example, was never able to transcend heavy-handed imitations of Van Gogh and Matisse, while later he turned to a coarse form of cubification derived from Cézanne. Derain, on the other hand, had greater natural gifts as a painter. Yet even he never developed the 'primitivizing' devices, which he borrowed for a while from Picasso, beyond the stage of superficial mannerisms and also relapsed quite soon into an uncreative, *Pls. 58, 59* post-Cézannesque cubification.

The origin of the confusion stems from the fact that the Fauve movement broke up while Picasso was working on the *Demoiselles* and that at the same time young French painters gave up trying to follow Matisse and fixed their attention, as had Picasso, on Cézanne. Undoubtedly, word went round the studios of Paris in the winter of 1907–8 that Picasso was effecting a revolution in painting, but that told the young artists nothing about Cubism. Nor could they learn anything from the handful of close friends who were privileged to see the *Demoiselles* in Picasso's studio, and it was never publicly exhibited. The one artist who saw and quickly understood what Picasso had achieved in the *Demoiselles* was Georges Braque, who was brought to Picasso's studio by Guillaume Apollinaire in the late fall of 1907. The effect on Braque was to make him renounce Fauvism and decide to follow Picasso's lead, from which time the early phase of Cubism became the joint creation of these two artists.

Braque's *Nude*, 1907–8

Pl. 5

*The daring innovations of the *Demoiselles* had come as a shock to Braque, although once he had recovered he set to work in December 1907 to apply the understanding he had gained in a big painting of a *Nude*. This, his most ambitious work to date, was to occupy him for several months, but at the end he had painted another early Cubist picture. Nothing in the *Nude* has been literally taken over from the *Demoiselles*, nevertheless, Braque's indebtedness to Picasso is explicit, notably in the mask-like face, in the color scheme of pink, blue and ocher, and in the faceted handling of the background. The influence of Negro art is less visible than in the work of Picasso. Yet it is innately present, for Braque himself spoke about becoming acquainted with Negro sculpture at this time through Matisse and Picasso, and claimed that it opened up for him 'a new horizon. It permitted me (he continued) to make contact with instinctive things, with direct manifestations, which were in opposition to the false traditionalism which I abhorred.'

* E. Fry, *Cubism*, 1966, pp. 16, 53.

Edward Fry* has recently discovered that this *Nude* was preceded by a drawing in which Braque had grouped

Pl. 6

three crudely simplified female figures in complementary views: back, front and profile. And some time in 1908 he said, very significantly, of this drawing to an American interviewer, Gelett Burgess, that 'it was necessary to draw three figures to portray every physical aspect of a woman,

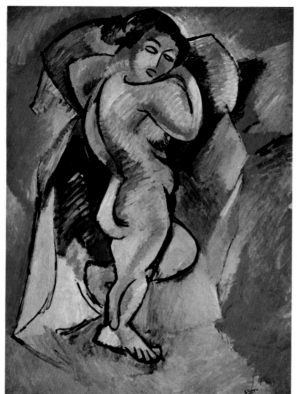

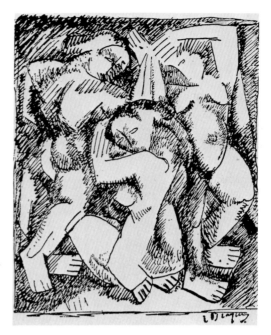

Plate 5

Georges Braque
Nude, 1907–08
Oil, 55³/₄ × 40 in.

No. 14

Pl. 3

just as a house must be drawn in plan, elevation and section.' Already, therefore, the Cubist idea was forming in Braque's mind, so it is relevant to note that in the same interview he also said of the *Nude*, which derived from one of the three figures in the drawing: 'I want to expose the Absolute, and not merely the factitious woman.'

More evident than the Negro influence in Braque's *Nude* is that of Cézanne and even of the *Blue Nude* of Matisse, painted a few months previously. These influences emerge particularly in the pose, in the accented rhythm of the curving outlines, and in the broad parallel brush-strokes which create the modeling. The picture as a whole is not entirely successful: for example, some of the distortions are clumsy, some parts of the body are left vague, the proportional relations are awkward. However, it is important for the innovatory characteristics it displays: the way Braque has twisted and spread the figure outwards to escape from a simple profile view, the way the figure is projected from and not absorbed into the background, and the deliberately inconsistent handling of light.

Georges Braque
Three Figures, 1907
Ink drawing, dimensions and
whereabouts unknown.

Reproduced from The Architectural
Record (New York) 1910.

Pl. 7

This *Nude* was the start of revolutionary developments in
Braque's painting, for during the summer of 1908, part
of which he spent in Cézanne's countryside at L'Estaque,
he began to evolve Cubism proper in landscapes and still-
lifes. The landscape motifs are Cézannesque, but Braque
outstripped Cézanne in that he did not allow the landscape to impose itself on him as an organized set of forms,
but instead consciously imposed his own sense of reality
on the landscape. Discussing this moment in his evolution,

Plate 7

Georges Braque
Trees at L'Estaque, 1908
Oil, 31 × 23⅝ in.

No. 15

Plate 8

Raoul Dufy
Green Trees at L'Estaque, 1908
Oil, 28½ × 23½ in.

No. 79

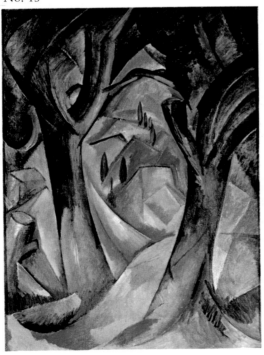

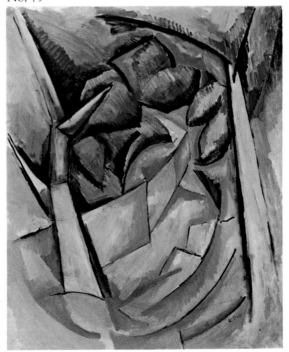

Braque once said that the Fauve painting he had done earlier was 'physical painting' and that this had appealed to him at the time because of its 'novelty.' But on this occasion, his third visit to L'Estaque, he no longer felt 'the exaltation which had overwhelmed him before' and instead '*saw* something else.' This 'something else' was, of course, the solid tangible reality of things, the permanent element in nature, which he then set out to represent in a new spirit of realism and without eye-fooling illusion. In his L'Estaque landscapes, therefore, we find Braque treating buildings as simple cubes and using a neutral palette of greens, ochres and black instead of the bright colors of Fauvism. He also cut out the sky, the source of general irradiation; created volume by faceting; induced a sense of volume in space by a series of planes tilted at varying angles to the picture surface; and used beams of light to pick out aspects of forms which would otherwise have been half-lost. Line was used purely as a structural element in the composition and not for creating perspective.

Developments in Picasso's Painting, 1907–9

Pls. 13, 14, 19

The course of Picasso's development after painting the *Demoiselles* appears somewhat zig-zag—that is to say, he does not pursue any one line consistently—until it culminates in a brilliant and homogeneous group of early Cubist paintings executed at Horta de San Juan, in Spain, in the summer of 1909. During these two years, Picasso was wrestling with one central problem, that of essential form, which he proceeded to master by repeated changes in his method of attack. Just as Picasso took over certain figures which had appeared in many of his drawings and paintings during 1905–6 and used them in the composition of the *Demoiselles*, so in 1907–8 we find him continuing to use a limited number of familiar figures, heads and poses, and

writing (as it were) postscripts to the great painting by
varying their treatment. At this time Picasso alternated
between a painterly and positively sculptural approach
characterized by the boldness with which he hacks out
his forms and emphasizes their volume. His brushwork
too varies from fine to much heavier strokes. This
procedure of treating a limited range of figures in a
variety of ways is characteristic of Picasso's working methods, for no single solution satisfies him absolutely and each
repetition of a motif with which he is familiar is a challenge
to extract from it a new formal and expressive solution.

In the severely frontal, hieratic *Woman in Yellow*, painted
in the summer of 1907, the reduction of the body to
elementary, geometrical forms and the strict formal balance
of their arrangement illustrate what the Douanier Rousseau
must have had in mind when he referred to Picasso as a
master of the 'Egyptian style.' But Cubism enters this
picture through the way in which Picasso broke
down and faceted the two arms to arrive at a more
complete formal expression of them. Picasso thus obliges
the eye, with the help of the mind, to take in the whole
form as it would a piece of sculpture. In other pictures

Pl. 11

of the autumn of 1907, such as *Three Nudes* or *Friendship*,
we find Picasso carrying this procedure of faceting still
further. But in these paintings the 'negro' influence dominates in the 'primitive' simplifications and in the substitu-
tion of masks for personalized faces. Picasso adopted this
latter device as a means of detaching himself emotionally
from the figures as human beings and from such considerations as beauty or ugliness (which then as now he always
refused to recognize). André Salmon, a great friend of
the artist at the time, has written that Picasso particularly
admired Negro sculpture because it seemed to him

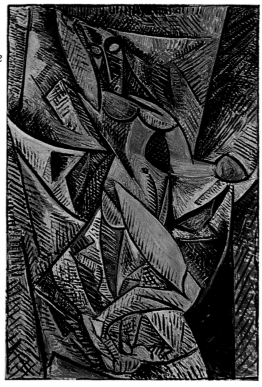

Plate 9

Pablo Picasso
Nude with Draperies, 1907
Oil on canvas, 59⁷/₈ × 39³/₄ in.

No. 228

Plate 10

Pablo Picasso
Nude with Drapery, 1907
Watercolor, 12 × 9¹/₄ in.

No. 263

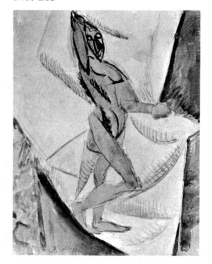

'rational.' Picasso, he adds, was 'struck by the fact that Negro artists had attempted to make a true representation of a human being, and not just to present the idea, usually sentimental, that we have of him.' What Picasso meant—and the similarity with Braque's statement to Burgess is striking—was that Negro sculpture is not visually but conceptually true and offers a clarified image, without embellishments, composed only of essential features.

But Picasso did not merely draw stylistic lessons from 'primitive' sculpture. He himself carved a few 'primitive' figures in wood, while several of the figures in his paintings are treated as though they were pieces of sculpture. This is the case, for example, with a *Standing Female Nude*, painted in the summer of 1907, and no less emphatically with the great *Nude in a Forest* painted in the winter of 1908. But a more extreme, and at the same time more Cubist example, is provided by that complex painting *Nude with Drapery* painted in the fall of 1907. Here Picasso has treated the various parts of the body individually in terms of cylinders and cones surrounded by heavy black contours. Within these he has evoked volume by colored striations

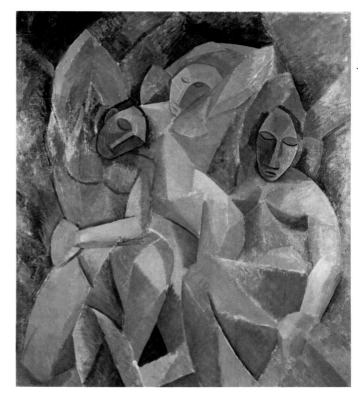

Plate 11

Pablo Picasso
Three Women, 1908
Oil, 78³/₄ × 70¹/₂ in.

No. 229

Plate 12

Pablo Picasso
Standing Figure (Study for 'Three Women'), 1907–08
Watercolor, 24³/₁₆ × 16 in.

No. 264

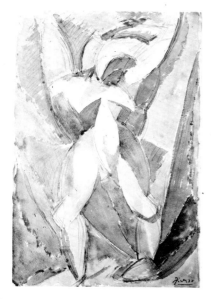

going in different directions, though the flat picture-surface is never violated. Furthermore, Picasso has created a semblance of space around the body by setting it against a series of faceted and variously orientated planes, which are colored differently according to the artist's need for light or shadow. This major painting reflects yet another of Picasso's sculptural preoccupations, for it seems to bear out his expressed hope that, if he had succeeded in truly representing his subject, one should be able 'to cut up' his canvas and having reassembled it 'according to the color indications . . . find oneself confronted with a sculpture.'

The group of figure paintings discussed above illustrates the different forms of sculptural approach which enabled Picasso during the period 1907–8 to advance progressively towards the creation of Cubism. But at this point we are bound to ask why a painter like Picasso should be thinking in sculptural terms at all. The most likely explanation is that sculpture is a three-dimensional art-form where, from the point of view of the spectator, light functions purely as an external and not at all as an internal factor. That is to say, light serves to make a sculpture visible but, as opposed to a *motif* in nature, plays no active part from within in determining the appearance of the thing seen. For Picasso, who wanted to represent what he knew to be there and not what nature made him see at certain moments, this was of vital importance. For it meant that instead of wrestling with natural effects of light which—as Impressionist painting showed—eat into form and involve the painter in problems of tonal modulation, Picasso could use local color and handle light like a display electrician, directing it wherever needed.

We have now dealt with the important influences of 'primitive' art and sculpture in Picasso's work during the early phase of Cubism. But two other important influences still remain to be discussed: those of Henri Rousseau, le Douanier, and of Cézanne. And here we must begin by making a distinction, for whereas the first two influences are visible in Picasso's figure paintings of the time, the two last influenced above all his painting of landscape and still life. Picasso first became acquainted with the painting of Henri Rousseau through seeing and buying one of his finest works in a junk-shop in Montmartre in the winter of 1907. Soon after, he met this living Parisian 'primitive' painter, through his friends Alfred Jarry and Guillaume Apollinaire. The profit which Picasso drew from Rousseau's paintings was more in the nature of an encouragement than a real influence, because what captivated him was the extraordinary realism which Rousseau could produce by ignoring visual conventions and adopting an unsophisticated factual approach. In landscapes such as those painted at La Rue-des-Bois in the summer of 1908, Picasso's bold literal way of representing a tree, a house, foliage or a surrounding wall, undoubtedly owes something to the example of Rousseau, and the same spirit is at work

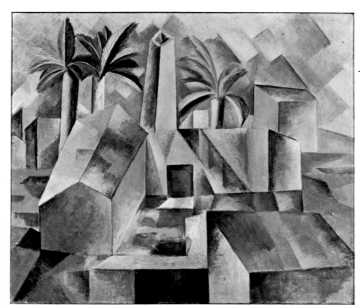

Plate 13

Pablo Picasso
Horta de San Juan: Factory, 1909
Oil, 20⁷/₈ × 23⁵/₈ in.

No. 230

in a still life such as *Flowers and Glass* or *Bowls* of the same date.

Cézanne was the source of the painterly element in early Cubism, and his influence may be said to counterbalance the 'primitivizing' elements. Cézanne's feeling for the underlying geometrical forms in nature was based on intuition and sense data, not on intellectual understanding, so he did not set out to give an ideated vision of nature but to make its greater reality evident in what the Cubists called 'purely pictorial terms.' Picasso took in all of this, and in his search for the most direct pictorial method of representing reality attempted to combine the shifting perspectives of Cézanne with the conceptual formulations of the 'primitive' idioms. Sometimes, therefore, we find him making a bold, literal statement of basic forms 'completed' with only slight visual inconsistencies. In other works of 1908–9, on the contrary, Picasso adopted a more painterly approach and followed Cézanne in changing his viewpoint to arrive at a fuller expression of forms and volumes in space. The reconciliation of the two procedures was to come in 1909 through perfecting and elaborating the technique of faceting.

During the winter and spring of 1908–9, Picasso continued to work in an experimental vein. He was, however,

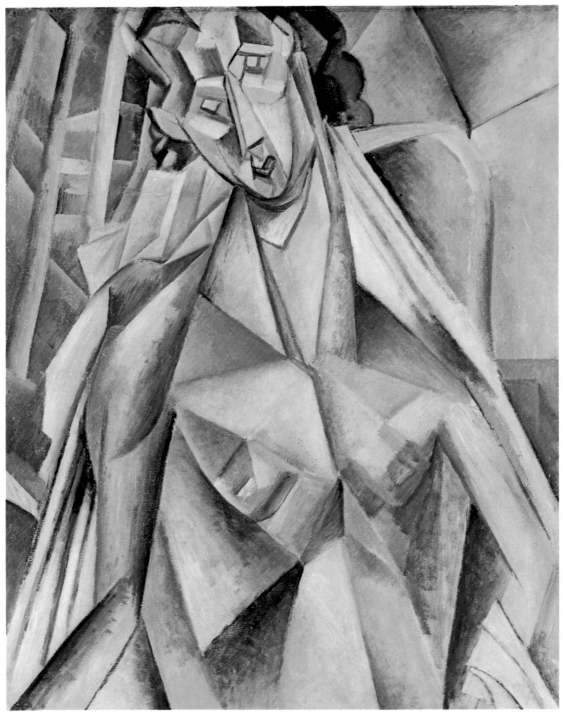

Plate 14

Pablo Picasso
Seated Woman, 1909
Oil, 36¹/₄ × 29¹/₂ in.

No. 231

Pls. 13, 14

progressively able to blend stylistic discoveries and inventions and arrive at an early Cubist language. But it was at Horta de San Juan, where Picasso went to work for several months in May 1909, that the style at last crystallized in a succession of masterly 'analytical' canvases such as *The Factory* and *Seated Woman*.

Developments in Braque's Painting, 1908–9

Pl. 7

When Braque returned to Paris from L'Estaque in the fall of 1908, he submitted a group of recent landscapes to the Salon d'Automne and the jury rejected them. So he exhibited these and some other paintings at the Kahnweiler Gallery in November, and it was on this occasion that Louis Vauxcelles, writing in *Gil Blas*, first referred to his manner of reducing 'everything, sites, figures and houses to geometric outlines, to cubes.' A few months later, this same critic writing of the paintings Braque had shown at the Salon des Indépendants in March 1909 referred to his '*bizarreries cubiques.*' And so the new style of painting came to be popularly know as Cubism.

Braque's progress towards Cubism from his Cézannesque landscapes of L'Estaque was continuous and rapid, but while Picasso stated forms and volumes in their basic simplicity, flattening their spatial setting to counteract recession, Braque brought objects up to the surface of the canvas so that the depth of space around them became ambiguous and largely lost. He was not quite ready to tackle the problem of representing space without perspective, yet he was as much aware as Picasso that this had to follow once they were able to represent things as though they were tangible in the round. 'It is not enough to make people see what one has painted,' Braque once said, 'one must also make them touch it.' Thus already the dialectic between those two realities which determined the evolution of Cubism—the reality of objects in space and the reality of the flat painted surface—was engaged.

Pl. 8

At this point, it is instructive to look at *Green Trees at L'Estaque* (1908) by Raoul Dufy, who had worked beside Braque during part of the summer. For Dufy, probably because he was more influenced by Matisse than by

Cézanne, did not have the same impulse towards realism
and did not get to grips as Braque did with either a spatial
or a tactile reality. Dufy's composition is made up of
stylized natural forms arranged with decorative effect in
a shallow setting: thus its effect is comparable with a
tapestry. But in their paintings, Braque and Picasso
showed a common concern for an accurate representation
of reality, and this was to distinguish them increasingly
Pls. 15, 16   from their friends' efforts. Significantly, Dufy dropped his
flirtation with Cubism at this point.

Braque's next step was to seek a solution through formal
analysis and abstraction, both in his handling of objects
and space, which he treated alike. In *Fishing Boats* and *Harbor
in Normandy*, painted in the spring of 1909, Braque (anticipating developments in Picasso's painting by a few months)
at last took full possession of what he saw and invented

Plate 15

Raoul Dufy
Factory, 1908
Oil, 36 × 28¹/₂ in.

No. 80

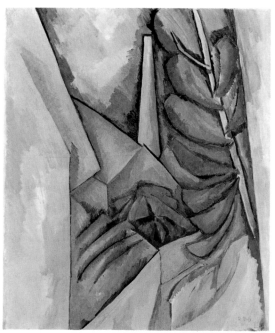
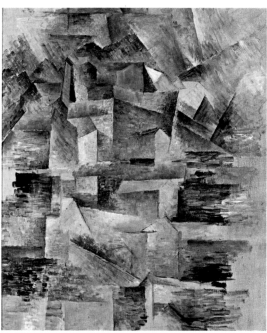

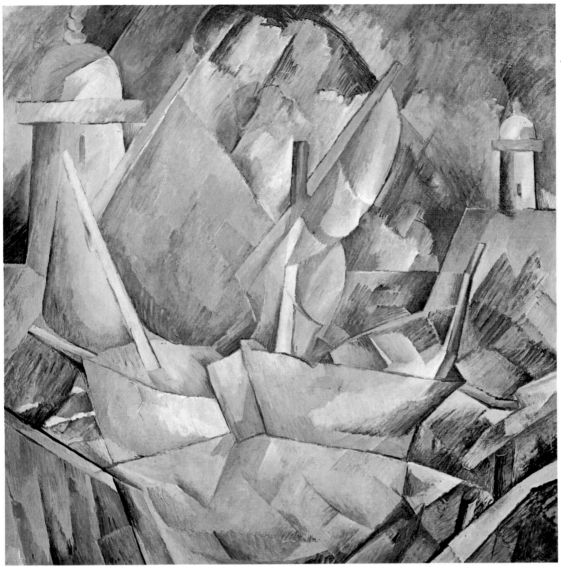

Plate 17   Georges Braque, *Harbor in Normandy*, 1909   No. 16
Oil, 32 × 32 in.

◄ Plate 16

Georges Braque
Rio Tinto Factories, 1910
Oil, 25⁵/₈ × 21¹/₄ in.

No. 20

a non-naturalistic way of representing things and expressing spatial relationships. Thus these two canvases are
among the first truly Cubist paintings. In the *Harbor*,
the sky and distant sea are treated as a continuous limiting
background plane, which is flat although its tonal intensity
varies. Light and space are treated together in a palette of
neutral tones, tonal variations representing degrees of
luminosity. Color is nowhere used descriptively, nor
atmospherically. Distances between one point and another
are expressed by lines, which form a structure of verticals,

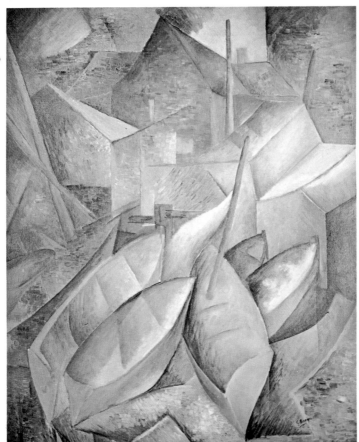

Plate 18

Georges Braque
Fishing Boats, 1909
Oil, 36 × 28³/₄ in.

No. 17

Plate 19 ▶

Pablo Picasso
Landscape with a Bridge, 1909
Oil, 31⁷/₈ × 39³/₈ in.

No. 232

diagonals and horizontals to guide the eye and hold the composition together. The boats, breakwaters and lighthouses are piled together in a shallow foreground plane, volumes being expressed by faceting and tonal gradations. And Braque has seen to it that where a facet leads the eye backwards into the pictorial space this is countered by one which brings it forward again. In this way, Braque makes the solid reality of things simultaneously visible and tangible, and prevents their receding from the eye (as they do with one-point perspective).

The *Harbor* was painted in Paris and from imagination, but in the summer of 1909 Braque worked again from nature at La Roche Guyon, in the Seine valley, another site frequented by Cézanne. On this occasion he began to create an easier spatial continuity by merging one form into another; he also discovered that he could articulate these forms by directing light where he needed it. These

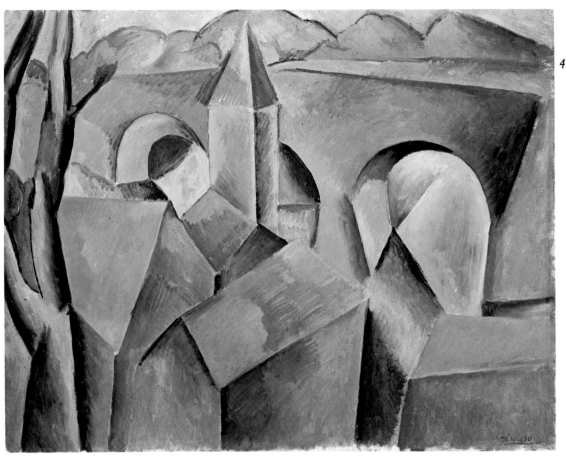

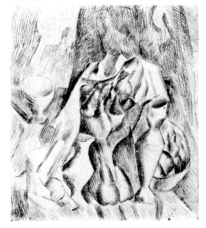

Plate 20

Pablo Picasso
The Fruit-Dish, 1909
Drypoint, $5^1/_8 \times 4^3/_8$ in.

No. 280

La Roche Guyon landscapes represent Braque's last assault on the natural scene for some years. From then on he worked in his studio, concentrating on still life subjects and occasionally painting a figure. Braque's development throughout the crucial years of Cubism was to be more meditated and gradual than that of Picasso, a passionate painter who likes to tackle a problem from several angles simultaneously. Braque's approach to painting was always more tentative: he was also much less interested in the human figure and concerned himself less with landscape. As a result, the total number of works executed by Braque between 1909 and 1914 is considerably less than half of the output of Picasso.

Now while Braque was painting at La Roche Guyon, Picasso was working at Horta de San Juan in Catalonia, where his Cubist style first crystallized in an analytical form. So when the two artists compared their recent

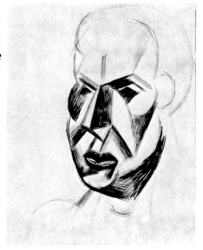

Plate 21

Pablo Picasso
Woman's Head, 1909
Ink, 25 × 19³/₈ in.

No. 265

Plate 22

Pablo Picasso
Woman's Head, 1909
Ink, 24³/₄ × 18⁷/₈ in.

No. 266

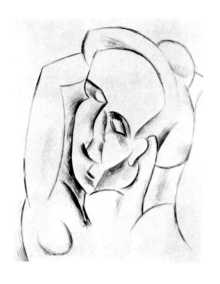

works they realized that there were not only affinities of style but, more important, also of aim between them. Nevertheless, there existed the difference that where Braque was already concerned with giving 'material form to his awareness of a new type of space'—the space between things—Picasso still saw Cubism primarily as a means of dealing with forms. Braque could achieve continuity in his handling of space and volumes, whereas Picasso was still chopping up the natural scene into block-like forms— *Pl. 19* as in *Landscape with a Bridge*—and creating spatial articulation with lines of direction. Each therefore had something to offer to the other, and from then on Braque and Picasso pooled their pictorial understanding and experience. So the evolution towards 'high' Cubism which followed was to be a joint progress.

From Early to High Cubism: The Painting of Braque and Picasso, 1909–12

From the time that Braque and Picasso joined forces and became 'rather like two mountaineers roped together,' as Braque was to say, the evolution of Cubism was the expression of a continual give-and-take between their two different temperaments. Both tried to sublimate their individualities and realize a sort of mutual anonymity for the sake of the style, which is also expressed in their reluctance in those days to sign their names on the painted surface. We cannot therefore make a clear distinction between their respective contributions—at least not before 1914— or weigh the relative importance of the one

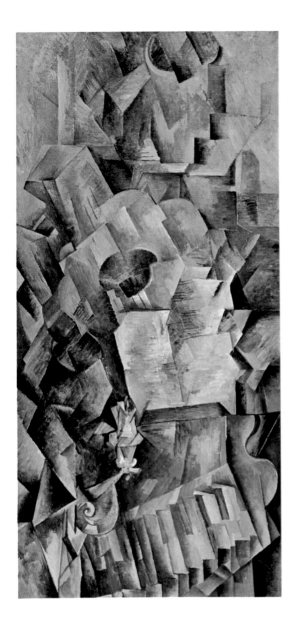

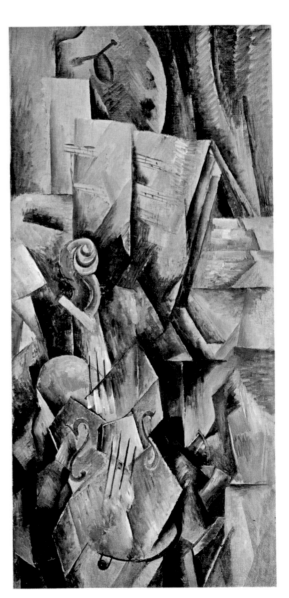

Plate 23   43

Georges Braque
Piano and Mandola, 1909–10
Oil, $36^1/_8 \times 16^7/_8$ in.

No. 18

Plate 24

Georges Braque
Violin and Palette, 1909—10
Oil, $36^1/_4 \times 16^7/_8$ in.

No. 19

against the other. Yet, with the hindsight of today, their paintings appear less impersonal than they perhaps believed, and the trained eye will distinguish between them instinctively. Suffice it to say, in the most general terms, that whereas Picasso's Cubist paintings tend to be more pronouncedly linear, angular, immediate in their presentation, even sculptural in conception, Braque's are more painterly, lyrical, suave and cohesive.

The effect of the alliance between the two men soon showed in Braque's work, notably in two superb still lifes, *Pl. 23, 24* *Violin and Palette* and *Piano and Mandola*, painted during the winter of 1909–10. Here, coming closer to Picasso, Braque was much bolder in his formal analysis, so that his faceting is more elaborate and he has broken the continuity of outlines in order to express volume through a series of interlocking cubes. Nevertheless the objects represented remain legible. The significance of this fragmentation was later accounted for by Braque when he said that it was a means of getting closer to objects 'within the limits that painting would allow' and of establishing 'space and movement in space.' In other words, it was a way of reconciling his knowledge of a given three-dimensional order in nature with his determination that the equivalent pictorial order should not violate the two-dimensional surface of the canvas. But it is important to add that neither in the work of Braque nor in that of Picasso were any preliminary mathematical calculations involved in their cubifying process. Their analysis of forms, which involved combining different aspects of a single object, so that the eye would be led to take in its total mass, has tempted some writers to read into it an implication of the 'fourth dimension,' the passage of time. Such an interpretation is certainly false, for neither Braque nor Picasso imagined

Plate 25

Pablo Picasso
Nude, 1909–10
Oil, 36^1/$_4$ × 28^3/$_4$ in.

Tate Gallery, London.

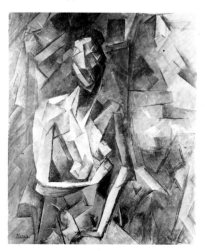

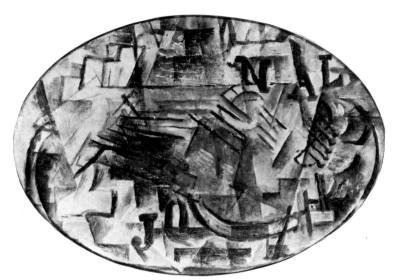

Plate 26

Georges Braque
Guitar, 1910–11
Oil, $9^{1}/_{2} \times 13^{3}/_{4}$ in. (Oval)

No. 25

either himself or a spectator walking around or among the objects they were representing. The various facets of a form are meant to exist and be seen simultaneously as elements disposed on a flat surface, where although no optical illusion has been attempted there co-exists an autonomous representation of space.

Pl. 14 Braque's two still lifes and Picasso's *Seated Woman* represent the point when the development of the technique of faceting—by which they were able to create volumes and make space tangible—caused the two artists to realize that they had to decide how they intended in the future to use color and light. In these three paintings both had used a limited but modulated palette of green, ochre and grey and had lit parts of objects from different angles. That is to say they had paid no heed to local color and had imposed their pictorial will both on form and on light. Braque even underscored the resulting inconsistencies and stylistic innovations of Cubism by his ironic treatment of *Pl. 24* the nail on which the palette hangs at the top of the canvas. For he painted it in *trompe-l'œil*, completed by a regular shadow, thereby pointing a contrast between his own invented method and the familiar eye-fooling method of representing reality. Now faceting produced a complex structure of planes at different levels and going in different directions, in addition to which Braque used a network of small interpenetrating planes to unite objects with the space around them. It therefore became essential for the

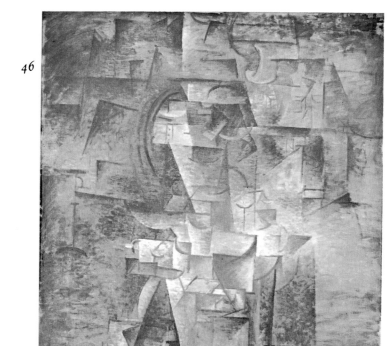

Plate 27

Pablo Picasso
Woman, 1910
Oil, 39¹/₂ × 32¹/₄ in.

No. 235

two artists to be able to differentiate spatially between one plane and another. To do this with contrasts of strong colors would probably have upset the subtle spatial structure. Yet even if they resorted to light they were faced with the problems of color modification and the erosion of form, that is to say violations of reality. Therefore, while they were concentrating on the representation of objects and elaborating the spatial notation of Cubism, Braque and Picasso limited the role of light and reduced their palette to a neutral range of greys and ochers.

Pls. 281, 21 It was at this stage, in the winter of 1909–10, that Picasso again turned to sculpture and produced a bronze *Woman's Head*, highly faceted like those in many of his paintings. He was, as it were, testing in three dimensions and in the light of reality, the validity of his newly invented pictorial methods for evoking a complete form and its volume. This *Woman's Head* was followed by a succession of works in which Picasso came to represent both objects and space with an

Plate 28

Pablo Picasso
Nude, 1910
Oil, 38¹/₂ × 30 in.

No. 233

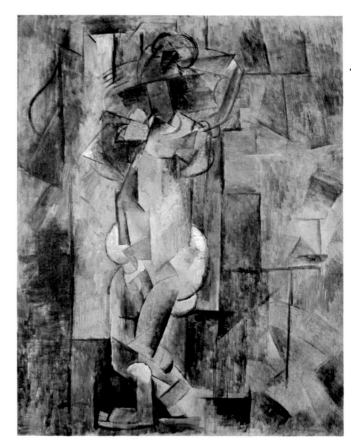

Plate 29

Georges Braque
The Table, 1910
Oil, 15 × 21¹/₂ in.

No. 21

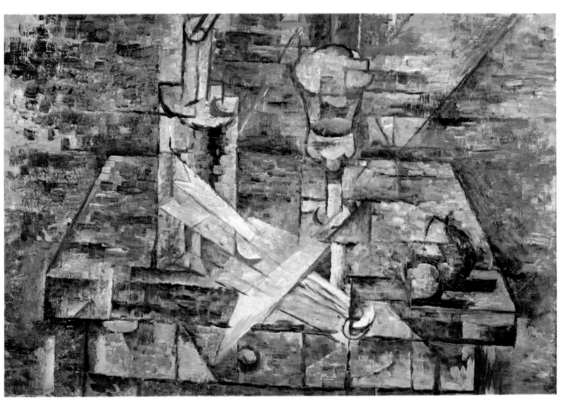

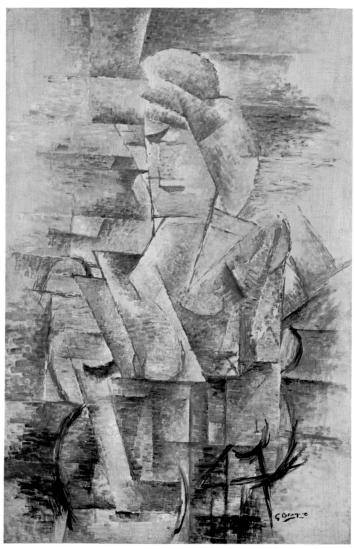

Plate 30

Georges Braque
Female Figure, 1910–11
Oil, 36 × 24 in.

No. 22

Pl. 28 elaborate arrangement of planes and facets. Figures (*Nude*, 1909–10) as well as objects were submitted to this process of abstraction and lost their individuality. Picasso made planes and forms open up into each other so that he could penetrate to the inner structure of things. Then by extending the planar structure over the whole surface of the canvas he was better able than before to relate the figure or the still life to the Pl. 29 background and the space around them. In *The Table* and Pl. 30 *Female Figure* we see Braque using the same means, though he carried abstraction less far and his objects remain more legible. There is a subtle difference between the painting of Braque and Picasso all through these years in the way that Picasso seems to focus on a figure or a still life and keep

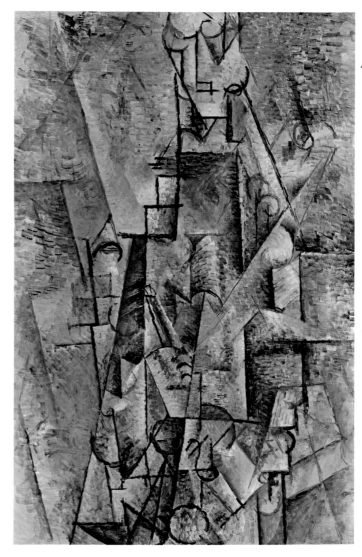

Plate 31

Pablo Picasso
Clarinet Player, 1911
Oil, 41³/₈ × 27¹/₈ in.

No. 240)

it half-detached from the background plane, whereas Braque aimed at a smoother, more integrated image.

The basic intention of Braque and Picasso in creating Cubism was not merely to present as much essential information as possible about figures and objects but to recreate visual reality as completely as possible in a self-sufficing, non-imitative art-form. They had not yet succeeded in working out a comprehensive system of spatial notation, so this was the next problem which they had to resolve. At this point, particularly in the work of Picasso, Cubism approached the frontier of total abstraction, because in the middle of 1910, while this aspect

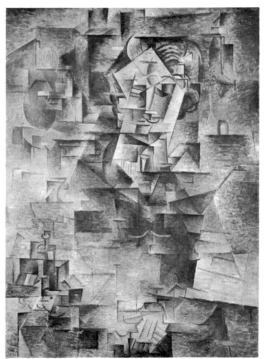

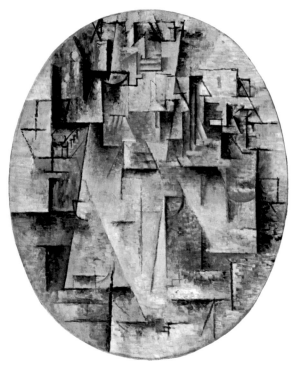

Plate 32

Pablo Picasso
Portrait of D. H. Kahnweiler, 1910
Oil, $39^5/_8 \times 28^5/_8$ in.

No. 234   *Pls. 27, 31*

absorbed their attention—as it did again in 1911—Braque and Picasso for a while allowed the objective content (which had hitherto been manifest) of their pictures to be only faintly suggested beneath an assertive structure of lines and planes (Picasso, *Clarinet Player*, 1911). Here we reach the most austere moment of 'high' Cubism, the phase which has been called 'hermetic,' an adjective which means airtight or impenetrable and is therefore wholly inappropriate. Admittedly an untrained eye may at first have difficulty in reading these paintings, but they can be interpreted none the less. It is only matter of understanding that the lines and planes represent different features and parts of the body or objects and pass through angles which, though they sometimes correspond with natural facts, are primarily dictated by spatial considerations and pictorial necessity. And we can measure the strength of will to keep in touch with reality which animated the two Cubist painters by the steps they took to prevent their painting becoming wholly abstract and non-figurative. For they devised a repertory of abbreviated signs which they incorporated, like hieroglyphs, into their pictures to make particular features identifiable and provide clues to the build-up of the composition as a whole. Thus in the

Pablo Picasso
*La Pointe de la Cité (The Point of
the Ile de la Cité, Paris)*, 1911
Oil, 35¹/₂ × 28 in. (Oval)

No. 239

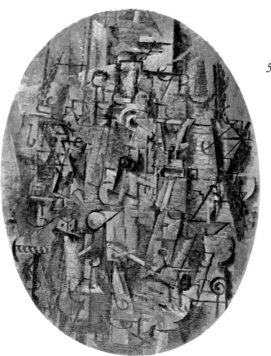

Plate 34

Georges Braque
Still Life with Dice and Pipe, 1911
Oil, 31¹/₂ × 23 in. (Oval)

No. 24

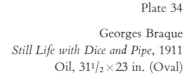

Pl. *32* *Portrait of Kahnweiler*, painted in the fall of 1910, Picasso was at pains to elucidate his planar structure by writing in descriptive details such as the eye, the nose, the well-brushed hair, the watch-chain, the clasped hands and the still life groups beside and behind the sitter.

Plate 35

Pablo Picasso
*Absinthe Glass, Bottle, Pipe and
Musical Instruments on a Piano*,
1910–11
Oil, 19³/₄ × 51¹/₄ in.

No. 236

Pl. *33* Both Braque and Picasso (*La Pointe de la Cité*, 1911) reached the frontier of non-figuration more than once between the summer of 1910 and the spring of 1912, though Braque never came as close to total abstraction as Picasso. On each occasion, both artists recoiled. We must, however, consider why this problem recurred. The answer seems to be that the

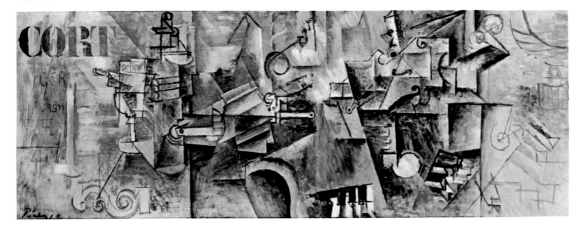

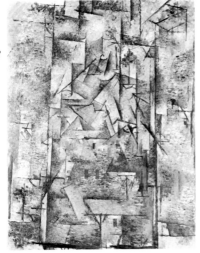

Plate 36

Georges Braque
Rooftops at Céret, 1911
Oil, 32³/₈ × 23¹/₄ in.

Ralph Colin, New York.

Plate 37

Pablo Picasso
Bottle of Marc, 1911–12
Drypoint, 19¹¹/₁₆ × 12 in.

No. 281

Pl. 36

Pls. 37, 38

more elements of reality Braque and Picasso managed to incorporate into their pictures (Picasso, *Absinthe Glass, Bottle, Fan, Pipe and Musical Instruments on a Piano*, 1910–11; Braque, *Still Life with Dice and Pipe*, 1911), the more they found that the clarity of their spatial structure became obscured by descriptive detail, formal complexities and an elaborate play of light and shade. Yet whenever they reacted against this complication and tried to make things clearer, they found themselves losing touch again with tangible reality.

It was during the summer of 1911, when Braque and Picasso were working together at Céret in the Pyrenees, that the two artists at last found a way to clarify things and went on to produce compositions which were more concentrated but more legible. A linear scaffolding (clearly visible in their two great prints *Bottle of Marc* and *Fox*,

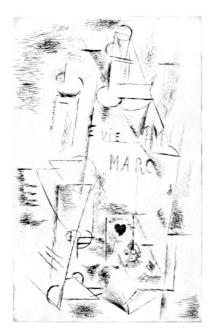

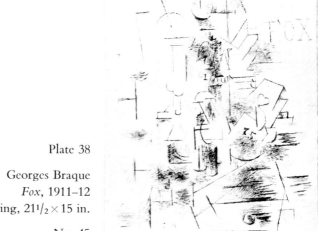

Plate 38

Georges Braque
Fox, 1911–12
Etching, 21¹/₂ × 15 in.

No. 45

Pls. 26, 33, 34, 44

1911–12) was made to indicate distances and to hold the composition together, while an associated structure of planes and cubes, over which realistic details were inscribed, gave volume and served to integrate spatially the foreground with the background. The use of an oval canvas is also characteristic of this phase of Cubist painting because, said Braque, it enabled him 'to rediscover a sense of verticals and horizontals.' But Braque and Picasso also found oval canvases useful because they had no corners, where the definition of space tended to become ambiguous, and thereby helped them to concentrate around the subject and create a more compact pictorial structure. Another feature of this phase is the broken brushwork which they used to create a luminous palpitation, to differentiate between planes and to make the surface of the canvas more vibrant and tactile. All of these procedures can be observed in still lifes such as Braque's *Violin and Candle-*

Plate 39

Pablo Picasso
Man's Head, 1911–12
Charcoal 24½ × 19 in.

No. 269   *Pl. 42*

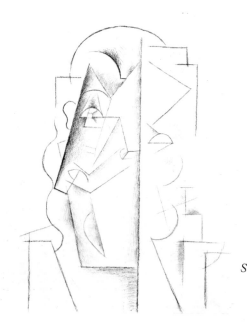

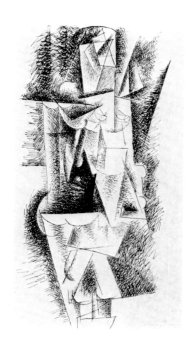

Plate 40

Pablo Picasso
Standing Woman, 1911
Ink, 12½ × 7½ in.

No. 268

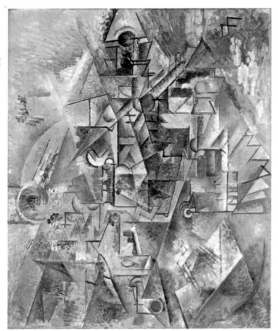

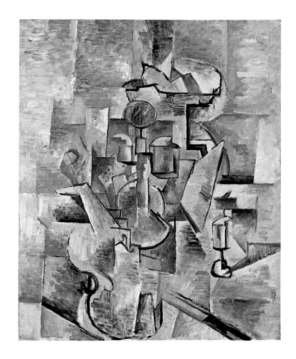

Plate 41

Pablo Picasso
Still Life with Clarinet, 1911
Oil, 24 × 19³/₄ in.

No. 238

Plate 43

Georges Braque
The Portuguese, 1911
Oil, 46¹/₈ × 32¹/₄ in.

Kunstmuseum, Basel.

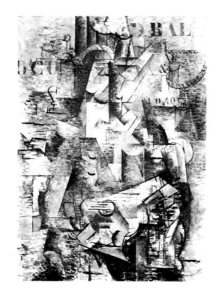

stick, 1910, or Picasso's *Still Life with a Clarinet* of 1911. But it is even more evident in figure compositions such as Picasso's *Man Smoking a Pipe* or Braque's *The Portuguese*, both of 1911, the latter being probably the first painting in which stenciled lettering made its appearance. This innovation—an unexpected application of a painter-decorator's stock-in-trade—was certainly made by Braque. In a still life by Braque of early 1910 a newspaper appears with its mast-head spelled out, but there the lettering serves simply to identify the form and plays no structural role in the composition. From the summer of 1911 on, however, Braque, and almost immediately Picasso, began to use words, letters and figures as an active pictorial element. That is to say, they treated them not simply as ornamental additions but chose those with an associative relevance to the subject of the picture, so that they contributed to the realism of the presentation. They also played a comparable role to the *trompe-l'œil* nail in Braque's 1909 still life by paradoxically emphasizing the schism between painting and reality. This lettering, Braque said, was a group of 'forms which could not be distorted because, being themselves flat, they were not in space, and thus by

Georges Braque
Violin and Candlestick, 1910
Oil, 24 × 19³/₄ in.

No. 23

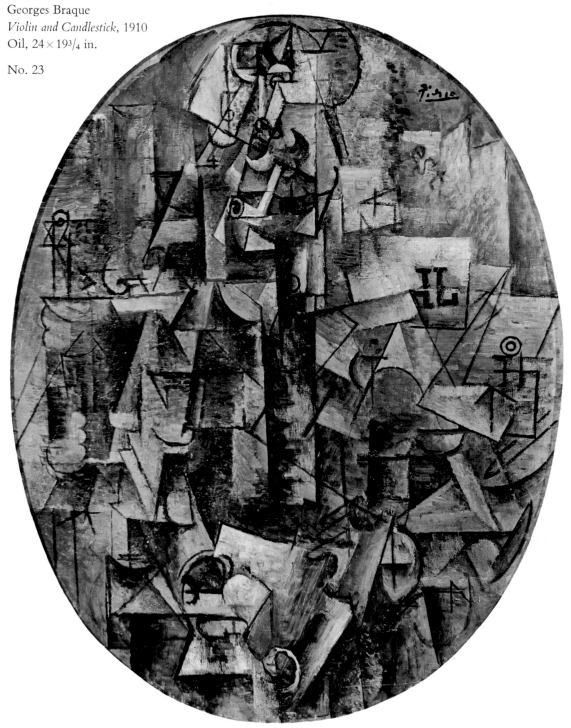

Plate 44 Pablo Picasso, *Man Smoking a Pipe*, 1911 No. 237
Oil, 36 × 28¹/₄ in. (Oval)

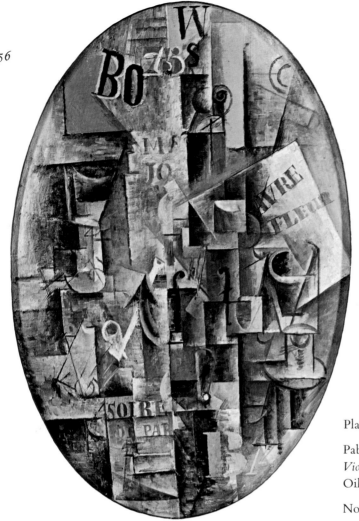

Plate 45

Pablo Picasso
Violin, Glass and Pipe on Table, 1912
Oil, $31^7/_8 \times 21^1/_4$ in. (Oval)

No. 241

contrast their presence in the picture made it possible to distinguish between objects situated in space and those which were not.' In other words, the lettering emphasized the two-dimensional nature of the painted surface yet acted as a *repoussoir* in reverse to make the objective content assume a spatial connotation.

With some other changes which occurred in the painting of Braque and Picasso in the first half of 1912, the language of 'high' Cubism reached its fullest expression; soon after, the artists embarked on a wholly new cycle of development which constitutes the 'late' phase of Cubism. Thus the year 1912 marks the end of one long evolution and the initiation of another. After their return from Céret in the

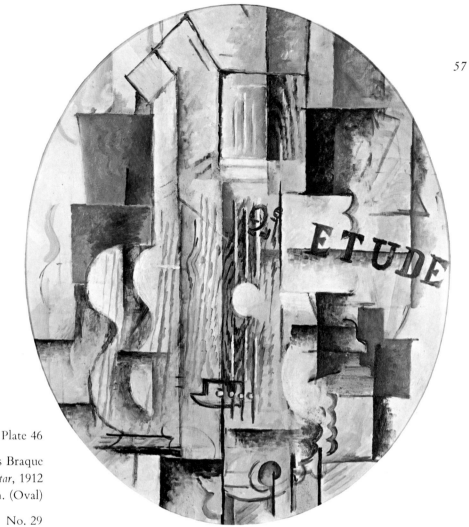

Plate 46

Georges Braque
Guitar, 1912
Oil, 29 × 24 in. (Oval)

No. 29

fall of 1911, both artists seem to have become aware that so far as the handling of form and space was concerned they had carried the 'analytical' language as far as possible and that it was time to begin enriching it. The introduction of color still remained an unsolved problem, but in

Pl. 45   Picasso's *Violin, Glass and Pipe* of 1912—there are comparable works by Braque—we see a tentative move in this

Pl. 51   direction. Simulation of different textures, which Braque (again drawing on his painter-decorator's training) was the first to try, occurred at the same time and we therefore find both artists using craftsmanly methods to imitate veined marble, the graining in wood and even the strands

Pl. 47   of human hair (Braque, *Homage to Bach*, 1912). Braque also went further and thickened his paint with sand and other matter. This was to prove even more telling because, as he was to say later, with the experience of *papiers collés* behind him, it revealed to him 'the extent to which color is related to substance . . . Now this intimate relationship between color and substance is inevitably more delicate when it comes to painting. So my great delight was the "material" character which I could give to my pictures by introducing these extraneous elements.' This statement is yet another proof of the realistic—indeed materialistic— intentions which animated Braque and Picasso while they were creating Cubism. Going on from here, however, Picasso made a still more important innovation, in a small picture of May 1912, when he stuck a piece of American cloth over-printed with a design of chair-caning on to his canvas and used it to represent the seat of a chair, painting a still life on and around it. This was the first *collage*, and once again it embodied several paradoxes. For by introducing a ready-made 'real' element with a literal connotation into an otherwise painted representation of reality, Picasso called the bluff of the eye-fooling technique, offered the challenge of the Cubist way of recreating reality and left the spectator to make his own terms with an illusion of reality (chair-caning) which had been given a false reality by the pictorial simulation of the objects he had painted around it.

The creative possibilities of this last innovation were not to be fully realized or followed up by either Braque or Picasso for a few months. But in the meanwhile Braque took another constructive step on his own when, in the summer of 1912, he cut pieces of paper and cardboard and made some models of objects (guitars, violins) which he then painted. These have now disappeared, but since a few of those made by Picasso (who followed his example) have

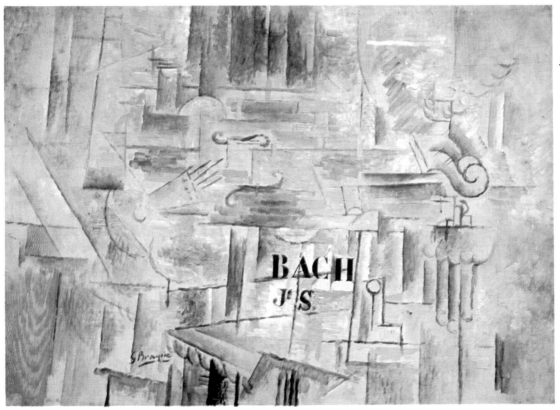

Plate 47 Georges Braque, *Homage to Bach*, 1912 No. 26
Oil, 21¹/₄ × 28³/₄ in.

survived we know more or less what they looked like.
With a ready wit, Picasso was soon referring to Braque as
'*mon cher Vilbure*,' a topical allusion to the recently
deceased Wilbur Wright behind which also lay a private *jeu
d'esprit*. For the two artists had sometimes likened their
own efforts in the pictorial realm to those of the early
aeroplane designers, so that there was already a *double
entente* in Picasso's use of the banner headline '*Notre Avenir
est dans l'Air*,' which appears in some of his paintings
of 1912. 'If one plane wasn't enough to get the thing off
the ground,' I have heard Picasso say, 'they added another
and tied the whole thing together with bits of string and
wood, very much as we were doing.'

At this point, which immediately preceded the invention
of the technique of *papiers collés* (pasted papers), through
which the idiom was to be transformed, it is
necessary to interrupt the development of Cubist painting

as created by Braque and Picasso in order to sum up their achievements thus far and discuss the Cubist movement which had grown up in France since 1910 and was already spreading to other countries.

Summary

Pls. 48, 49

In considering the development of true Cubism between 1908 and 1912, it is essential to bear in mind that Braque and Picasso kept themselves largely apart from other painters. Close friends such as Guillaume Apollinaire, Max Jacob, André Salmon and Maurice Raynal, all of them writers, as well as artists such as Derain and of course Juan Gris, came often to their studios and saw their latest works. Other artists and writers came more occasionally and were undoubtedly shown less, but those interested could always see a selection of paintings by Braque and Picasso hanging in the Kahnweiler Gallery. So it was never very difficult for anyone in the Paris art-world to discover,

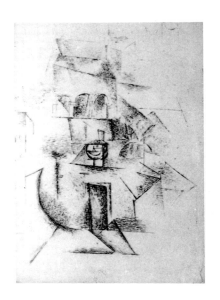

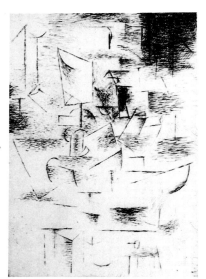

Plates 48, 49

Pablo Picasso
Max JACOB: Saint Matorel,
1910
Etchings,
Plate II, 'The Convent,'
$7^3/_4 \times 5^1/_2$ in.
Plate IV, 'The Table,'
$7^3/_4 \times 5^9/_{16}$ in.

No. 286

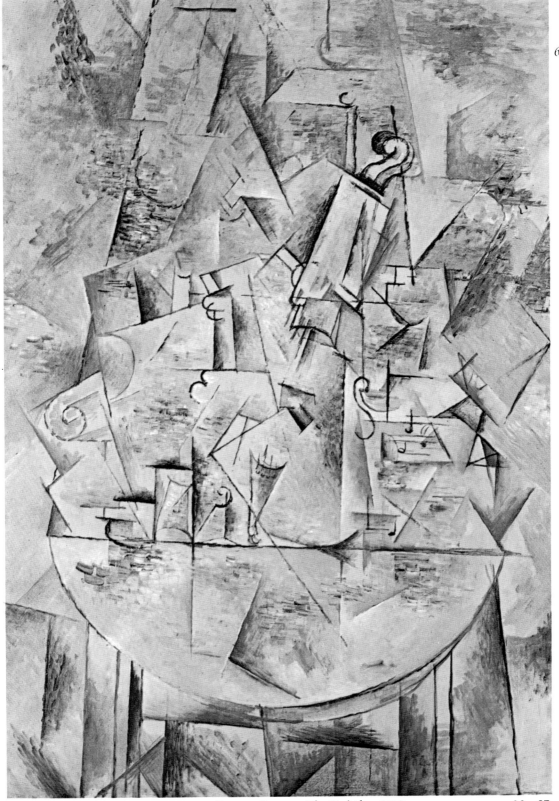

Plate 50   Georges Braque, *The Guéridon*, 1912   No. 27
Oil, $45^5/_8 \times 31^7/_8$ in.

Plate 51

Georges Braque
Still Life with Pipe, 1912
Oil, 13³/₈ × 16³/₈ in.

No. 28

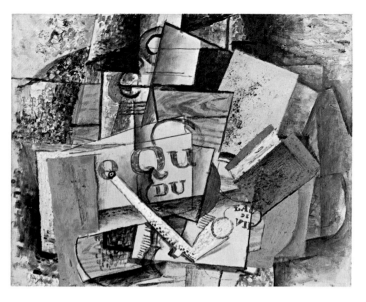

Plate 52

Pablo Picasso
Man's Head, 1912
Etching, 5¹/₈ × 4⁵/₁₆ in.

No. 282

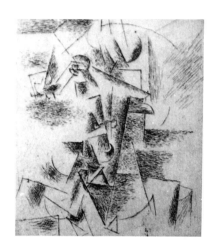

more or less, what they were doing. Braque and Picasso never aspired to be leaders of a movement, nor to attract a following, and they shunned the regular Salons. No exhibition of recent paintings by Picasso was held in Paris after 1902; Braque on the other hand showed recent works at Kahnweiler's in November 1908 and two more paintings at the Salon des Indépendants of 1909. After that, neither artist had a formal exhibition until both had one-man shows at Léonce Rosenberg's gallery, L'Effort Moderne, in 1919. This self-isolation was deliberate and calls for no explanation. True Cubism, as created by Braque and Picasso, was not the outcome of a theory or a mathematical exercise which had to be demonstrated: it derived from a wholly fresh conception of what true painting should be, and flowered creatively in the privacy of the studio. Moreover, thanks to the intuitive and inventive genius of Braque and Picasso it developed as a vital force without ever tending to become doctrinaire.

Cubism has often been accused of being formalist and divorced from life, probably because most people have seen it as an art dealing with prosaic everyday objects and anonymous figures. Of course the major effort of Braque and Picasso went into solving the strictly pictorial problems arising out of their intention to find a wholly new and precise way of recreating tangible reality on canvas. That is to say, they thought more about forging the language

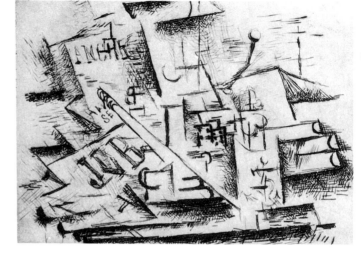

Plate 53

Georges Braque
Job, 1911
Drypoint, $5^7/_8 \times 7^7/_8$ in.

No. 43

Plate 54

Georges Braque
Guitar on a Table, 1909
Etching, $5^1/_2 \times 7^7/_8$ in.

No. 42

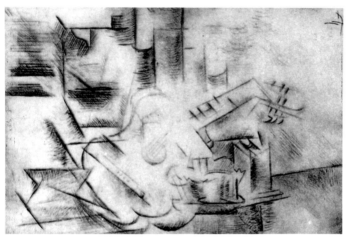

Plate 56

Georges Braque
Cubist Still Life II, 1912
Drypoint and etching,
$12^{15}/_{16} \times 17^7/_8$ in.

No. 47

Plate 55

Georges Braque
Bass, 1911–12
Drypoint and etching, $18 \times 12^{15}/_{16}$ in.

No. 46

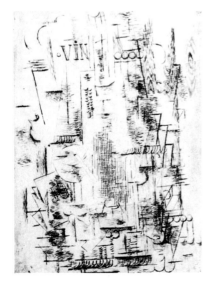

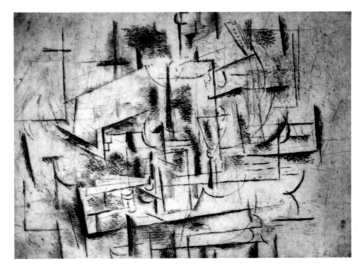

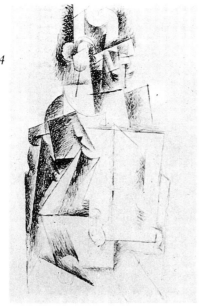

Plate 57

Pablo Picasso
Seated Man, 1912
Ink, 12¹/₈ × 7³/₄ in.

No. 270

of Cubism than about the aesthetic value of their subject-matter. So it was a great advantage for them to be able to use wholly familiar objects whose simple forms made them easy to represent. And they were rewarded for doing this by the rapidity (1907–12) with which they mastered the means for creating such a full but clear statement of form, space and volume.

Yet we must not overlook the personal relevance and time-bound significance which this seemingly banal subject-matter also had for Braque and Picasso: not for nothing is the iconography of Cubism replete with intimate and often topical references. The daily life of Braque and Picasso is enshrined in their still lifes: things to eat, drink, smoke, read and discuss. Pipes, packets of cigarettes, jugs, fans, newspapers and musical instruments lay around in their studios; bottles of Bass, Rum, Anis or Pernod, playing-cards and dice were on the tables of the bars and cafés they frequented. The violins, guitars and sheets of music are tokens of their personal pleasures. Braque's *Portuguese* was inspired by a man he saw in a bar in Marseilles. Picasso made portraits of friends and mistresses: Sagot, Vollard, Uhde, Kahnweiler, Fernande Olivier. And at a later stage (1912) when he could not be concerned with physical resem-

Pl. 217   blance, he would write on his canvas *J'aime Eva* or *Ma Jolie* so that his private emotions could visibly enter into the work. In other paintings we find personal letters, the names of hotels and cafés which Braque and Picasso frequented and souvenirs of bullfights. And lastly, both artists painted views from their studio windows in Montmartre and Céret. Thus even though the artists seem to have neglected the human element, we find on examination that Cubist painting was in fact a very real record of their private lives and experiences.

2 The Cubist Movement in Paris: 1906—1914

Derain, 1906—10

Writing in *Le Temps* in October 1912, on 'The Beginnings of Cubism,' Guillaume Apollinaire rather casually noted that it was as a result of the friendship which grew up between Picasso and Derain in 1906 'that almost immediately Cubism was born.' A few months later, in an article of February 1913 in *Der Sturm*, this first vague statement was changed into: 'The Cubism of Picasso was born of a movement originating with André Derain.' But Apollinaire modified even this claim in his famous booklet *Les Peintres Cubistes*, published in March 1913, where he wrote that while 'the new aesthetic first originated in the mind of André Derain, the most important and daring works which it produced forthwith' were created by Picasso and Braque, who should therefore be considered as co-originators, with Derain, of the style. This is all that Apollinaire has to say about Derain's role as an originator of Cubism: he never refers to specific works in which Derain anticipated the revolutionary steps taken by Picasso in *Les Demoiselles d'Avignon*, nor does he say what Picasso took from Derain in the way of new aesthetic ideas. What is more, Apollinaire had never discussed Derain's work in this light in any of the separate articles, written between 1908 and the end of 1912, which he used to make up the text of *Les Peintres Cubistes*, and even there he felt obliged to explain that he could not then 'write anything valid about a man who deliberately keeps himself apart from everything and everyone.' This sudden and unsupported claim is so curious that it requires discussion.

It is certainly true that in 1906–07 Derain was on very friendly terms with Picasso, as well as with Braque, whom he had known through the Fauve group, and that between 1907 and 1910 Derain painted some pictures which

★ André Salmon, who had known
both Picasso and Derain since 1906,
writing early in 1912 said: 'André
Derain—let's get this clear at once—
was to join (Picasso) by following
his own paths and then move away
from him without having overtaken
him.' See *La Jeune Peinture Française*,
p. 52.

relate rather timidly to 'early' Cubist developments.
Yet it is difficult to assign a definite place to Derain either
as an originator of Cubism or as an artist who contributed
to the Cubist movement. His paintings of the time show
him always following and *never anticipating* what Picasso did,
and never making a stylistic innovation of his own.
Moreover, Derain never painted a Cubist picture. Derain
was neither a revolutionary artist nor a pioneer: he was not
even the creator of fauvism, though he was certainly a
splendid executant. However, when in 1906 he discovered
Negro sculpture, together with Matisse and Vlaminck, it
was Derain (then painting in a Cézannesque manner), so
Apollinaire tells us, who in particular admired 'the artistry
with which the image-makers of Guinea and the Congo
succeeded in reproducing the human figure without using
any element borrowed from direct observation.' Yet
it was not until 1907–8,★ that is to say after Picasso had
abandoned *Les Demoiselles d'Avignon*, that Derain modified
his style and produced a group of works with Cézannesque

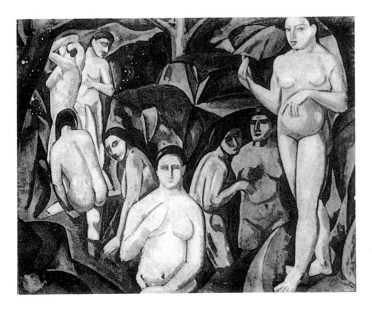

Plate 58

André Derain
Bathers, 1908
Oil, $70^3/_4 \times 98^1/_2$ in.

Present whereabouts unknown.

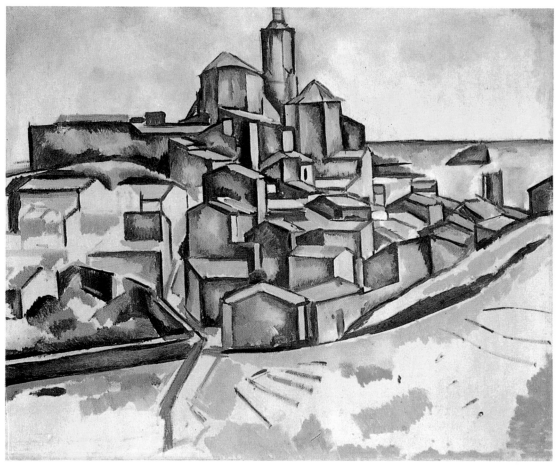

Plate 59   André Derain, *Cadaqués*, 1910   No. 70
Oil, 23⁵/₈ × 28³/₄ in.

Pl. 58   subjects (*Bathers, Nudes*) in which he treated the figures in a simplified, 'primitivizing' manner. In other words, Derain's painting reflected the 'negro' influence which had already become apparent in Picasso's work in the same
Pl. 3   way that it was reflected in Matisse's *Blue Nude* (1907) and
Pl. 5   Braque's *Nude* (1907–8). But Derain made no attempt, as Braque and Picasso did, to invent new ways of handling form and space, and did not share their conception of pictorial realism, so that his 'primitivizing' paintings were heavy-handed and lifeless. Moreover, Derain never went on to recreate forms in their totality through the technique of faceting. Instead, he abandoned all thoughts of Cubism and, when he spent part of the summer of 1910 at Cadaqués with Picasso, contented himself with a stylized, post-Cézannesque naturalistic idiom. True, Derain used little

Pls. 59, 60

perspectival distortions and differently inclined planes to evoke mass, and showed a liking for cubic forms, but his vision and his use of perspective in paintings such as *Cadaqués* and *Still Life on a Table* was fundamentally conventional. The cubes are descriptive, the use of light is consistent and the space recedes. Thus, although it is unquestionable that, like Braque and Picasso, Derain was profoundly influenced by Cézanne, he never attempted, as they did, to pursue Cézanne's inventions towards new creative ends. Of course he was aware of and must have understood—since they discussed it at length—the full purport of all that Braque and Picasso were attempting to do. But in his own work he followed another line of development.

Le Fauconnier, Gleizes and Metzinger, 1910–14

The first references to a school of Cubist painters occurred in the French press in 1910. At the Salon des Indépendants, and again at the Salon d'Automne of that year, Jean Metzinger, Henri Le Fauconnier, Robert Delaunay, Albert Gleizes and Fernand Léger showed a number of paintings in a post-Cézannesque idiom which the critic of *La Presse* described as 'geometrical follies,' while Apollinaire hailed them as signifying 'the rout of Impressionism.' But on the second occasion Apollinaire wrote more precisely: 'There has been some talk of a bizarre manifestation of Cubism. Ill-informed journalists ended up by seeing it as plastic metaphysics. Yet it is not even that. It is a flat, lifeless imitation of works not on view and painted by an artist with a strong personality who, what is more, has not let anyone share his secrets. This great artist is called Pablo Picasso. The Cubism at the Salon d'Automne was only the jackdaw in borrowed plumage.' No doubt Apollinaire was mainly concerned with making the point that this was

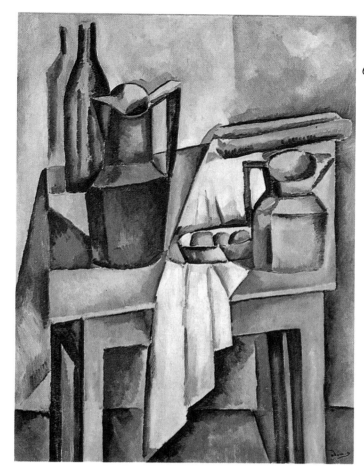

Plate 60

André Derain
Still Life on a Table, 1910
Oil, 36^1/$_4$ × 28^1/$_8$ in.

No. 69

not true Cubism, but he certainly exaggerated. Admittedly Metzinger was trying to imitate the pictorial methods used by Braque and Picasso in 1909, but the near-Cubist style of both Léger and Delaunay was eminently personal, whereas there was nothing Cubist at all about the works exhibited by Le Fauconnier and Gleizes.

Bearing in mind the increasing influence of Cézanne on the young artists of Paris since 1904, it seems at first surprising that in 1910 critics should have felt that Impressionism still lingered on. But it is easy to lose sight of the great quantity of colorist painting, in the form of belated Fauvism and Neo-Impressionism, that still appeared at the Paris Salons because most of it was undistinguished and much has disappeared. At the Indépendants of 1907, for example, the critic Louis Vauxcelles counted twenty-five painters whom he felt had been affected by Fauvism. And in fact most of the artists who took up Cubism

between 1909 and 1913 had worked during the past few
years in a colorist tradition: Le Fauconnier, Gleizes and
Lhote painted in a sub-Impressionist manner; de La
Fresnaye followed Gauguin and the Nabis; Metzinger,
Delaunay, Léger and Picabia painted under Neo-Impressionist influence; Braque had been a Fauve painter. So it
was perhaps natural that, when faced with a wave of
Cubist-type painting in 1910–11, the critics should have
felt that a new movement was being born. At all events, this
passage from one style to the other so confused Apollinaire
that he wrote in 1911 of Fauvism and Cubism as 'two art
movements which followed each other and fuse so well,
giving birth to an art that is simple and noble, expressive
and restrained.'

Many of these painters had known each other for a few
years already—though only Metzinger knew Braque and
Picasso—but when they saw their works hanging together
at the Salon d'Automne of 1910 they became aware of
stylistic affinities, and as Gleizes writes in his *Memoirs*: 'It
seemed essential to us then that we should form a group,
see more of each other and exchange ideas.' This they
proceeded to do throughout the winter of 1910–11. Then
just before the opening of the Indépendants, in the spring
of 1911, they managed to overthrow the established
Hanging Committee and take over the job themselves.
This gave them the chance to exhibit as a Cubist group in
a separate gallery, while in a gallery nearby they hung works
by de La Fresnaye, Lhote, Marchand and de Segonzac, with
whom they thought they had something in common. Such
was the official launching of the Cubist movement in Paris.

Le Fauconnier was at first the leading personality and his
enormous painting *Abundance*, shown at the Indépendants

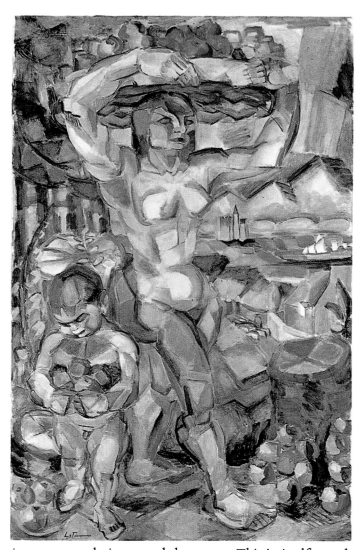

Plate 61

Henri Le Fauconnier
Abundance, 1910–11
Oil, 75¹/₄ × 48¹/₂ in.

No. 174

in 1911, greatly impressed the group. This in itself reveals how little most of these painters were concerned with true Cubism in its essential aspects. There is really nothing Cubist about *Abundance:* the use of light is consistent, the perspective is traditional, the cubes and facets are not arrived at by formal analysis, nor do they serve to recreate space and volume. Le Fauconnier has simply disguised a conventional allegorical subject by giving it a superficially Cubist look. It is not surprising therefore that within two years, after trying other Cubistic experiments, he had turned into a representational academic painter of no consequence.

Gleizes was an intelligent, sensitive man, with a theoretical turn of mind, who continued to paint under the influence

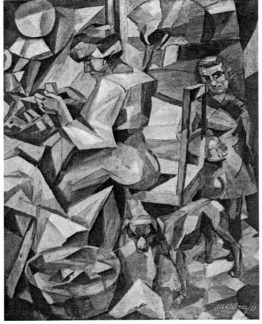

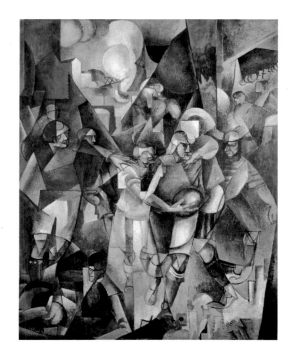

Plate 62

Albert Gleizes
Women in a Kitchen, 1911
Oil, 46⁵/₈ × 37¹/₄ in.

No. 95

Pl. 62

★ See the following passage in *On Cubism* by Gleizes and Metzinger, Chapter I: 'Formerly the fresco incited the artist to represent distinct objects, evoking a simple rhythm, on which the light was spread at the limit of a synchronic vision, rendered necessary by the amplitude of the surfaces; today painting in oils allows us to express notions of depth, density and duration supposed to be inexpressible, and incites us to represent, in terms of a complex rhythm, a veritable fusion of objects, within a limited space.'

of the Fauves and Cézanne until the end of 1910, when he started to give his pictures a more pronounced geometrical structure through elementary formal simplifications. In late 1910 Gleizes came under the influence of Le Fauconnier, discovered the analytical paintings of Braque and Picasso and adopted some of the external aspects of Cubism in paintings such as *Woman with Phlox* (1910) and *Women in a Kitchen* (1911). The latter is a conventional genre scene painted in a restricted neutral palette, like that of Braque and Picasso, but Gleizes has not used faceting and an element of Cubism to recreate reality more completely, nor has he renounced traditional perspective. His painting therefore makes no contribution to the development of Cubism in any of those essential aspects which preoccupied Braque and Picasso. Like his friends Metzinger and Delaunay, Gleizes was primarily concerned with subjects which had a communal significance—the buzz of the modern city and the calm of the countryside, factories, work, leisure, sport, and flight. In short he chose conventional subjects but handled them with modern pictorial means to produce a sense of multidimensionality and contemporary activity.★ Thus in the large *Harvest Threshing* (1912) the landscape setting, the receding views, the modern agricultural machinery and the peasants at work are locked into a

Plate 63

Albert Gleizes
The Football Players, 1912–13
Oil, 89 × 72 in.

No. 98

Plate 64

Albert Gleizes
Landscape at Toul, 1913
Oil, 35³/₄ × 28¹/₂ in.

No. 97

Plate 65

Albert Gleizes
Harvest Threshing, 1912
Oil, 106 × 138⁷/₈ in.

No. 96

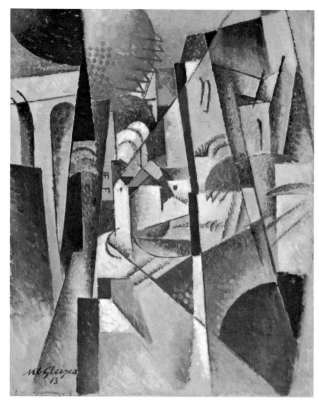

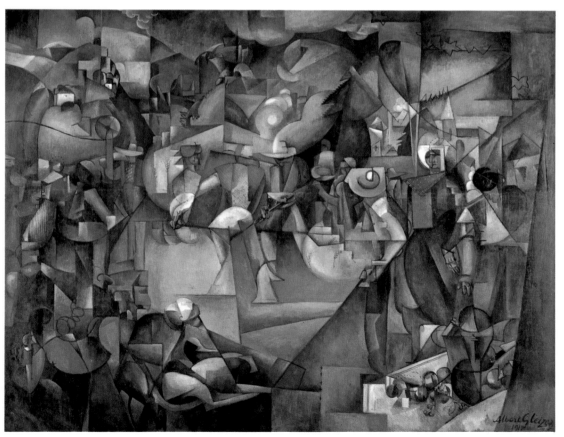

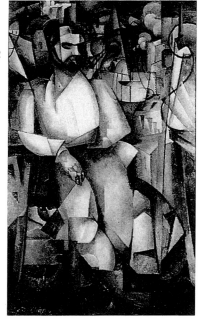

Plate 66

Albert Gleizes
Man on a Balcony, 1912
Oil, 77 × 45¹/₄ in.

Philadelphia Museum of Art,
Philadelphia, Pa.

geometrical and predominantly linear structure whose rhythms and formal contrasts create space and a dynamic effect. But nowhere are the geometrical forms derived from the objects represented, nor do they serve to create volumes: sometimes they are awkward stylizations, often their significance is ambiguous. The best analysis of the artist's intentions in this composition is that by Daniel Robbins, who describes it as 'a multiple panorama celebrating the worker, his material life and his collective activity in securing that life on a permanently changing land. Gleizes confronts us not with one action or place but with many; not with one time, but with past and future as well as present.' In 1913–14, Gleizes clarified his pictorial structure and greatly reduced the role of space, under the

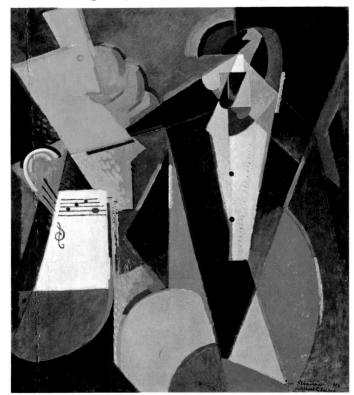

Plate 67

Albert Gleizes
Portrait of Igor Stravinsky, 1914
Oil, 51 × 45 in.

No. 99

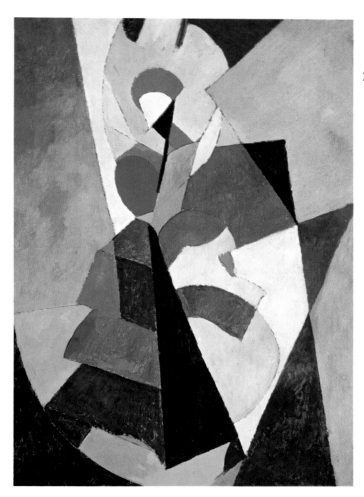

Plate 68

Albert Gleizes
Dancer, 1917
Oil, 39¹/₂ × 30 in.

No. 101

Pls. 94, 95, 225, 227

Pls. 67, 239

Pl. 68

joint influences of Léger (*Landscape at Toul*, 1913), Gris, the *papiers collés* of Braque and Picasso, and even Futurist painting (*Portrait of Stravinsky* [1914], *Broadway* [1915]). Yet while using certain Cubist procedures, Gleizes came more and more to disregard visual reality and evolved a predominantly decorative, formalized style of painting (*Dancer*, 1917) which was virtually abstract.

Metzinger, who was co-author with Gleizes of the first theoretical volume (1911–12) about Cubism—as they envisaged it—was referred to by Apollinaire in his review of the Indépendants of 1911 as 'the only adept of Cubism in the proper sense.' This was an unmerited compliment. For although Metzinger had met Picasso toward the end of 1909 and had written an informed article on the Cubism of Braque and Picasso in 1910, his own painting showed no evidence of a desire or ability seriously to follow them in

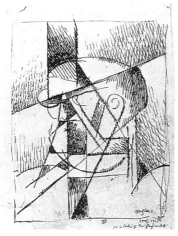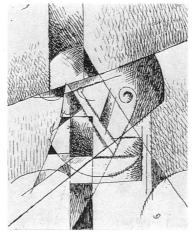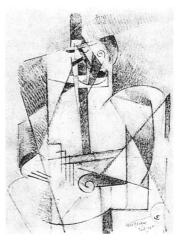

Plates 69–71

Albert Gleizes

Studies for 'Portrait of an Army Doctor', 1915

No. 1, Ink, 11³/₄ × 9 in.

No. 2, Ink, 7 × 5¹/₂ in.

No. 5, Ink, 9⁵/₈ × 7³/₈ in.

Nos. 102–104

their pictorial quest. Metzinger was a painter of little imagination and no originality, who seized on the planes and faceting in the analytical painting of Braque and Picasso and tried to use the same technique himself (*Nudes*, 1910). Here was a real case of a 'jackdaw in borrowed plumage,' for Metzinger did not properly comprehend the pictorial logic or structural significance of Picasso's

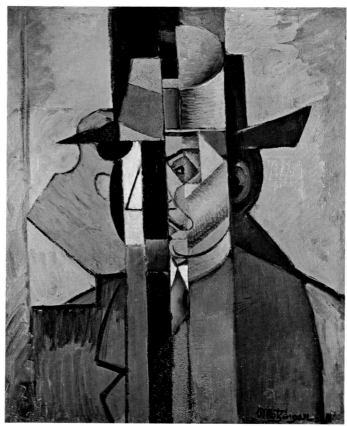

Plate 72

Jean Metzinger
Portrait of Gleizes, 1912
Oil, 25¹/₂ × 21¹/₄ in.

No. 213

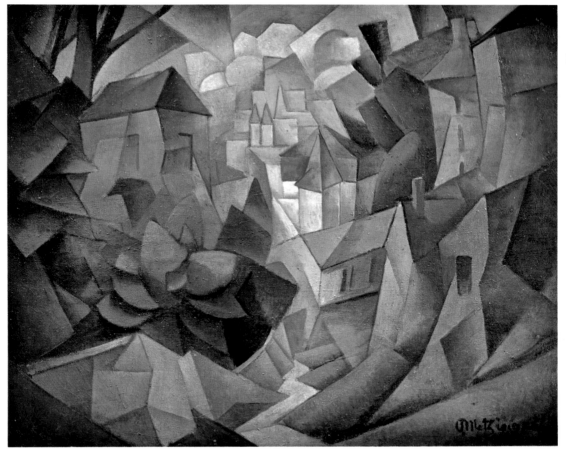

Plate 73

Jean Metzinger, *Cubist Landscape*, 1911   No. 212
Oil, 32 × 39 in.

Plate 74

Jean Metzinger
Head of Woman in a Hat, 1912
Charcoal, 21^1/$_4$ × 18^1/$_2$ in.

No. 216

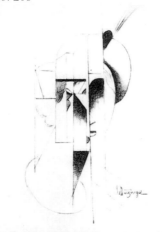

methods, with the result that his own paintings, like Le Fauconnier's *Abundance*, are only Cubist through the mannerism of having spattered the figures with cubic forms. Metzinger's vision was basically naturalistic, yet he imposed over it a system of proportions, planes and angles, which were mathematically calculated; he did not want to recreate reality in its totality using pure pictorial means, so his painting ended up by being artificial and schematic. We can see this in his *Cubist Landscape* (1911) which, despite a busy planar structure and geometric simplifications, is perspectively cleft by a receding diagonal leading off into deep space. In 1912, Metzinger was greatly influenced by the Cubist inventions of Juan Gris, as can be seen in the *Portrait of Gleizes*. But here again the way in which he dissected the naturalistic image is both

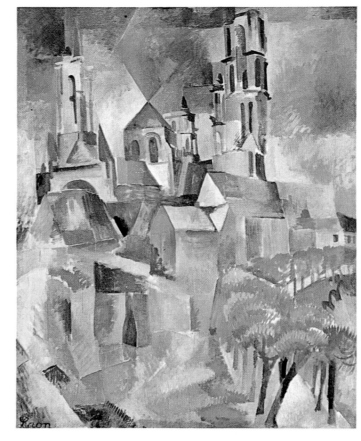

Plate 80

Robert Delaunay
The Towers of Laon, 1912
Oil, $63^3/_4 \times 51^1/_8$ in.

No. 63

Plate 81

Robert Delaunay
Window on the City II, 1912
Oil, $15^3/_8 \times 11^3/_8$ in.

No. 64

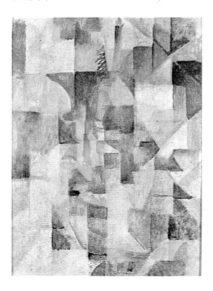

it instead inconsistently to illuminate different parts of the work. Yet even in this group of paintings Delaunay diverged significantly from true Cubist painting in his use of sharp formal contrasts—many of the forms having an ambiguous significance—to create a dynamic effect, and especially in the way he applied a layer of dots over the basic composition to simulate atmospheric vibration and create a decorative effect. 'Every area of space,' Delaunay said, 'is broken down in all directions into the smallest possible dimensions. This is the most complete type of dynamic dissolution, the liquidation of the recognized artistic means such as line, values, volumes, chiaroscuro and so on.' These paintings thus mark an advance toward, as well as a parting of the ways from, the true Cubists, because in them Delaunay began to abandon a concern with the material aspects of reality in favour of an interest in the immaterial. But before he did so completely, Delaunay turned back again to Cézanne for guidance in *The Towers of Laon* (1912), a painting in which the cubification of space and form resembles that

Pls. 7, 17 in Braque's landscapes of 1908–9. But again here Delaunay did not follow the true Cubists, because he worked with a palette of bright colors and used the curving avenue of trees on the right to create a perspectival effect which is in contradiction with the spatial flattening of the rest of the composition. From there Delaunay went on to sum up the experience he had gained in his paintings of the *Pl. 82* past three years in a vast allegorical composition *The City of Paris* (completed early in 1912), which is anti-Cubist by virtue of the unreality of its conception. For this is a Salon-type homage to Paris expressed through an uncomfortable cubified synthesis of, on the left, a Rousseau-like view of the Seine with a sailing-ship and houses, on the right a fragmented Eiffel Tower with clouds and a building, and in the center a highly elongated representation of a pseudo-classical group of Three Graces, set in an indeterminate foreground space. The whole composition has then been given a decorative, agitated and false life by gay colors, fragmentation, formal contrasts and a skillfully contrived geometric structure. But as a pictorial recreation of reality it deals with another world than that of the *Eiffel Tower*.

Plate 82

Robert Delaunay
The City of Paris, 1912
Oil, 104$^1/_2$ × 158$^1/_2$ in.

Musée National d'Art Moderne,
Paris.

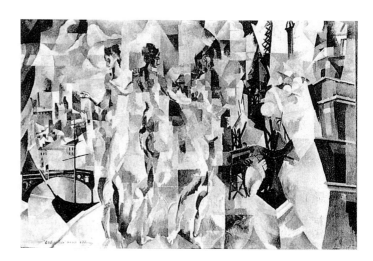

Pl. 81

Delaunay's next move, which marked the beginning of what he was to call the 'constructive' period of his work, took him still further away from true Cubism. For in the summer of 1912 he painted a new series of *Windows* in which he reinterpreted his earlier city views in terms of transparent, interacting planes of pure color which do not correspond to material objects. It is possible in several of these still to discern vaguely a suggestion of the Eiffel Tower, of a façade of a house or of a ferris-wheel, but their real subject is light and space. 'My eyes can see to the stars,' he was to write in 1913. 'Line is limitation. Color gives depth—not perspectival, not successive, but simultaneous depth—as well as form and movement.' In these paintings, Delaunay went back technically to his Neo-Impressionist beginnings. But instead of using the Neo-Impressionist technique of complementary and contrasted colors which are meant to blend in the eye of the spectator, he used what he called 'simultaneous' contrasts, that is to say colors which were intended to be seen simultaneously and independently without blending. This, Delaunay claimed, was a form of 'pure' painting, which was also 'realistic' because it expressed a visual experience. Nevertheless, abstraction here gained the upper hand over representation and Delaunay abandoned tangible reality for a visionary metaphysical reality. He still retained, in a modified fashion, the planar structure and faceting of Cubism, but used it for a wholly different purpose. This was the style which Apollinaire christened Orphic Cubism. However, it was but the prelude to the complete break with Cubism which occurred in Delaunay's next series of paintings, the *Circular Forms*, *Homage to Blériot* and *Discs* (1912–13), which even he referred to as non-figurative. These later paintings have no objective content, are based on concentric circles of color, inspired by the planets, are

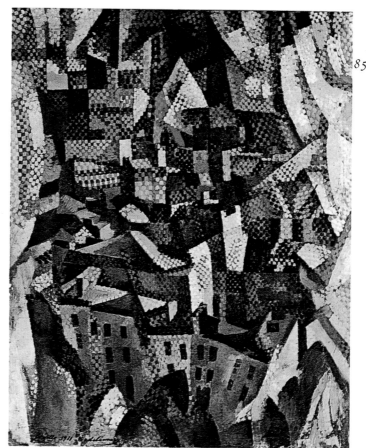

Plate 83

Robert Delaunay
*The City Seen From an
Open Window*, 1911
Oil, 57¹/₂ × 44¹/₈ in.

No. 62

supposed to develop in time and space, and mark the point at which Delaunay finally crossed the frontier into an art of total abstraction.

Léger, 1909–14

Léger was the first of the group to abandon the colorist tradition and in two paintings executed in the first half of 1909 resorted instead to a limited and rather dark palette: *The Bridge* and *Woman Sewing*. The seated figure is represented with a 'primitivizing' directness—comparable with that of Picasso's sculptural figures of 1907–8, which Léger had not seen—which owes a lot to Cézanne but also something to Henri Rousseau. The mass of the woman's body is composed of greatly simplified, angular but unbroken forms, which are coarsely faceted and heavily modeled, so that its volumes take on the fullness of a relief. Light comes from a single source, and Léger has used a palette

Pl. 84

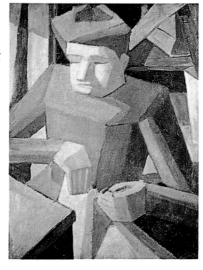

Plate 84

Fernand Léger
*Woman Sewing (Portrait of The
Artist's Mother)*, 1909
Oil, 28³/₈ × 21¹/₄ in.

No. 175

of dark blue, gray and light brown. Léger always claimed, correctly, that his own artistic conceptions derived directly from Cézanne, so it is interesting to see how nearly this painting relates to Cézanne's *Woman in Blue* of about 1897 (Venturi 705), though Léger has brought the figure closer to the surface of the canvas and aimed at a simpler, more monumental effect. Unlike Braque, who began by following up the subtle articulations of Cézanne's method, Léger was inspired by Cézanne's feeling for defining forms and his sense of volume in space, as is also evident in *Table and Fruit* (1909). 'Cézanne taught me to love forms and volumes, he made me concentrate on drawing. And then I realized that drawing had to be rigid and in no way sentimental,' he said in a lecture in 1913. Thus, in terms of style, Léger was close at this point to the early Cubism of Braque and Picasso but far removed from the pictorial methods of Delaunay, who took as his point of departure the fragmentation of form.

Léger next undertook a large and complex composition of *Nudes in a Landscape*, finished in the spring of 1910, in which everything—figures, trees and the other landscape elements—was reduced to basic geometric forms. Again his handling of these forms was in effect sculptural, although now he faceted and partially broke them down by a sort of analytical process. A reasonable comparison can be made between this picture and Picasso's *Three Nudes* of 1908, for both are surface-conscious paintings, executed in a neutral palette, in which the solid tangible aspects of reality are forcefully rendered, space is flattened, one-point perspective disregarded and faceting used to evoke volume. But whereas the figures in Picasso's painting have a sculptural unity and are static, while the setting is neutral, Léger's whole composition is based on an arrangement of dis-

Pl. 85

Pl. 86

Pl. 11

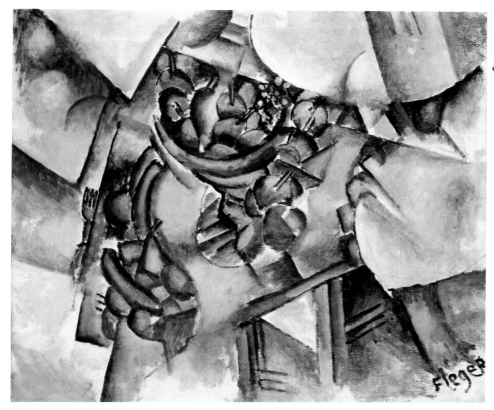

Plate 85   Fernand Léger, *Table and Fruit*, 1909   No. 176
                    Oil, 33 × 39 in.

Plate 86   Fernand Léger, *Nudes in a Landscape*, 1909–10   No. 177
                    Oil, 47¼ × 67 in.

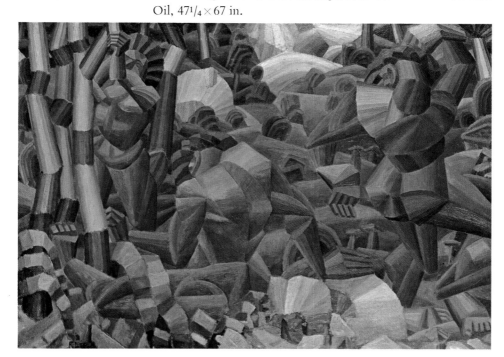

jointed cones, cylinders and cubes, which serve a representational purpose and at the same time create, by their directional slant and formal oppositions, a dynamic movement in space. Thus already at this stage Léger's pictorial aims were realistic in a sense that Braque and Picasso would have understood. And when he said that for himself the *Nudes* were 'only a tussle with volumes' because much as he would have liked to introduce color he 'felt that he could not control it,' Léger revealed that he was working with the same single-mindedness as they were. It was, however, only after he had completed this painting that Léger and Delaunay first saw the early Cubist paintings of Braque and Picasso at the Kahnweiler Gallery.

The influence of this experience is visible in a group of virtually Cubist cityscapes, comparable with those executed by Delaunay at the same moment in the spring of 1911. Here Léger abandoned imaginary subjects for everyday reality. In the finest and most resolved of these (coll. McMillan, Minneapolis) the buildings and their roofs provided Léger with rectangular cubic forms and several flat planes which he used to recreate space by pointing them in varying directions. He defined each of these elements with lines, which thus provided him with a structural framework, and he limited the depth of his pictorial space by vertical planes in the background which arrest the inward movement set up by those in the foreground. The roof planes form an ellipse around a central space, but this is also flattened by the use of varying perspectives, while by tilting the planes Léger has repeatedly brought the eye back to the picture surface. In all of this, Léger has respected a certain degree of visual logic, but it is equally significant that he has not 'analyzed,' faceted or

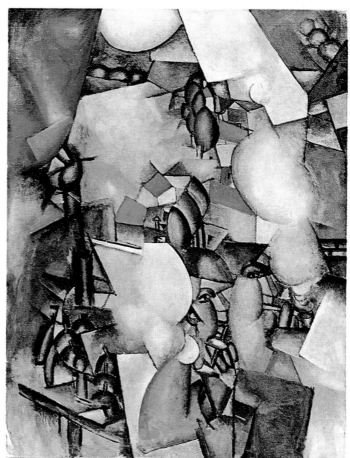

Plate 87

Fernand Léger
Smokers, 1911
Oil, 51 × 37⁷/₈ in.

No. 178

fragmented his forms. Léger has thus succeeded in representing space without recourse to eye-fooling devices and has recreated an experience of reality with purely pictorial elements. This is therefore a predominantly static painting—only a slight movement is evoked by the rising coils of smoke—because Léger has omitted the active formal contrasts which played a part in his preceding works. All of this proclaims that his painting was Cubist in spirit. Where Léger diverged from the practice of Braque and Picasso, however, was in giving an active role to light—which emanates from a hidden source between the buildings—and in using primary colors on some of the planes, often with a descriptive significance.

This was the closest Léger ever came to true Cubism because, after that, although he continued to represent reality in its solid, tangible aspects, he modified his

Pl. 87

pictorial methods to express also a dynamic experience.
That is to say, that while Léger went on using basic
geometric forms and primary colors to represent reality,
he completed his picture with oppositions of form and
color to evoke movement in space and express a more
dynamic twentieth century vision. Léger had already
begun to use this method tentatively in *Three Figures*
(1910–11), which he painted shortly after *Nudes in a
Landscape*, and more explicitly in *The Smokers* (1911), where
the stylized puffs of tobacco smoke create an interplay
on the picture surface with some flat, angular planes of
color which have no representational significance. Again
in these paintings Léger had no recourse to scientific perspective and recreated space chiefly by a contrast in size
between the figures and still life in the foreground and
the landscape with trees and houses behind, but secondly
by the way objects and the planes of color mount rhyth-
mically up the surface of the canvas. The contrasts
between the different types of forms and between the
primary colors—angular with curving, flat with rounded,
solid with opaque, red with green, blue with ochre—
which send the eye backwards and forwards (since they
are not meant to be seen 'simultaneously'), also induce a
sense of movement. Now both *Three Figures* and *The
Smokers* can be properly regarded as Cubist paintings,
personal though they are. But when in the *Woman in
Blue* (1912) Léger allowed the formal and tonal contrasts
of abstract planes of color to play a much more dominant
role, so that the aim of recreating reality suffered, he had
moved away from the aesthetic of Cubism. Unquestion-
ably Léger was still concerned up to a point in that
painting with representing a known reality, though neither
with making it tangible nor with recreating it in its
entirety. The figure, seated in an armchair and with hands

Plate 88

Fernand Léger
Study for 'Woman in Blue,' 1912
Oil, 51¹/₂ × 39 in.

No. 179

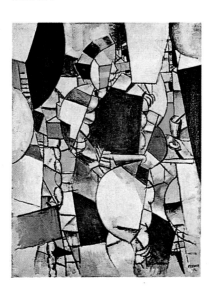

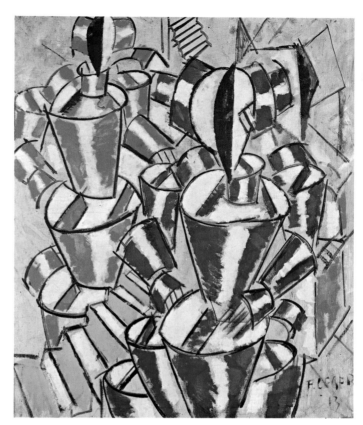

Plate 89

Fernand Léger
TheStairway, 1913
Oil, 56³/₄ × 46¹/₂ in.

No. 181

clasped, is represented in the foreground plane, in front of a table on which a glass is visible, and against a flat background plane. Space therefore plays very little role in this painting. Descriptive details have been largely dispensed with and the objective content of the picture is composed of basic geometric forms, insistently modeled to evoke volume, which have been arrived at not through formal analysis but through pictorial determinism. On top of this figurative element, Léger has imposed a second composition consisting of bold unfaceted planes of color whose role is partly descriptive—the chest and lap, for example—and partly arbitrary. Thus Léger injected vitality into his painting through the way he contrasted, but yet integrated, two different sets of elements and made color play a decisive constructive role.

However, Léger seems to have felt that this type of composition was too complicated to pursue because, in 1913, in *The*

Pl. 89 *Stairway* for example, he abandoned the use of arbitrary

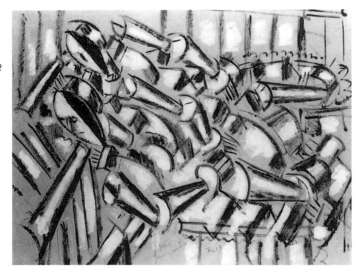

Plate 90

Fernand Léger
Two Reclining Women, 1913
Gouache, 19³/4 × 25¹/8 in.

No. 187

Pls. 90, 91, 94, 97

Plate 91

Fernand Léger
House Among Trees, 1912
Gouache, 17¹/2 × 13 in.

No. 185

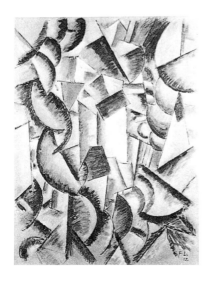

colored planes in order to give greater value to the objective content of his paintings—either figures, a still life or a landscape. At this stage Léger dehumanized his figure completely and reduced everything—bodies, buildings, trees, still life objects—to an articulated structure of the same basic geometric forms. Each of these forms is given bold unbroken outlines, is emphatically rounded and painted in a primary color, and as before Léger uses the contrasts between them and their rhythmic progression up the canvas to create space and movement in space. This may seem to indicate a flight from reality, and of course Léger was not attempting to use pure pictorial means to recreate visual reality. But he did aim at evoking another type of reality, for as he himself explained: 'Contrasts = Dissonance, that is to say a maximum of expressive effect. Consider the visual effect of the balls of smoke curving up between the houses and the way to transpose this into plastic terms, for it is one of the best examples of how to arrive at a heightened intensity. Throw your curves off-centre with as much variation as possible, though without breaking their continuity, then set them off against the hard, dry planes of the houses, dead planes which will take on a sense of movement by virtue of being differently colored from the central mass and opposed to forms which are animated.'

Léger's realistic intentions proclaim his affiliation to the principles of true Cubism. But unlike Braque and Picasso,

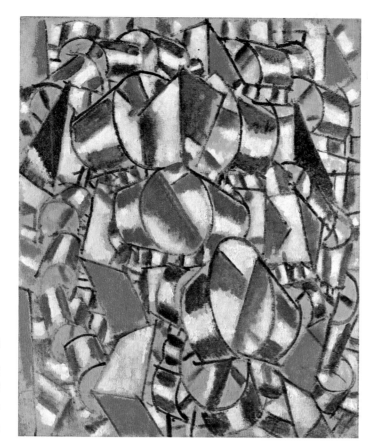

Plate 92

Fernand Léger
Contrast of Forms, 1913
Oil, 39^1/$_2$ × 32 in.

No. 180

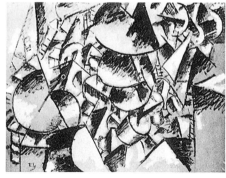

Plate 93

Fernand Léger
Drawing for 'Contrast of Forms
No. 2,' 1913
Wash drawing, 19 × 25 in.

No. 186

whose realism consisted in recreating reality as fully and as literally as possible by new pictorial methods, Léger's conception of realism began with rejecting symbolical or romantic trappings in order to be free to use basic pictorial elements to evoke the throbbing intensity, the opposing rhythms, the dynamism and the human involvement of modern civilization. This explains why for a while, in *Pls. 92, 93* 1913–14, he experimented in a series entitled *Contrasts of Forms* to discover how strong an expressive effect he could achieve by using his habitual repertoire of geometric forms and primary colors without any representational

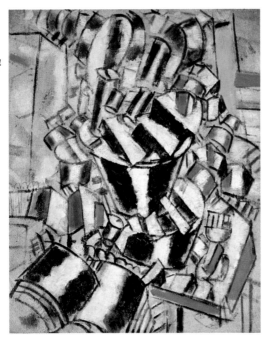

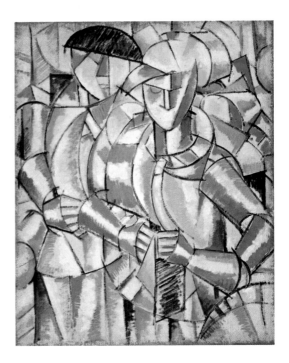

Plate 94
Fernand Léger
Still Life on a Table, 1914
Oil, 35³/₄ × 28 in.
No. 184

Plate 95
Fernand Léger
Two Figures, 1914
Oil, 31⁷/₈ × 25⁵/₈ in.
No. 183

Plate 96

Fernand Léger
Woman and Still Life, 1914
Gouache, 15¹/₄ × 12¹/₂ in.

No. 188

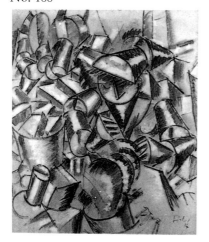

signification whatever. But this non-figurative venture failed to satisfy Léger, and in the last group of paintings he executed before receiving his mobilization orders in August 1914—for example, *Houses among Trees, Still Life* and *Two Figures*—Léger returned to using conceptual means to recreate solid, tangible aspects of reality. It was at this point, however, that Léger's affiliation to Cubism was to be abruptly broken, because while he was at the front he was deeply affected by a first-hand experience of the beauty of modern precision engineering, and when he came back he adopted a wholly different aesthetic.

In *Les Peintres Cubistes*, Apollinaire classified Léger with Delaunay as an Orphist because, as he makes clear, the 'lightness' and clarity of his colors appealed to him. In fact the aims, interests and methods of these two painters could hardly have been more different, for where Delaunay was drawn into the realm of light and space, Léger remained obstinately earth-bound. But there are certain

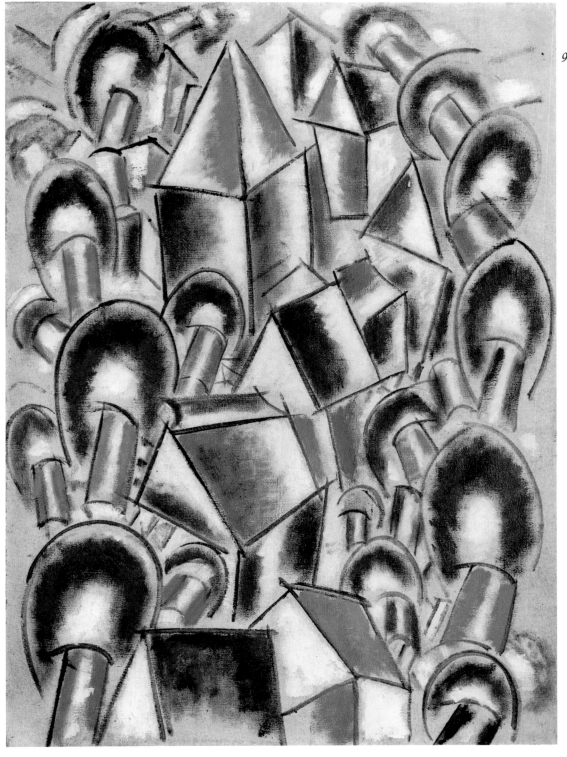

Plate 97   Fernand Léger, *Houses Among Trees*, 1914   No. 182
Oil, 51^1/$_4$ × 38^1/$_4$ in.

similarities which must be considered between Léger's
work and that of other painters who were also concerned
with representing movement and dynamic experiences,
namely the Italian Futurists and Marcel Duchamp whom
he counted among his friends. At no point did Léger ever
try to follow the Futurists in representing crowd scenes,
the sensation of being in a moving vehicle, or the violence
of modern life, because to him their pictorial interests
smacked of illustration and sensationalism. Yet Léger did
have something in common with the Futurists in his
understanding of modern reality, for like them he spoke
of the visual consequences of mechanization and speed. In
a lecture of 1914, for example, justifying his own expressive methods, Léger said: 'The thing depicted is less
stationary, even the object in itself is less discernible than
it used to be. A landscape broken into and traversed in a
car or an express train loses in descriptive value but gains
in synthetic value; the window of the railroad carriage or
the windshield of the car, combined with the speed at
which you are traveling, have changed the familiar look
of things. Modern man registers one hundred times more
impressions than did an eighteenth century artist.'
However, what distinguishes the painting of Léger not
only from that of the Futurists, but also from that of
Delaunay and Duchamp, is the fact that Léger never
wanted to represent movement continuing or evolving
in space. Léger's subject-matter, like that of Braque or
Picasso, is always static: such movement as there is in
his pictures is generated by the compositional elements
themselves, which pile upwards on the picture surface in
an undulating and often sharply punctuated rhythm. How
could it be otherwise when, like the true Cubists, Léger
limited his pictorial space and had no recourse to eye-
fooling perspectives?

The Movement Gathers Momentum, 1911–14

An outline has now been provided of the types of painting being produced by, and the variety of ideas current among, the small group of Parisian artists who were looked upon in 1910–11 as the first representatives of a Cubist school of painting. Once the movement had been launched at the Salon d'Automne in 1910, it rapidly gained adherents, and throughout 1911 there were repeated Cubist displays at the Salon des Indépendants in the spring, at the annual exhibition of the Société des Artistes Indépendants in Brussels in June, and again at the Salon d'Automne in October. The new recruits who began to show with the original group during the year included de La Fresnaye, Lhote, Dunoyer de Segonzac, Duchamp, Villon, Moreau, Picabia, Mare, Laurencin, Duchamp-Villon, Archipenko, and Gris (first appearance at the Indépendants of 1912). By this time the movement had become more self-conscious, while for the public its existence became more real when Apollinaire, in an open-handed preface to the catalogue of the Brussels exhibition, stated that these 'new painters' accepted the 'name of Cubists which has been given to them. However, Cubism is not a system, and the differences which characterize not only the talents but even the styles of these artists are an obvious proof of this.'

At once the Cubist movement began to receive more notice in the press, where it was often laughed at. The principal critics who defended Cubism and were closely involved through friendship with the artists concerned were Guillaume Apollinaire, André Salmon, Roger Allard, Olivier Hourcade★ (who in 1912 wrote 'there is no Cubist school') and Maurice Raynal. These men were behind the idea of the Cubist gallery at the Indépendants of 1911 and were to continue to be active as exhibition organizers and as contact-men, keeping the lines open between the various

★ Author of the most meaningless of all comments: 'The real definition of Cubism it seems to me is: A reassertion of a sense of style through a more subjective vision of nature (sometimes expressed by a more definite notation of mass). The prime interest of Cubism is the absolute difference between one painter and another.' (*Paris-Journal*, 23 October 1912.)

Pls. 48, 49, 254, 255

★ Léger said of Cendrars: 'We were on the same wave-length. Like myself, he picked things up in the streets.' Cendrars was also a close friend of Chagall.

factions as they formed or broke away, and above all with related groups outside France. The only two, who, because of old and close friendships, enjoyed a freedom to visit all the studios were Apollinaire and Raynal; the others moved in more limited circles. But apart from these men, who wrote regular art criticism in newspapers and reviews, there were other men of letters who frequented the studios. Picasso, for instance, had as close friends the poet Max Jacob and Pierre Reverdy, the latter also being very friendly with Braque and Gris. Delaunay and Léger had a close friend in Blaise Cendrars.★ Gleizes and Metzinger, on the other hand, had as their entourage the writers Jacques Nayral' and Alexandre Mercereau, who had formed part of the Symbolist circle around Paul Fort. Thus Cubism spread into the world of literature, writers dedicated books and poems to the painters, and they in turn not only illustrated their friends' books but referred to them visibly in their paintings.

This close connection between writers and artists soon gave rise to the idea that Cubism also existed in a literary form, a notion which gained ground among the artists when, in the spring of 1912, Blaise Cendrars returned to Paris from a visit to America with a long poem entitled *Easter in New York*, which he read in Delaunay's studio to a group of friends including Apollinaire. All those present, it seems, felt that Cendrars' poem was realistic in the way Cubist painting was meant to be. As this reading occurred soon after the opening of the first Futurist Exhibition in Paris (February 1912) and contained lines such as:

Already the city is echoing with a tremendous noise.
Already the trains are leaping, groaning and rolling past,
While the subway is rumbling and thundering underground.

The bridges are shaken by the railroad trains.
The whole city is atremble.

it is not difficult to understand how the idea arose. This novel use of everyday reality as the stuff of poetry struck the members of the Cubist group as similar to their own use of cityscapes and everyday objects as the subject-matter of painting. But here they were confusing Cubism with Modernism. For where Braque and Picasso were intent on creating a new pictorial language and were happy if, despite their technical preoccupations, they could incorporate contemporary elements into their paintings, the painters of the Cubist school, and particularly the Italian Futurists, used Cubist discoveries to give their paintings a sensational modernism. Thus it was not so much the revolutionary technical innovations of the poets which caused them to be thought of as Cubist writers as their lack of fine sentiments, use of a conversational tone and the realistic modernism of their subject-matter. *Easter in New York* undoubtedly influenced Apollinaire's famous poem *Zone,*★ in which he openly rejected 'the old world' and opted for:

★ Written in the fall of 1912.

> *A charming street whose name I forget.*
> . . . .
> *In the morning a siren wails there three times*
> *An angry bell barks out at mid-day.*
> *The inscriptions on the walls, the street-signs*
> *The notices, the name-plates shriek like parrots.*
> *I love the grace of this industrial street.*

Shortly after completing this poem, Apollinaire wrote another entitled *Fenêtres* (Windows) in celebration of the 'orphic' paintings of his friend Delaunay.

★ A painter and a close friend of Léger.

★ Marie Laurencin was pushed into the Cubist group because she was the mistress of Apollinaire. Her painting was not Cubist in any way whatever.

★ The Futurists had heard about what Braque and Picasso were doing from Severini, who lived in Paris but had visited Milan that summer, as well as from the writer Soffici; presumably they had also seen some reproductions of Cubist paintings.

★ Significantly, the only Cubist works by a French painter exhibited before 1914 in Italy was a small group by Gleizes at the Fine Arts Society in Florence in April 1913. By this time the Futurists were claiming to have had their original ideas plagiarized by the French, and in particular by Delaunay.

★ The paintings by Braque and Picasso at all these exhibitions were either lent by the Kahnweiler Gallery in Paris or by private collectors in the different countries.

The year 1912 witnessed the rapid expansion and internationalization of Cubism. The group appeared again in mass at the Indépendants and the Salon d'Automne, where in two large galleries the work of over twenty so-called Cubist painters was hung, among new recruits at this time being Gris, Marcoussis, Herbin, Mondrian, Rivera, and Kupka. A group of Cubist paintings was also on view at the Salon de Juin in Rouen, where Apollinaire delivered a lecture. Then too there was the novelty of Cubism spreading into architecture and interior decoration, for a feature of the Salon d'Automne was a Cubist House, organized by André Mare★ (interior) and Duchamp-Villon (architecture), with paintings and wall-decorations by Léger, de La Fresnaye, Villon, Duchamp, Metzinger, Gleizes and Laurencin.★

In February 1912, the Italian Futurists, who had begun to adopt certain Cubist procedures in their own painting during the fall of 1911★—after seeing the Salon d'Automne in October and doing a round of Parisian studios where for the first time they saw true Cubist works in those of Braque and Picasso—held an exhibition at the Bernheim Gallery. Apollinaire seized the opportunity to point out in his articles for the press not only what they owed to Picasso but also in what respects their painting differed from that of the new generation in France. The show then moved on to London, Berlin, Amsterdam, Vienna, Dresden, and Moscow spreading the knowledge of Futurist and cubistic techniques.★

Germany also suddenly became aware of Cubism at this time. Works by Braque, Picasso, Metzinger, Delaunay and others had already been shown at *avant-garde* Salons in Düsseldorf, Cologne, Berlin, and Munich since 1910.★

But now the newly formed Blaue Reiter group in Munich sponsored the showing of Cubist paintings by Braque, Picasso, de La Fresnaye and especially Delaunay at its inaugural exhibitions in December 1911 and February 1912. Then Marc, Macke, and Klee went to Paris, visited Le Fauconnier, Delaunay and Picasso in their studios, and on their return to Germany began to refer to themselves as German Cubists.

In May 1913, at the exhibition of the *Group of Avant-Garde Artists* in Prague,★ Cubist works by Braque, Picasso, and Gris were shown, while at the same Group's show in 1914 there were Cubist works by Villon, Metzinger, de La Fresnaye, Gleizes and Marcoussis. A second exhibition of modern art, organized by Mercereau for the Mánes Group, was also held in Prague in 1914, and included works by Delaunay, de La Fresnaye, P. H. Bruce, Friesz, Gleizes, Lhote, Metzinger, Marcoussis, Mondrian, Rivera, Villon, and Duchamp-Villon.

★ The artists in control of this more advanced Group had broken away from the Mánes Group in 1911 and were already painting under Cubist influence, having seen original paintings in Paris and in the Kramář collection.

Meanwhile, Cubism had also penetrated to Russia, where between December 1910 and the spring of 1913 Lentulov, Falk and Larionov organized four exhibitions ('*Jack of Diamonds*' Society) in Moscow which included works (selected by Mercereau) by Gleizes, Le Fauconnier, Léger, and Metzinger.★ More important still, however, was the very large collection of Cubist works by Picasso which was being amassed in Moscow between 1908 and 1914 by the merchant Shchukin.

★ Delaunay was also invited, but his paintings never arrived. Paintings of 1908–09 by Braque were seen at the *Golden Fleece* exhibition in Moscow in the spring of 1908 and in January 1909.

Cubist paintings by Braque and Picasso were included in the Second Post-Impressionist Exhibition in London in October 1912, but in the dead artistic climate of England they were laughed to scorn. Cubist paintings by

Gleizes, Gris, Léger, Le Fauconnier, Duchamp, and Metzinger were shown at the Galeries Dalmau in Barcelona in April 1912. In 1911 and 1912 the Circle of Modern Artists in Amsterdam, of which Mondrian was an active member, showed Cubist works by Braque, Picasso, Léger, Gleizes, Le Fauconnier, and Metzinger. New York had its first sight of Cubist works (drawings) by Picasso at the Photo-Secession Gallery in 1911, but its great awakening to Cubist painting did not come of course until The Armory Show of February 1913, which included recent works by Braque, Picasso, Delaunay, Duchamp, Gleizes, de La Fresnaye, Léger, Picabia, Villon, and Archipenko.

The result of this spreading of the movement—which was accompanied by certain hostile demonstrations—was to encourage artists everywhere to look long at Cubism and think about what it had to offer. And this opening of a debate inevitably led to restless experimentation. Cubism could surely be improved on or put to other uses, they seem to have decided. And so between 1912 and 1914 we find the Cubism of Braque and Picasso—which to many artists seemed cold, colorless, static, reasonable or convention-bound—providing the impetus for new movements which assumed a wholly different character: Orphism, Futurism, Cubo-Futurism, Rayonnism, Vorticism, Suprematism, Dadaism and ultimately (1919) Purism. These movements ran the gamut from those which tried to represent movement, or ultra-modern experiences of speed and flight, to others whose aims were non-figurative or involved total abstraction in one form or another, and thus onwards to an art of stylized decoration, to an art compounded of mockery and nihilism (Dada), and at last to the reaction of Purism.

As the Cubist movement spread through Europe, so confusion grew. Each new idea had to be publicized, manifestos in several languages made their appearance, and each new faction laid claim to better, greater and more significant achievements. Small wonder, then, that not only the public but even the artists themselves were bewildered. So in 1912–13 the Parisian critics and writers started to make a great effort to explain what Cubism was all about and to classify its different manifestations. First in the field was André Salmon, already an old friend of Picasso, whose volume *La Jeune Peinture Francaise*, published in the fall of 1912, contained an informative, sharply discriminating chapter entitled 'Anecdotal History of Cubism,' which was based on personal observation of the events related. Next came Gleizes and Metzinger with a largely theoretical exegesis entitled *Du Cubisme*,★ published at the end of 1912. It was at the beginning of this year that Apollinaire had published his two articles on Futurist painting, distinguishing it from Cubism. But in October 1912, he brought out a slight, though very personal, account of Cubism proper, entitled *The Beginnings of Cubism*, and he followed this up in December 1912 with a much more serious article on the painting of Delaunay in which, using the artist's own words, he demonstrated how he too had diverged from true Cubism. Then finally in his booklet *Les Peintres Cubistes: Méditations Esthétiques*, published in the spring of 1913, where the text consisted of a re-working of passages from articles which had appeared during the past four years, plus some freshly written additional chapters, Apollinaire produced what has long passed for the first serious analysis of Cubist painting as it was understood by those participating at the time. Today we know that many of the ideas put forward in these various publications were misguided, also that

★ English language edition *Cubism* published (London) in the spring of 1913.

they enshrine many errors of fact. But they are of interest because they reflect certain notions which were in the air and are symptomatic of the belief in Cubism as a new artistic force.

As the number of self-styled adherents to Cubism grew and groups of different nationalities—all with different ideas—attached themselves to the Parisian nucleus, so the semblance of unity disappeared. Delaunay was the first to break away openly when, in the summer of 1912 (after painting *The City of Paris*), he formed a small coterie of his own which included his old friend Apollinaire, Cendrars, and two new painters, Chagall and Patrick Bruce, an American. Gleizes and Metzinger tried to counter this break and preserve the appearance of a coherent militant movement by forming their own new discussion group, *Les Artistes de Passy*, in October 1912, to which they attracted de La Fresnaye, Picabia, Villon and Duchamp-Villon, as well as certain critics. It was, however, Apollinaire, the perfect fixer, who in the name of friendship and The Modern Movement, was the most adept at glossing over irreconcilable differences of outlook, by finding room for everyone in his Cubist embrace. He even went so far as to suggest that Matisse, Rouault, Laurencin, and Van Dongen were Cubist painters at heart.

A serious division of opinion developed in the Cubist group in the summer of 1912 over the question of whether realism or abstraction was the real goal of Cubist painting. The principal champions of abstraction gathered in the suburban studios at Puteaux of a mathematically and scientifically minded trio of brothers: Jacques Villon, Marcel Duchamp, and Raymond Duchamp-Villon. The three brothers gave a scientific twist to Cubism and drew into their circle a few kindred spirits such as Gleizes, Léger, Picabia, Lhote, Kupka, and Gris. It was this group which thought up the idea of organizing an independent Cubist exhibition under the title *La Section d'Or*, which opened to the accompaniment of considerable press publicity at the Galerie la Boëtie in October 1912. A special periodical edited by Reverdy was produced for the occasion with articles by Apollinaire, Salmon, Raynal, Nayral and Hourcade. Some two hundred works by thirty artists were put on view, among newcomers being Marcoussis, Marchand, Dumont, Archipenko (who was to announce two months later that he had severed all connection with the Cubist group), and such near-academic artists as Girieud, Tobeen, Luc-Albert Moreau, Le Beau, Valensi and Dunoyer de Segonzac. The one obvious absentee (apart from Braque and Picasso) was of course Delaunay. The idea behind this exhibition was to 'present the Cubists, no matter of what tendency . . . as the most serious and most interesting artists of this epoch' (Apollinaire). To this end, each artist was invited to send not only his most recent works but a group illustrating his development over the past three years. Thus this exhibition represented yet another attempt to clarify the situation and was important for establishing the prestige of the Cubists.

Despite Delaunay's secession from the group, Apollinaire was not prepared to desert his friend, more especially since at this time Delaunay's 'Orphist' theories began to have a considerable influence on painting in other European countries. So in January 1913 he accompanied Delaunay to Berlin for the opening of his one-man show at the Sturm Gallery, publishing a long new poem on his *Windows* in the catalogue and an explanatory article in

★ e.g. Zervos Catalog, Vol. II, Nos. 303, 353 (1912).

the Gallery's monthly periodical *Der Sturm*.★ The Sturm Gallery was an international *avant-garde* center run by Herwarth Walden, which embraced Expressionism, Futurism, Cubism, Orphism and Abstract Art, and where the German impresario-dealer hopefully tried to bring the multifarious strands of the modern movements in Germany, France, Italy, Holland and Russia into a meaningful relationship. But, alas for Delaunay and Apollinaire, the outcome of their trip was to bring the Cubist movement into still greater disrepute with the public. For on their return to Paris '*le Cubisme*' soon began to be referred to as '*Der Kubismus*'—helped perhaps by the fact that the letters '*KUB*' (a brand of soup cubes) appeared in pictures by Picasso★—and for a long while to come the suspicion persisted that Cubism was in some way unpatriotic.

By the early months of 1913, the Paris school of Cubists was in ferment, no coherent style had evolved, and the idiom which Apollinaire and others had for so long proclaimed to be both reasonable and French was felt to be developing dangerous international affiliations. This provided an excuse for the bourgeoisie, who could not recognize what was represented pictorially and had already decided that Cubism was simply flaunting accepted aesthetic principles, entrenched conventions and even the recognized use of the technical means, to bring its fear and resentment into the open. In the tense atmosphere of these pre-war months, feeling began to mount, so that just after the opening of the *Section d'Or* a Municipal Councillor of Paris, named Lampué, published in the *Mercure de France* (16 October 1912) an Open Letter to the Under-Secretary for the Fine Arts protesting against the admission of the Cubists to the Salon d'Automne. Then in December a Socialist Deputy, Jean-Louis Breton, made a similar interpellation in the Chamber, protesting that it was outrageous for 'buildings belonging to the nation to be used for demonstrations of such an unmistakably anti-artistic and anti-national character.' Fortunately, another Socialist deputy, Marcel Sembat, who was in sympathy with the new art, was on hand to reply tartly that Breton had no need to look at what he did not like, but no right whatever to think of calling in the police. Even so, feelings were not calmed.

Apollinaire had become converted to a belief in the great future awaiting Cubism and the new art during 1911. Since then he had made every effort to present and explain the unruly elements of the *avant-garde* to the public as part of one great constructive movement. But despite his manoeuvres he was unable to keep the Cubist movement together. The outbreak of war in 1914 thus resolved many an awkward situation by consummating the break-up of the group, both in France and elsewhere. However, by that time the essential aesthetic battle had been won, fruitful and unfruitful artistic experiments had opened doors to new possibilities, and the true Cubists had entered upon a great constructive period which was to carry the style forward for several years to come. The Renaissance tradition seemed then a thing of the past, and all young painters in Europe—even in America—were ready to profit by the outcome of the Cubist revolution, which had already laid the foundations of a new international pictorial language.

Types of Cubism

Before analyzing the stylistic variants and deviations which were nourished and inspired by the revolutionary achievements of the true Cubists, it is essential to repeat that

Braque and Picasso were not directly involved with any faction. They allowed their paintings to be exhibited outside of France alongside those of the other so-called Cubists, while maintaining their creative independence and never trying to assert any kind of authority. Indeed Picasso's aloofness made of him a somewhat legendary and prestigious figure. Few people were privileged to see the paintings in his studio, yet he got full credit for having invented Cubism because by some curious twist of fortune Braque—whose name had been just as prominent at the start—was rarely mentioned after 1909 except as one of his followers. Thus Cubism, so far as the French public was concerned, was what it actually saw and read about. And it is not unfair to say that this was largely the production of lesser talents and of a considerable number of artists who were not French by birth.

★ Metzinger, Gleizes, Delaunay, Léger, Le Fauconnier, Apollinaire, Mercereau, Nayral, and Salmon had all frequented Paul Fort's gatherings at the Closerie des Lilas on Tuesday evenings.

★ Braque is the one exception. He renounced the colorist art of Fauvism in 1907 when, after studying paintings by Cézanne, he 'saw something different' in nature.

Two factors have to be borne in mind when considering the art of The Cubist Epoch: first, that many of the artists and writers of the Paris group had once belonged to the Symbolist circle;★ second, that many others were by temperament anti-traditionalist above all and therefore predisposed to find in Cubism a convenient tool of destruction. All those coming from the Symbolist circle had a colorist past, so that unlike Braque and Picasso they were not attracted by the formal and realistic possibilities of Cubism.★ They did not want to arrive at a truer and more complete pictorial representation of reality but envisaged a 'pure' form of painting which would be a visual equivalent to music and poetry. Hence their predisposition to regard Cubism as a stage on the path towards an art of total abstraction. Other members of the Cubist group proceeded, on the contrary, by calculation and theory rather than by intuition: they believed in the intellectual appeal of proportions, shapes and a balanced design without regard for its visual meaning, so that they began by stylizing and later accepted an abstract design as a valid substitute for an image of reality. Then there were those who believed in the negation of all inherited notions about painting and regarded the Cubist breakthrough as only a first step towards new techniques to express a new vision of reality and new sensations as well. These artists saw themselves as the interpreters of novel experiences which should affect modern man not only in his life but in his imaginative outlook, and they tried to borrow from modern inventions, such as machinery and the motion picture, the means for doing so.

With this picture in mind of the different tendencies existing within the Cubist movement it is necessary to look back at the way in which Apollinaire proceeded to classify them in *Les Peintres Cubistes*. This classification no longer has any validity, but it must be recorded because it was the first. Apollinaire identified four tendencies in Cubism, two of which he described as being 'pure': 'Scientific Cubism' and 'Orphic Cubism.' The former he defined as 'the art of painting new structures with elements borrowed not from visual reality but from the reality of knowledge,' and cited as the representative artists Picasso, Braque, Gleizes, Metzinger, Gris, Laurencin, Marcoussis, and Villon. Next, Apollinaire defined 'Orphic Cubism' as 'the art of painting new structures out of elements which have not been borrowed from visual reality but entirely created by the artist and endowed by him with a powerful reality. The works of the Orphic artist must simultaneously offer a pure aesthetic pleasure, a structure which is self-evident, and a sublime meaning, that is to say the subject.' As representatives of this form of

Cubism, Apollinaire named of course first Delaunay, then Léger, Picabia, Duchamp, Dumont and Valensi. The confusions and contradictions underlying these first two categories are self-evident. Apollinaire's third type, 'Physical Cubism,' was defined simply as painting in which use is made of 'elements borrowed from visual reality,' and he named as representatives Le Fauconnier, Marchand, Herbin, and Véra. The link with Cubism here is obviously very tenuous. Apollinaire's last category, 'Instinctive Cubism,' is meaningless and was thought up to cover the work of any of his friends who showed *avant-garde* tendencies. Apollinaire defines it as painting in which use is made of elements borrowed 'from the reality suggested to the artist by instinct and intuition,' and cites as representatives Matisse, Rouault, Derain, Dufy, Chabaud, Puy, Van Dongen, Severini, and Boccioni. It is noteworthy that Apollinaire mentions only one artist who was not resident in Paris and had not taken part in any of the Cubist exhibitions: Boccioni. But then, he had been impressed by Boccioni's work and had written in February 1912 that 'Above all, Boccioni paints under the influence of Picasso, who today dominates the whole field of young painting, not only in Paris but throughout the world.'

Apollinaire's attempt at classifying the various tendencies of the Cubist movement was vague and unsatisfactory. Cubism as it was invented and practiced by Picasso and Braque was certainly not 'scientific,' since it was wholly guided by intuition—and this is by no means the only objection one can raise. I would propose, with today's hindsight, a more exclusive but I believe more meaningful classification of the forms of Cubism. First, True or Instinctive Cubism, a category reserved for the work of Braque and Picasso, the true creators of the movement, as well as of two other artists closely related to them in intention and method, Juan Gris and Fernand Léger. Next, it seems to me, we cannot make any valid distinction between the work of a great many artists who flirted with Cubism, or made of it a system, either by applying cubification as a stylistic formula or on the basis of mathematical calculation, and who in the end either relapsed into a dreary academicism or crossed the frontier into non-figuration. This second category, to which I would give the all-embracing name of Systematic Cubism, covers the work of Le Fauconnier, Gleizes, Metzinger, de La Fresnaye, Marchand, Herbin, Lhote, Marcoussis, Picabia, Férat, Rivera and later Hayden. Delaunay deserves a third category to himself. For although he was not a 'true' Cubist before 1911 and became a 'systematizing' Cubist in *The City of Paris*, he went on to create a Cubist derivative of his own, namely Orphism—for want of anything better, I accept Apollinaire's adjective—which inspired the artistic conceptions of the Blaue Reiter group, as well as of Larionov's Rayonnism and the work of Valensi, Kupka, and Chagall, and finally the American artists Patrick Bruce, Arthur Frost, Morgan Russell and Stanton MacDonald-Wright. This leaves us with works of a fourth and final category, which I call Kinetic Cubism, because the artists involved—Duchamp, Villon, the Italian Futurists and in America Joseph Stella—took over from true Cubism a certain formal vocabulary which they tried to apply in their paintings to represent actual movement.

Of course these classifications are not watertight, because the Cubist Epoch was a time of experiment and influences were easily exchanged. But at least they serve to isolate more clearly the salient characteristics of each of the four types.

The Puteaux Group and the *Section d'Or,* 1911–13

★ The middle brother, Raymond Duchamp-Villon, was a sculptor. His work will be discussed later.

★ G. H. Hamilton and William C. Agee, *R. Duchamp-Villon* (New York 1967), p. 12.

The three brothers Duchamp★ provided that thoughtful but provocative intellectual element that for a short while put a semblance of new life into the Cubist movement. They became friendly with Gleizes and Metzinger early in 1911, and within a few months had decided on the path that Cubism could, and should, follow and were trying to put it into practice in their own work. By 1913 they had already lost interest and abandoned Cubism. The brothers Duchamp were, as George Heard Hamilton has written,★ 'thinkers rather than doers, given to reflection on the nature of art and artists, and delighting as much in the formulation of problems as in their solution.' Eager talkers, they attracted round them a circle of artists who met in Villon's suburban studio at Puteaux, including Gleizes, Metzinger, Léger, Gris, and Archipenko.

Temperamentally, the two brothers Jacques and Marcel were different, Villon being cautious and methodical, Duchamp imaginative and impetuous, and this difference was reflected in their painting. Villon's artistic background was also different from that of Duchamp, who had been an undistinguished painter all along. Villon, on the other hand, had been a successful humorous illustrator for ten years, but when he took up Cubism his ideas on painting had recently been stimulated and formed by studying Pythagorean theory and reading Leonardo's *Trattato della Pittura*. This gave him the edge as a theorist over his brother and will account for their general idea that Cubism should evolve through analysis towards abstraction. The novelty of Cubism appealed to them, and like Apollinaire they believed that it could have lasting value. But they were competitive by nature, had no intention of becoming disciples of Braque and Picasso and even less of allowing them to establish exclusive rights over the form of an art which was intended to express the modern mode of vision. So the two brothers quickly came to the conclusion that what Cubism needed in order to fulfil itself was the discipline of mathematical calculation, a reasoned but vigorous use of color and the injection of expressive new ideas and techniques. Moreover, great individualists though they were, the Duchamp brothers also wanted to see these aims achieved through a communal effort.

The first group manifestation organized by the artists of the Puteaux Group was the creation of a Cubist House at the Salon d'Automne of 1912, which turned out to be a tame, uninspiring effort. The building was a symmetrical eighteenth-century-type pavilion which had angular, prismatic moldings in the place of swirling rococo curves, while the interior (to judge by photographs) was an uncomfortable blend of up-to-date *art nouveau* and the latest in painting. This venture would be difficult to account for unless we knew that the intention was to bring home to people that architecture was the framework holding the arts together, and that Cubism had come to stay and was destined to invade their daily life. Yet by this time, Duchamp had already abandoned Cubism, while there was still no suggestion of Cubist influence in Duchamp-Villon's sculpture. The second undertaking of the Puteaux Group was more interesting and of far greater significance: the *Section d'Or* Exhibition of October 1912. This was intended both as a declaration of independence from true Cubism and as a demonstration that the Cubist movement was already strong and creative enough on its own to embrace many different types of personality. All tendencies were represented in the show, from the near-academic and inept to the most experimental and daring. A great many of the works were brightly colored, and several large canvases represented elaborate traditional-type subjects having a general significance; for another ground on which the Puteaux Group criticized Braque and Picasso was that their type of Cubism lacked human interest. Gleizes was represented by *Women in a Kitchen* and *Harvest Threshing*, while Metzinger contributed the *Portrait of Gleizes* and *The Yellow Feather*. A more dynamic section included a large group of figure compositions and cityscapes by Léger, as well as Picabia's *Dances at the Spring*, Duchamp's *Portrait of Chess-Players* and *Nude Descending a Staircase, No. 2* and a convulsive suburban landscape with trails of factory smoke and flowering trees by Villon, as well as his *Young Girl*. True Cubism was represented only by a group of early and rather systematic works by Gris, including *The Watch* and *Man in a Café*. A more way-out tendency was represented by the work of the Czech painter, Frank Kupka, a friend of the Duchamp brothers, who had settled in Puteaux in 1904. He was the only representative of the Duchamp brothers' aspiration to see Cubism developing away from reality towards abstraction and musicality. Kupka fitted perfectly too with their real or assumed belief that it was time for intellect and imagination to assert their primacy over intuition. In 1911, Kupka had given up working in a representational idiom to adopt an invented, abstract, expressionistic style of his own based on parallel planes and interlocking discs of color. His purpose in doing this, he said, was 'to liberate color from form,' because he believed that the artist could not compete with the camera and was thus free to find in painting 'something that lies between the visible and that which can be heard.'

This aim of course had nothing to do with Cubism. But it is fascinating to note that contemporaneously Kupka

Pls. 62, 65

Pls. 108, 110

Pl. 100

Pl. 224

had the aim 'to liberate color from form' in order to approach musicality in painting, while Delaunay suppressed line in order to free color and create form in space by 'simultaneous' contrasts of tone. On the other hand, when Braque and Picasso separated the functions of line from those of color, in the first *papiers collés*, they went on to recreate objects with a more complete pictorial reality and physical independence.

Villon, Duchamp and Picabia, 1911–13

Jacques Villon was a restrained painter who never sought to make a striking effect, had a fine sense of line and a subtle personal sense of color. Indeed he once said he was 'the Impressionist Cubist,' and this description is apposite because a play of light and luminous tonalities were distinctive features of his work. Villon's tentative beginning on the path towards Cubism can be seen in a portrait of his brother Raymond Duchamp-Villon (1911), where the faceted, analytical treatment of the spot-lit head shows a will to represent the whole mass in the manner of Cézanne and 1909 Picasso. By 1912 Villon was, however, already attempting a freer and more lyrical style of painting based on transparent planes of color—the forms and volumes of objects being drawn over them—as in *The Dinner Table*. The subjects of these paintings are static. But later in 1912 Villon modified his style, under the combined influences it seems of Gleizes, Delaunay and the Futurists, in such a way that he broke up his forms, used overlapping planes of color to express volume and space, abandoned linear definition, but introduced lines of force and connected formal repetitions to evoke a vigorous sense of movement. Yet beneath the surface animation, Villon composed his picture in accordance with a predetermined geometrical scheme, so that in

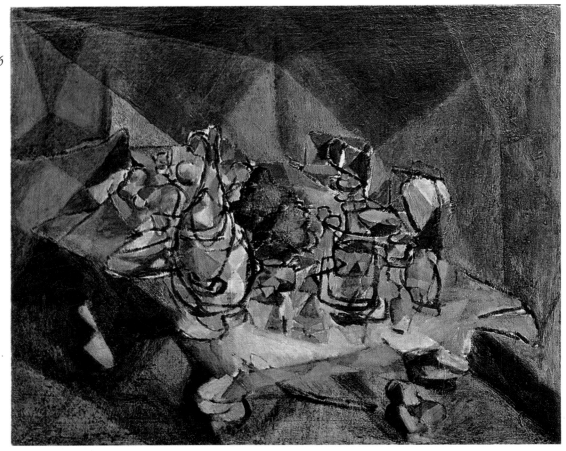

Plate 98

Jacques Villon, *The Dinner-Table*, 1912
Oil, $25^3/_4 \times 32$ in.

No. 311

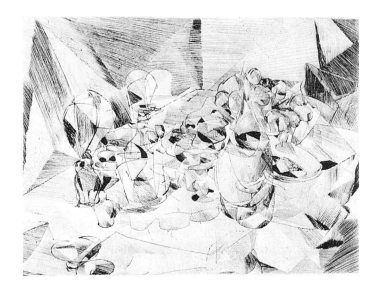

Plate 99

Jacques Villon
The Dinner-Table, 1913
Drypoint, $11^1/_8 \times 15^1/_8$ in.

No. 316

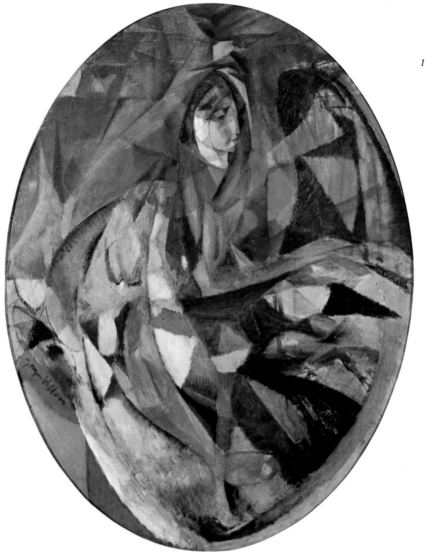

Plate 100

Jacques Villon
Little Girl at Piano, 1912
Oil, 51 × 38 in. (Oval)

No. 310

Pl. 100 *Young Girl* or *Little Girl at the Piano* (1912) for instance, the placing of the limbs and even the outlines of the figure were not determined by observed fact but by his preestablished mathematical division of the canvas. In both of these paintings, Villon indicated that the figure was not static by a simple kinetic effect: he repeated the forms of the arms, shoulders, body and feet in a short sequence. This represents a sincere attempt to apply the Cubist technique of separate aspects for a new purpose, and there is Cubist influence too in the way Villon used an analytical technique to represent forms and volume in a shallow *Pl. 104* pictorial space. Similarly the *Portrait of Mlle. Y. D.* (1913) is Cubist painting of a sort, though here the subject is

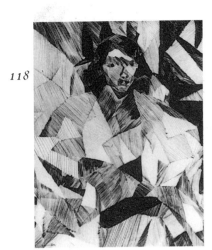
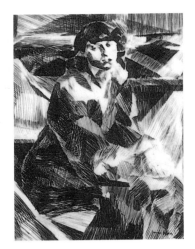
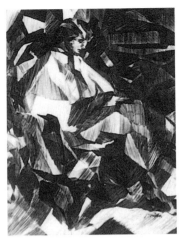

Plate 101

Jacques Villon
Mlle. Y. D., Full Face, 1913
Drypoint, $21^5/_8 \times 16^3/_8$ in.

No. 315

Plate 102

Jacques Villon
Portrait of a Young Woman, 1913
Drypoint, $21^1/_2 \times 16^1/_4$ in.

No. 317

Plate 103

Jacques Villon
Yvonne in Profile, 1913
Drypoint, $21^1/_2 \times 16^1/_4$ in.

No. 318

Pl. 110

again static, the faceting of forms correspondingly clearer (it is comparable with Gleizes' *Women in a Kitchen*) and the planar structure less complex. But with *Soldiers on the March* (1913), Villon came closer to Futurist painting. In this pale prismatic composition, Villon used line as an element divorced from color (which for the most part evokes space, but is also partly descriptive) to define primarily the stylized forms of the soldiers. These are outlined against an elaborate and mathematically determined structure of cubes and triangles which, by tonal and formal interplay, evoke the space through which the regiment moves. But again this is basically a static painting, because the movement is arrested. Therefore in order to suggest the forward movement of the soldiers Villon was obliged to introduce some accented lines of force. Thus it is not the movement which accounts here for the break-up of the forms (as it would in a Futurist painting) but the application of a cubistic system of analysis. Stylistically, therefore, *Soldiers on the March* represents an intermediate achievement in which Villon tried to bring elements both of Cubism and of Futurism together to serve a kinetic purpose. But from this point—and his brother Duchamp had abandoned kinetic Cubism over a year before, after painting the *Nude Descending a Staircase, No. 2*—Villon began to move towards the wholly abstract art which he was to practice after the war. For in his *Seated Woman* of 1914 reality was not merely stylized but suppressed in favour of a brightly colored

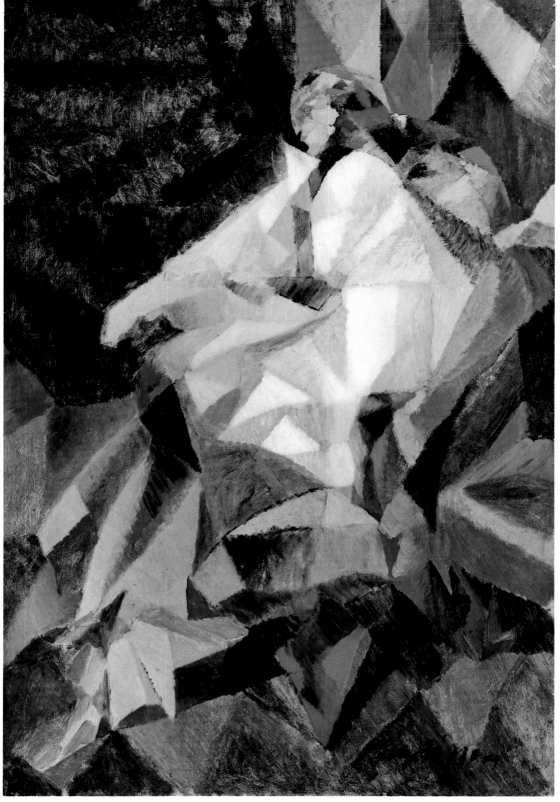

Plate 104 Jacques Villon, *Portrait of Mlle. Y. D.*, 1913 No. 312
Oil, $50^3/4 \times 35$ in.

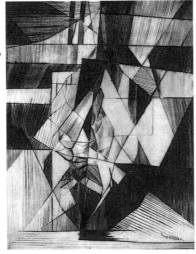

Plate 105

Jacques Villon
Tightrope Walker, 1913
Drypoint, 15³/₄ × 11⁷/₈ in.

No. 314

Plate 106

Jacques Villon
Portrait of an Actor (Felix Barré), 1913
Drypoint, 15³/₄ × 12³/₈ in.

No. 313

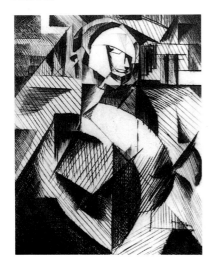

pattern of flat, shaped forms with only a faint representational signification.

Marcel Duchamp's contribution to the extension of Cubism is hard to evaluate, because it is not easy to separate what he intended as a serious contribution from what he intended as a mockery of what he feared might turn into a new convention. For Duchamp, who had a very clever, agile mind, had an uncanny knack of being able to exploit the absurd while seeming to be completely serious. When Duchamp began to interest himself in Cubism, at the end of 1911, he certainly had a good working knowledge of its aims and methods. Yet at the same time he had an ambition to outshine Braque and Picasso as a true Cubist or to create his own more realistic and impressive form of Cubism. On the other hand, as his work both before and after his Cubist interlude (1911–12) proves, Duchamp lacked the mastery as a painter which he would have liked to possess, and it was this shortcoming which drove him to submerge his creative talents in the sarcasm of anti-art before abandoning painting altogether. Sarcasm was a fundamental strain in Duchamp's character, and it is significant that among his favourite books in these Cubist years were the poems of Jules Laforgue, an early Symbolist but anti-romantic who wrote in a colloquial, sometimes coarse, inconsequent style about everyday happenings, and also the stories of Raymond Roussel, a disruptive, ironical personality who could describe supernatural happenings and fantastic inventions—for example, a painting-machine—in an impassive matter-of-fact tone.

Between 1907 and 1910, Duchamp was producing undistinguished paintings in the colorist tradition of the

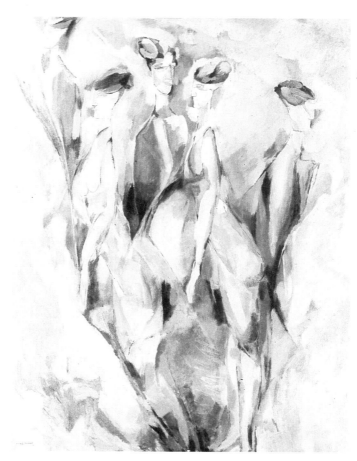

Plate 107

Marcel Duchamp
Portrait, 1911
Oil, 57⅝ × 44⅞ in.

No. 71

Nabis and Fauves. However, under the influence of his brother Villon, Duchamp began to be interested in Cubism in the spring of 1911 and adopted a limited palette of ochre, green and grey. In a short space of time, Duchamp produced a group of pictures in which he experimented with the Cubist device of 'simultaneous aspects'—which Braque and Picasso used to recreate form and volume—for a new purpose. Instead of forming one synthesized image out of several aspects, Duchamp in *Portrait* (1911) represented the same figure on different planes and in different attitudes to express more of the individual as well as the concept Woman. No movement was involved here. But at the end of 1911, Duchamp started to combine different aspects into a single image to represent a succession of evolving movements. Thus in *Portrait of Chess-Players* (December 1911) the two tense and thoughtful contestants are shown united, as it were, around the pawn which one of them holds in his hand in the foreground. Duchamp has

Pl. 107

Pl. 108

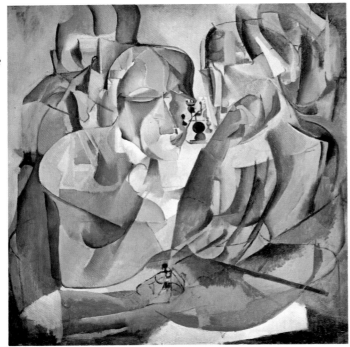

Plate 108

Marcel Duchamp
Portrait of Chess-Players, 1911
Oil, $39^5/_8 \times 39^3/_4$ in.

No. 72

then represented the head of each two or three times, on the same plane, in full-face and profile, and done the same with their arms and hands, to evoke their restless movements during play. Furthermore he has tried to symbolize what is going on in their minds by representing other chess-men on a narrow plane which hovers between their two heads. This is not a painting in which the artist has tried to represent reality in its solid tangible aspects: indeed nothing seems stable, the figures dissolve into their surroundings and are painted as though they were transparent. Yet Duchamp's idea—and he was an intellectual in art—was to find an equivalent realism in non-imitative painting to express the tenseness engendered by a game of chess. Of course, he drew on the pictorial ideas of the Futurists for his kinetic effect.* But in his conceptual approach, in his use of an analytical procedure, in the effort he made to arrest the movement and keep the composition flat and on the surface of the canvas, Duchamp was animated by a Cubist spirit. His pictorial solution is not wholly successful, but *Portrait of Chess-Players* can be accepted as a valid attempt to extend the language of Cubism. And this is also true of *The Coffee-Grinder* of the same date.

* The Futurist Manifesto of Painting had been published in the French press in 1909. Several of the Futurist painters had visited Paris in October 1911. But no Futurist paintings were exhibited in Paris before February 1912.

Pls. 109, 110

Pl. 109

The Coffee-Grinder must however be considered together with the *Sad Young Man in a Train* and the first two versions of *Nude Descending a Staircase*, all four painted between November 1911 and January 1912. The interest of these four paintings, which complement each other, is that they reveal how shallow Duchamp's interest in Cubism was and how quickly he was in reaction against it. All four involve (though on an imaginative not a visual plane) the representation of movement by new pictorial means: in the first, the functional rotation of a household gadget; in the second, a figure standing, swaying and being jolted in the coach of a moving train; and in the last two, the successive movements of a walking figure. Another interesting aspect of these four paintings is that they illustrate the passage in Duchamp's work from images of Man to Machine images. *The Coffee-Grinder* is a witty schematic diagram, but inspired by Cubism in so far as Duchamp recreated the gadget conceptually, and in two dimensions. This is still partially true of the first version of the *Nude Descending a Staircase*, where the successive stages of the abstract figure walking down a staircase are represented as a continuous image as in a stroboscopic photograph. But there is a pictorial dichotomy in this experimental picture which makes it much less Cubist. For whereas the abstract, modeled forms of the figure exist on a single plane and have only an ambiguous anatomical connotation, the staircase and the space through which the figure moves are represented naturalistically. The *Sad Young Man* represents a greater pictorial innovation, for there Duchamp was more interested in representing movement than in representing a figure, and he achieved his purpose by a repetition of abstract forms swaying to left and right from a pivotal point (legs) in the center foreground. However, his most astonishing innovation occurred in the second

124

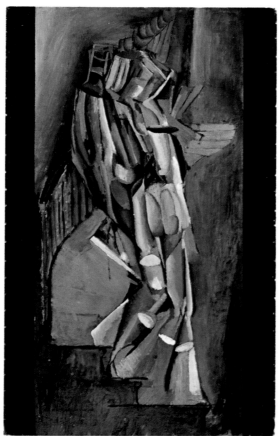

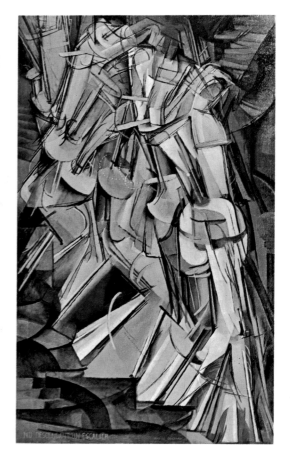

124

Plate 109

Marcel Duchamp
Nude Descending a Staircase No. 1,
1911–12
Oil, 37³/₄ × 23¹/₂ in.

No. 73   *Pl. 110*

version of *Nude Descending a Staircase* (January 1912). For there Duchamp rejected any suggestion of representing reality and turned the figure into a symbolic but seemingly powerful machine—a sort of descending-machine, in fact—which rattles its metallic structure and devours the staircase as it descends. This second *Nude* is an intensely clever but equivocal painting, part serious, part ironical, part revolutionary, owing something both to Futurism and to the cinema, but fundamentally anti-Cubist. For there is no doubt that Duchamp intended to produce an ultra-modern subject-picture which would be understood as an assault on the seriousness and static realism of the Cubist painting of Braque and Picasso, but which would also shake up the Cubist pretensions of his friends. At all events, the challenge proved so devastating that Duchamp's *Nude* was rejected by the jury of the Indépendants in 1912. Two years later, during which time Duchamp made no play with Cubism at all, he abandoned serious painting to become a Dada funster. Thus his

Plate 110

Marcel Duchamp
*Nude Descending a Staircase No. 2
(Definitive version)*, 1912
Oil, 58×35 in.

No. 74

activity in the Cubist movement lasted barely one year, although before passing on to other things he attempted to make a fruitful contribution but ended up making a subversive comment.

The third painter closely associated with the Duchamp brothers was Francis Picabia, a Cuban of French and Spanish descent, who was a less serious artist but almost as fertile in ideas as Duchamp himself. He too had begun painting in a Neo-Impressionist manner, but in 1911 Picabia had been introduced to the Cubist group by Apollinaire and soon after began to experiment with Cubist techniques. Picabia's flirtation with Cubism lasted only a few months and he made less constructive effort to extend its range than did Duchamp. Yet *Dances at the Spring* and *Procession in Seville*, both painted in

Pl. 111

Plate 111

Francis Picabia
Procession in Seville, 1912
Oil, 48×48 in.

No. 224

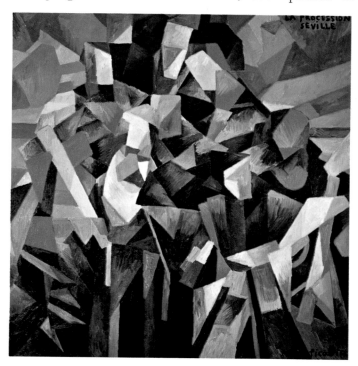

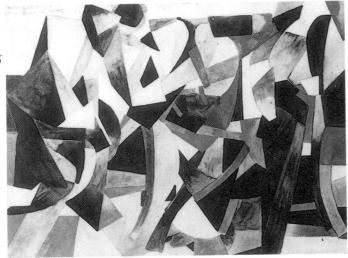

Plate 112

Francis Picabia
Star Dancer and Her School of Dancing, 1913
Watercolor, $21^7/_8 \times 29^7/_8$ in.

No. 225

the spring of 1912, are curious if somewhat naïvely jazzed-up variants on early Cubist compositions. Both of these paintings derived from a visual experience of reality—peasants dancing in a landscape near Naples and an Easter procession of flagellants in Seville—but Picabia was not concerned to re-create this pictorially either in physical or in spatial terms. He aimed simply at transposing the forceful rhythm of the scene into half-abstract pictorial terms. In order to achieve this he drew on Picasso's sculptural paintings of 1907 and, to a lesser degree, on the technique of Léger in his paintings of 1910. For Picabia employed block-like, crudely faceted forms, disposed in contrasted but interlocking rhythms spreading across the surface of the canvas, and enhanced the movement thus established with sharp color contrasts of blue, orange and brown reinforced with a violent play of light and shadow. These cannot be considered as Cubist paintings, even though certain forms have a figurative reference, because they are basically conceived in non-figurative terms. What is more, they were followed in 1913 by some wholly non-figurative paintings in which Picabia abandoned any suggestion of Cubist borrowings, so that to represent *Physical Culture*, for example, he chose a series of defined and contrasted abstract shapes revolving and evolving in a pictorially ambiguous space. And from there on, Picabia joined Duchamp as a leading Dadaist.

Pl. 112

Lesser Painters of the Cubist Movement, 1911–13 : de Segonzac, Moreau, Marchand, Lhote, Herbin, Rivera, Férat, Chagall, Marcoussis and de La Fresnaye

Many painters chosen to exhibit in the collective manifestations of the Cubist group were men of limited talents, who remained on the fringe of the movement and had no ambition to make a creative contribution. Most of them even clung to a basically naturalistic vision: they were caught up in the general reaction against the formlessness of Impressionism and had come under the spell of Cézanne in 1910–11. To these men, Cubism was no more than a modern 'constructive discipline' which could be imposed on reality. That is to say, their appreciation of true Cubism was barely skin-deep and they employed a timid sort of faceting and cubification as a pictorial system. This sort of flirtation with Cubism could, inevitably, be only of short duration. Apollinaire, who encouraged these artists, also judged them correctly when he said that theirs was not a pure art, because in it 'what is properly the subject— that is to say painting itself—is confused with images,' that is to say genre scenes, allegorical figures and visions of contemporary life.

André Dunoyer de Segonzac and Luc-Albert Moreau, who were close friends, cannot be considered as Cubist painters at all. The most that can be said to explain and justify their inclusion in Cubist exhibitions is that in 1911–12 they used a predominantly dark and earthy palette, simplified their forms and resorted to elementary formal analysis. It was, of course, Apollinaire who had brought these men into the Cubist milieu in order to increase the numbers of adherents.

Jean Marchand was painting in a post-Cézannesque manner already in 1910, and in 1912 was for a while influenced by Futurist painting. Yet he too was at heart a naturalistic painter, as he showed in all his later work. André Lhote

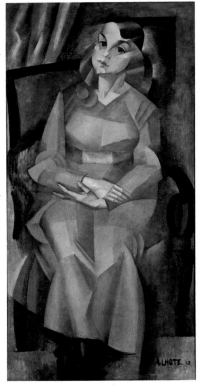

Plate 113

André Lhote
Portrait of Marguerite, 1913
Oil, 63³/₄ × 33¹/₂ in.

No. 189

discovered the work of Cézanne in 1911 and a year later was practicing an ineffective, mannered form of cubification. He continued to work in this style for a year or two (*Portrait of Marguerite*, 1913) before establishing himself subsequently, in his writings as much as in his paintings, as 'the academician of Cubism' (Rosenblum). Auguste Herbin, another member of the Cubist entourage, installed himself in 1909 in a studio in the '*bateau-lavoir*' in Montmartre, where Picasso and Gris lived. At the time he was still painting under the influence of Gauguin and the Fauves, though with heavy-handed stylizations. In 1911–12 Herbin adopted a coarse type of cubistic stylization, which he applied in landscapes and still lifes. But his interest in Cubism never developed further, and by 1917 he had arrived at a decorative idiom composed of stylized elements drawn from reality and assembled (as in the later work of Metzinger) with little representational logic. Later still Herbin evolved an art of total abstraction.

Diego Rivera too came late to Cubism, since he did not adopt the idiom until after his return to Paris from Mexico at the end of 1911. But for a few years (*Portrait of Lipchitz, Still-Life*) he showed an understanding of what it was about and handled the idiom deftly, though he gave no signs of an original vision in his Cubist paintings. Serge Férat, who met Picasso in 1910, was a close friend of Apollinaire and co-editor with him of the influential Cubist review *Les Soirées de Paris* (1912–14). He painted a number of colorful cubistic compositions in which fragments of objects are assembled with more regard for decorative effect than for logic. Cocteau once said of these paintings that Férat had 'removed a source of embarrassment by taking the insulting sting out of the word "charming".'

Pl. 115

Pl. 235

Marc Chagall, always at heart a fabulator, presents the more curious case of an artist wholly opposed in spirit to Cubism who became for a brief moment involved in the movement. After arriving in Paris from Moscow in 1910, Chagall set about improving the heavy folk-idiom which he had acquired in Russia by injecting into it more sophisticated colorist and formal techniques borrowed from various artists of the School of Paris. He was in short a real eclectic. Thus in *Cubist Still Life* (1912) he borrowed from Gauguin and Cézanne ways of handling form. In 1911 Chagall had met Delaunay, and under his influence he had transformed his use of

Pl. 116

Plate 114

Auguste Herbin
The Village, 1911
Oil, 32 × 25¹/₂ in.

No. 147

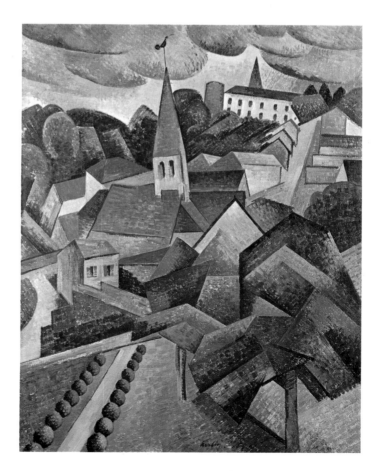

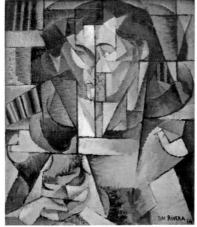

Plate 115

Diego Rivera
Portrait of Jacques Lipchitz, 1914
Oil, 25⅝ × 21⅝ in.

No. 294

color. Then, under the influence of Gleizes and Metzinger, Chagall attempted for a while to make use of Cubist formal and spatial procedures. This is apparent in several of his paintings of 1911–13 (*Golgotha; Russian Village, from the Moon*) where there is a tendency to crude faceting, and where Chagall animated the surface of his canvas by breaking the pictorial space down with geometrical divisions, which enabled him to situate different parts of the scene at different levels. Chagall's use of transparent, superimposed planes also derived from the Cubists. Chagall's most elaborate essay in the Cubist manner is *Adam and Eve*, where the fragmentation and faceting of forms derives from Metzinger's *Nudes* of 1910–11. There Chagall also used faceting to evoke the forwards movement of Eve as she moves in to pluck the fatal apple and seize the raised hand of the bashful Adam. This painting is difficult to read because the Cubist structure of the bodies is confused, the spatial arrangement ambiguous, and the yellow-green-red tonality wholly arbitrary.

Pl. 117

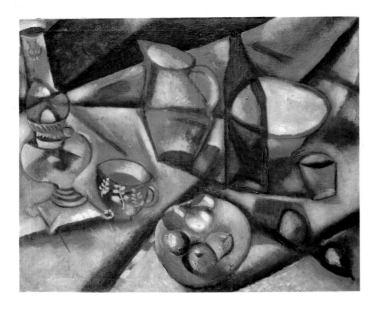

Plate 116

Marc Chagall
Still Life, 1912
Oil, 25 × 30¾ in.

No. 58

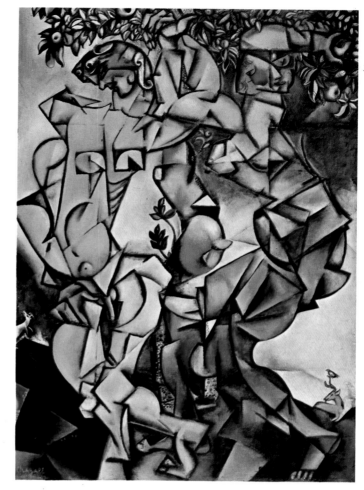

Plate 117

Marc Chagall
Adam and Eve, 1912
Oil, 63³/₁₆ × 44⁷/₈ in.

No. 59

Plate 118

Louis Marcoussis
Portrait of Gazanion, 1912
Ink, 25 × 19¹/₄ in.

No. 206

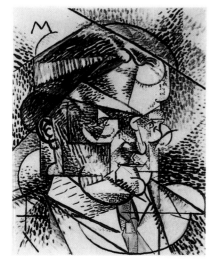

The naturalistic handling of the foliage and fruit at the top is also stylistically inconsistent. But Chagall never aimed at realism in his painting; he was only concerned with the upside-down world of fable and folklore. Cubist fragmentation seemed, however, to offer a technique which could serve his sense of fantasy, and even as late as 1918 Chagall produced in Vitebsk a very disjointed *Cubist Landscape* in which the compositional elements and the way they are assembled derive from the technique of *papiers collés*.

Louis Marcoussis, a Polish artist, was earning his living making humorous drawings when he met Apollinaire and Braque in 1910, and through them became friendly with Picasso. He had abandoned painting three years previously, but in 1911 Marcoussis took it up again, launched straight into a Cubist idiom and first exhibited

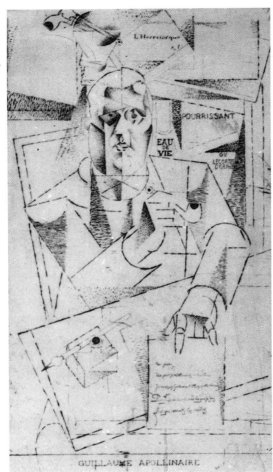

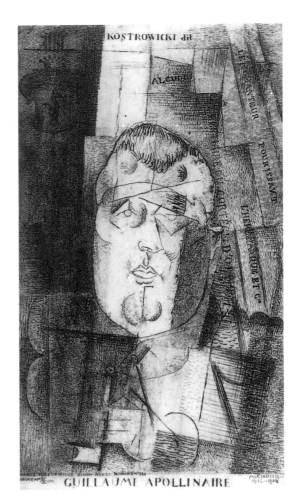

GUILLAUME APOLLINAIRE

GUILLAUME APOLLINAIRE

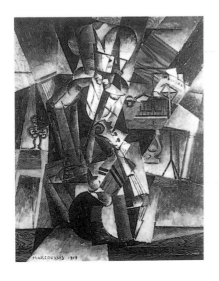

Pl. 118

with the Cubist group at the *Section d'Or* in October 1912. Marcoussis was a sensitive and gifted artist who was intelligent enough to understand and interpret in his own way the painting of Braque and Picasso. He was not a prolific artist, but in the small group of Cubist works —especially the prints— which he produced before joining the French army in 1914 he proved himself an accomplished Cubist disciple. In 1912, Marcoussis fell briefly under the spell of Delaunay, but the strongest influence on his pictorial methods seems to have been that of Juan Gris. Marcoussis began tentatively in 1912 making a wall-decoration (*The Checker-Board*) for a restaurant frequented by artists and writers in Montmartre. But his portrait drawing of the poet Edouard Gazanion (1912) and his engraved portrait of Apollinaire (1912) show—especially when compared with Metzinger's *Portrait of Gleizes* of the same date—that although Marcoussis was concerned with preserving a

Plate 122

Louis Marcoussis
The Beautiful Martiniquaise, 1912
Drypoint, 15³/₄ × 11⁷/₈ in.

No. 208

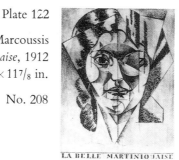

Plate 123

Louis Marcoussis
Head of a Woman,
1912
Drypoint,
11¹/₄ × 8⁵/₈ in.

No. 211

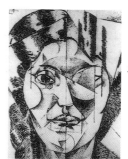

◀ Plate 119

Louis Marcoussis
Portrait of Guillaume Apollinaire, 1912
Drypoint, First version, 19¹/₂ × 11 in.

No. 209

◀ Plate 120

Louis Marcoussis
Portrait of Guillaume Apollinaire,
1912–20
Etching and Drypoint, Second
version, 19³/₈ × 10¹⁵/₁₆ in.

No. 210

physical likeness, he also knew how to use Cubist methods to represent 'mass and volume. But Marcoussis failed to live up to the promise of these first works, and in *Bar du Port* (1913) his cubistic handling of a group of buildings and their spatial relationship is arbitrary, confused and schematic. This painting is a travesty of Cubism, because it cannot be intelligibly read. Even the lettering has been placed where it carries no constructive significance. Marcoussis was most successful in small still life compositions, though his canvas *The Habitué* of 1920, probably his most important work, shows him once again skilfully

Plate 124

Louis Marcoussis
Bar du Port, 1913
Oil, 31⁷/₈ × 20¹/₈ in.

No. 205

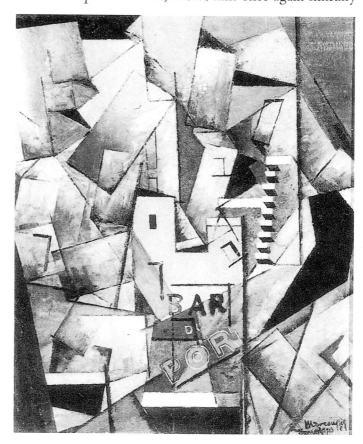

◀ Plate 121

Louis Marcoussis
Man Playing a 'Cello, 1914
Oil, 57¹/₂ × 44⁷/₈ in.

The National Gallery of Art,
Washington, D.C.
Chester Dale Bequest.

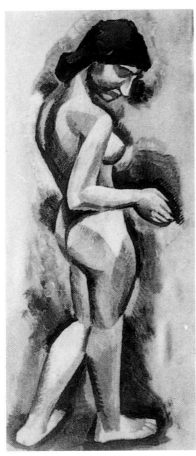

Plate 125

Roger de La Fresnaye
The Italian Girl, 1911
Oil, 50³/₈ × 21⁵/₈ in.

Philadelphia Museum of Art,
Philadelphia, Pa.

Pls. 125, 285
★ Some of these were exhibited with the Cubist group at the Salon d'Automne in 1911, and at the Section d'Or in 1912.

imitating Picasso in his later synthetic manner. After 1920, Marcoussis created a suave, but essentially decorative, personal idiom based on modified cubistic procedures.

Roger de La Fresnaye was the most considerable artist in this group of adherents to the Cubist movement, although he was never in a true sense a Cubist painter. Until the end of 1910, de La Fresnaye was painting in a flat somewhat stylized idiom influenced primarily by Gauguin and Sérusier. But at the end of 1910 de La Fresnaye met Raymond Duchamp-Villon, was drawn into the Puteaux Group, and during 1911 changed his style under the influence of Cézanne. This is apparent in *Italian Girl, in Profile* (May 1911), where volumes are more clearly defined and the body is treated sculpturally and faceted as in works by Picasso of 1907–8. This influence continued in a series of landscapes painted in the winter of 1911–12,★ in which buildings are reduced to simple cubic shapes, space is flattened by the adoption of a high view-point, and the landscape is built up in a series of flat planes aligned behind each other. There is however nothing conceptual or revolutionary about these landscapes: many of the forms are stylized and space is largely evoked by perspective. But de La Fresnaye extracted from a natural scene certain incomplete geometric descriptions which enabled him to give it an orderly, formal structure. De La Fresnaye's preoccupation, which is quite contrary to the spirit of true Cubism, was to remain faithful to the French tradition of painting while giving it a new look by the use of up-to-date methods of handling form and color. It did not take him long to discover that he could not satisfactorily marry the two. In 1911–13 de La Fresnaye painted some genre scenes in this manner which lack pictorial reality and are disconcertingly angular because

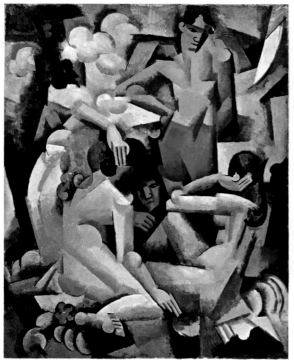

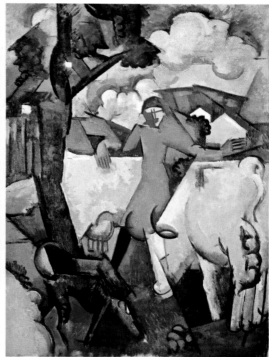

Plate 126

Roger de La Fresnaye
Bathers, 1912
Oil, 63¹/₂ × 50¹/₂ in.

No. 152

Plate 127

Roger de La Fresnaye
Marie Ressort, 1912–13
Oil, 58¹/₈ × 38 in.

No. 153

Pl. *127*

he lacked conviction in his handling of cubist methods. This is certainly the case with *Bathers* (1912), a Cézannesque subject in which de La Fresnaye carried fragmentation and formal analysis further than before. The cones, cylinders and spheres are not dictated by representational needs but are calculated, the figures have no solid reality and there is no attempt to recreate a spatial logic. Nor do the stylized white clouds (borrowed from Léger) function either as formal contrasts or as a source of light, while the tilted planes in the sky behind the young man have no spatial or structural signification. In short, nothing is quite what it should be in this painting.

In *Marie Ressort with her Cows* (1912–13), the influence of Delaunay is pronounced, both in the handling of color and in the suggestion of movement, while the more clearly defined planar structure derives from Léger's cityscapes of 1911. This is as near as de La Fresnaye ever came to true Cubism: the spatial structure is more logically represented, the style is consistent, and the handling more surface-conscious. But de La Fresnaye's cubistic paintings always have a brittle, disjointed quality which belies his aspiration to represent the solid earthy aspects

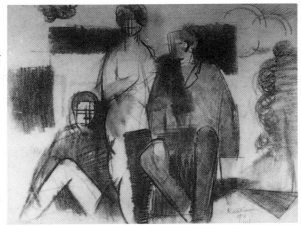

Plate 128

Roger de La Fresnaye
Three Figures, 1913
Charcoal, 19³/₄ × 25 in.

No. 154

Pl. 128

★ His brother Henri, represented with himself in the painting, was director of an aeroplane-manufacturing plant at Nieuport.

of reality. By 1913, de La Fresnaye had turned away from Cubism proper and come to accept the influence of Delaunay's 'Orphism,' although his way of simplifying the structure of his composition, based on large flat planes of color, also owed something to the technique of *papiers collés*. In these greatly flattened later works (1913–14, 1917–20) de La Fresnaye treated landscape elements, buildings, bodies, still life objects, water, the sky and clouds as though they were of similar consistency in terms of triangles, circles or rectangles. And by this means he arrived at a bold, colorful, eye-catching design where realism and spatial logic were lightly treated. Thus in *Conquest of the Air* (1913) for example, two tense but dehumanized figures, seated outdoors at a table, seem to be discussing France's aeronautical triumphs★ (balloon in the sky) and perhaps the future role of the aeroplane, as well as the pleasures of sailing (sail-boat on the river). Yet nothing here is real, solid or tangible: the corporeal forms are paper-thin, a white sail symbolizes an invisible boat, an unattached flag flutters in mid-air, the sky is cubically dissected, the men are seated—but on what?—and the landscape is so incoherent that one half of the village appears beneath the table, while the other half hovers in mid-air between the two figures. It is not to be denied that de La Fresnaye's composition is nicely painted and has both colorful charm and illustrative appeal—especially if one considers it as an allegory of open-air life or as a recruiting poster—but neither in this nor in any of his subsequent works did he make a serious contribution to the language of Cubism.

3

The Influence of Cubism Outside France

In Holland : Mondrian

Cubist painting was first seen in Holland at the exhibition of the newly-formed Circle of Modern Artists (*Moderne Kunstkring*) in Amsterdam in October 1911, where paintings by Cézanne, Braque and Picasso were included. Piet Mondrian, the only Dutch artist to be affected by Cubism, to which his contribution was more intelligent than most, was an exhibiting member of the Circle and saw this exhibition shortly before leaving for Paris in December 1911. The Circle's second exhibition, held in October 1912, while Mondrian was still in Paris, included works not only by Braque and Picasso, but also by Gleizes, Metzinger, Léger and Le Fauconnier.

Before his arrival in Paris—where he was to remain till his return to Holland in July 1914—Mondrian had been painting pictures of a Symbolist nature, executed in a post-Impressionist color technique deriving from Van Gogh, Seurat, the Neo-Impressionists and the Fauves, and had recently begun to simplify his forms and compositional design (e.g. *Church Tower at Domburg*, 1910–11). Mondrian had already exhibited at the Salon des Indépendants in the spring of 1911, and he went on exhibiting there for the next three years, his contribution in 1913 being specially noticed by Apollinaire as 'an offspring of Cubism . . . influenced by Picasso.' About the time of his move to Paris, or shortly before, Mondrian added another canvas to a series of paintings of a leafless tree, which he had started two years earlier. The first of these (1909) had been naturalistic in conception, though carried out in brilliant expressionist colors. In the *Horizontal Tree* painted in the winter of 1911, Mondrian dispensed with descriptive details, reduced the tree and branches to an expressive flurry of diagonal and curving lines, cut out strong colors, and introduced a planar notation borrowed

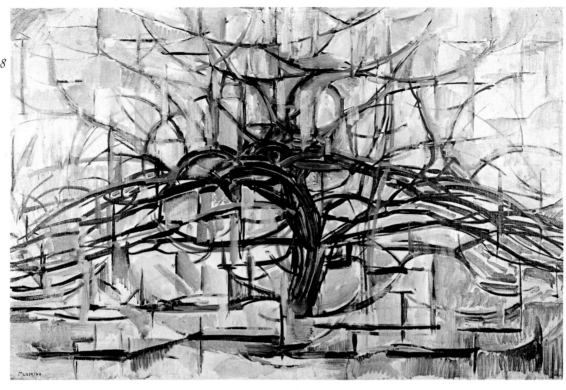

Plate 129   Piet Mondrian, *Horizontal Tree*, 1911   No. 217

Oil, 29⅝ × 43⅞ in.

Plate 130

Piet Mondrian   *Pl. 130*
Self-Portrait, *c.* 1911
Charcoal and ink, 25 × 19 in.

No. 221

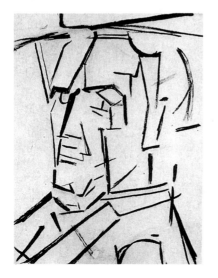

from Cubism to establish more exact spatial relationships. At the same time, Mondrian experimented in a *Self-Portrait* drawing with a faceted treatment of the head.

Shortly after this, in the second version of a *Still Life with a Ginger-Pot* (1912), a Cézannesque subject, Mondrian took to emphasizing the simple forms of objects with heavy black outlines, while building up over the rest of the picture-surface a network of straight lines and curves to give form to space and unify the composition. His method resembled that used by Metzinger and Gris in paintings of 1912, although he did not employ formal analysis or faceting but allowed objects to retain their natural form. Later, in *Female Form* (1912), Mondrian began to compose with block-like forms surrounding and engulfing the figure, which lost its corporeal reality but was thereby united with the surrounding space. And in a later version of the *Tree* (1912), the object itself and its

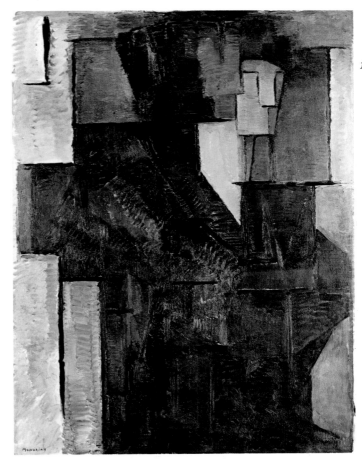

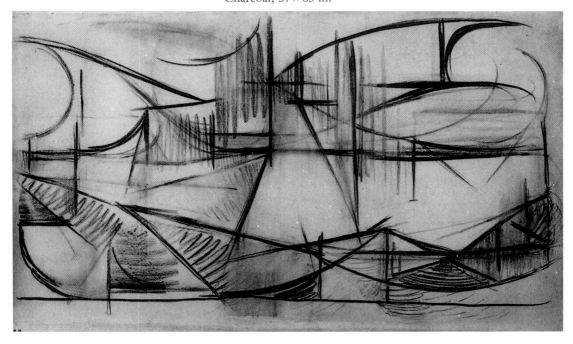

Plate 131

Piet Mondrian
Female Figure, c. 1912
Oil, 45¹/₄ × 34⁵/₈ in.

No. 219

Plate 132   Piet Mondrian, *Reclining Nude, c.* 1912   No. 223
Charcoal, 37 × 63 in.

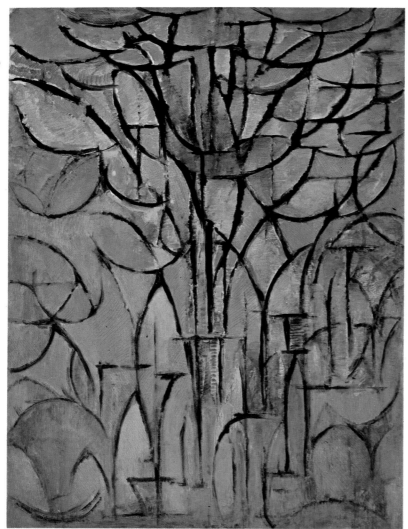

Plate 133

Piet Mondrian
Tree, 1912
Oil, $37 \times 27^1/_2$ in.

No. 218

existence in space were reduced to an all-over pattern of curves and straight lines, laid over a variously colored ground, which served to evoke the subject without describing or defining it. From there it was only a short step to the subsequent drawings of scaffolding, of a church façade and of the sea and sky, and to *Color Planes in an Oval* (1914?), in which there is no figurative subject but only an elaborate structure of cleverly balanced verticals and horizontals, curves and diagonals distributed in a single plane across the picture surface. Mondrian had, as it were, seized on the basic structural principle of Cubism and rejected the rest, for he believed that art was above reality and that the painter therefore should not be concerned with it. These paintings then are a sort of

Pl. 134
Pl. 135

Plate 134

Piet Mondrian
Church Façade, 1912
Charcoal, 39 × 24³/₄ in.

No. 222

Plate 135

Piet Mondrian
Color Planes in Oval, 1914(?)
Oil, 42³/₈ × 31 in. (Oval)

No. 220

intellectual shorthand with no representational purpose, for Mondrian's aim was to achieve a static balance of lines and colors which would satisfy the eye without troubling the mind, would evoke by intuition an experience of reality and at the same time induce a state of spiritual calm.

Cubism thus served Mondrian as a spring-board to jump from reality into non-reality, though he himself believed that he had carried Cubism to its logical and desirable conclusion. At all events, Mondrian's work from 1913–14 on amounts to a sort of elemental, ideal form of art which functions on 'a plane of direct and conscious spiritual

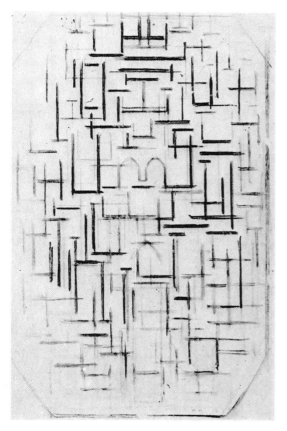

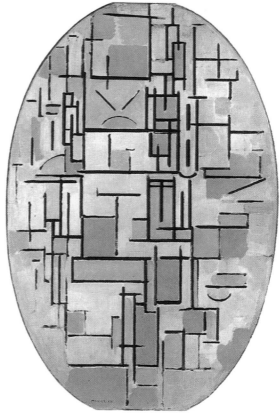

activity.' Being of a mystical turn of mind and influenced by theosophical beliefs, Mondrian's credo was that 'the interior of things shows through the surface, and as we look at the surface the inner image is formed in our soul.' The artist should therefore render no more than this 'inner image,' because 'things give us everything, but the representation of things gives us nothing.' No pictorial attitude could be more remote from that of the true Cubists. Yet a brief experience of handling the pictorial language of Cubism enabled Mondrian to pursue another type of reality through a personal non-figurative idiom, which he elaborated with a thoroughness which commands our fullest respect.

In Germany : Marc, Macke, Campendonk, Klee and Feininger

Germany was one of the first countries of Europe to open its Salons to later nineteenth and early twentieth century French art, so that from 1910 onwards Cubist paintings by Braque, Picasso, Metzinger, Delaunay and others were shown in Düsseldorf, Cologne, Berlin and Munich. But with their temperamental inclination towards an art of subjective emotionalism, involving distortions both of reality and of form, German artists at first found nothing meaningful to pursue in the clear structure, impassive realism and formal inventions of true Cubist painting. Among the artists of the Brücke group, to whom the paintings of Van Gogh, Munch, Gauguin and the Fauves were familiar, and whose own 'primitivizing' expressionist painting represented the first wave of modernism in Germany, Cubism found no echo. But between 1912 and 1915 Cubism played a small role in the painting of Franz Marc and some of his friends in Munich. Yet even then it was not the realistic impulse behind true Cubism which appealed to German artists but its new structural principles, which they adapted to a half-Orphist, half-symbolical use of color to evoke visual reality and give substance to their mystical insight into the reality of nature.

The first artist in Germany to make the discovery of Cubism's importance was Lyonel Feininger,★ an American-born German who had returned to Europe. In 1906–08 Feininger had spent some time in Paris, where he had known Delaunay. But when he returned there from Berlin in May 1911 and exhibited at the Salon des Indépendants, Feininger was impressed by the work of Cézanne, saw Delaunay's *Eiffel Towers* and *Windows*, found Paris 'agog with Cubism' and decided that in the painting of all three he had seen the sort of logical pictorial structure towards which he himself aspired. This marked a turning-point in Feininger's career, when he gave up expressing his feelings about mankind through bitter-sweet masquerade images and became instead a lyrical, romantic artist using confrontations between architecture, nature and the elements to symbolize the chasm between man's hopes and their realization. Feininger's principal subjects from then on were ships on a stormy sea, buildings on the edge of a cliff, soaring Gothic spires and tall buildings in the narrow streets of a city (*The Harbor*, 1913), images of strength and frailty, where man is dwarfed and yearns to escape from his isolation, just as the buildings seem to want to leave the ground and soar aloft. Feininger did not express himself by illustrative means any longer (he had started off as a humorous draughtsman), nor did he look to the technique of Cubism to give material reality to his buildings. Instead he used the technique of faceting and fragmentation, in conjunction with a complex structure of transparent, interpenetrating planes (*The Bridge I*, 1913), to dematerialize things and effect a fusion between the planes of physical

★ Feininger was not a member of the Blaue Reiter and did not exhibit there.

Plate 136

Lyonel Feininger
The Gate, 1912
Drypoint and etching, $10^5/_8 \times 7^3/_4$ in.

No. 87

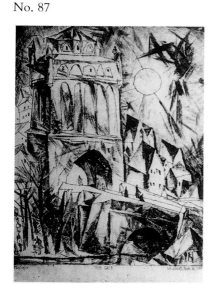

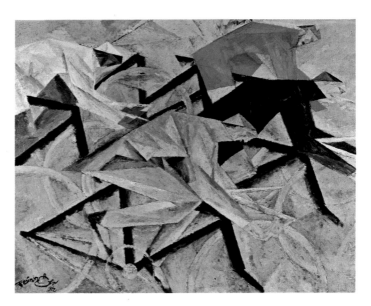

Plate 137

Lyonel Feininger
Bicycle Race, 1912
Oil, 31¹/₂ × 39³/₄ in.

No. 81

Plate 138

Lyonel Feininger
Gelmeroda IV, 1915
Oil, 39¹/₈ × 31¹/₄ in.

No. 83

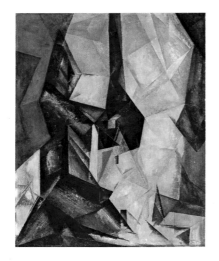

Pl. 137

Pl. 142

reality and those which carry onwards and upwards into the surrounding space and sky (*Gelmeroda IV*, 1915). Feininger's effects were subtly ordered and crystalline: like the true Cubists, Feininger disregarded linear perspective and kept his paintings surface-conscious. But unlike the Cubists, Feininger used multiple aspects and a contrasted play of light, with a harmony of unreal colors, to express the dynamic and transcendental workings of the competing forces—nature and man. Feininger's concern with the drama of light, like his sense of form in space, was no doubt enhanced by his contact with Delaunay, although he never used color in an Orphist manner. But a Cubist-like treatment of forms enabled him to evoke movement, as' in *The Bicycle Race* (1912), where cubistically stylized silhouettes and sharp arrow-like forms opposed to horizontals, diagonals and broken circles express momentum. However, in later works (1914) Feininger experimented with such Futurist techniques★ as 'lines of force' to heighten the clash of his planar and luminous encounters. But by 1916, having passed through this stage, Feininger adopted a bolder, simpler approach to formal analysis and planar structure which made his paintings more static and again more nearly Cubist (*Markwippach*, 1917).

The other German artists who borrowed from Cubism— Heinrich Campendonk, August Macke and Paul Klee— were all associated with Franz Marc in the Blaue Reiter

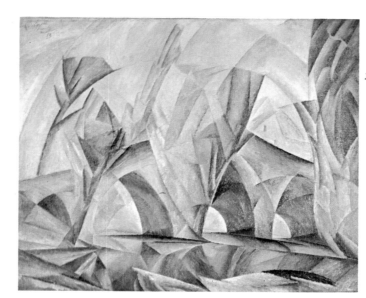

Plate 139

Lyonel Feininger
The Bridge I, 1913
Oil, 31¹/₂ × 39¹/₂ in.

No. 82

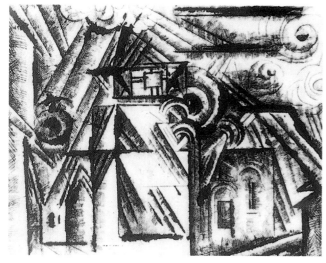

Plate 140

Lyonel Feininger
Vollersroda, 1918
Ink, 7⁷/₈ × 9⁷/₈ in.

No. 86

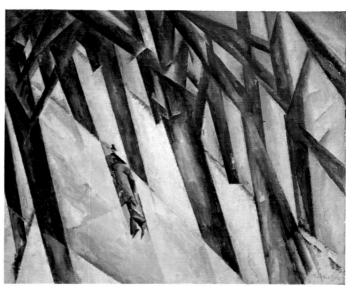

Plate 141

Lyonel Feininger
Avenue of Trees, 1915
Oil, 31³/₄ × 39¹/₂ in.

No. 84

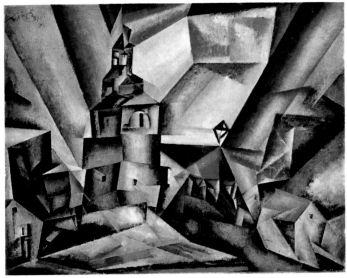

Plate 142

Lyonel Feininger
Markwippach, 1917
Oil, 31³/₄ × 39³/₄ in.

No. 85

and much influenced by his pictorial conceptions. The Blaue Reiter was a short-lived, loose association of gifted artists, presided over by Kandinsky and Marc, the former (who looked on Cubism as a curious but transitory phenomenon) advocating a so-called 'pure' type of abstract painting analogous to music, the latter seeking to convey through painting a 'pantheist empathy' with animals and nature. The first Blaue Reiter Exhibition, in December 1911, included only works by Henri Rousseau and Delaunay from France. For its second exhibition in February 1912 (graphic works only), Braque, Picasso, Derain, and de La Fresnaye were invited and their works were hung alongside others from Russia by Gontcharova, Larionov, and Malevich. The Blaue Reiter exhibitions brought together examples of those different types of art which interested its members—symbolism, mysticism, folk-art, expressionism, musicalism, Cubism and Rayonnism. Marc had first seen Cubist paintings by Braque and Picasso in September 1910 at the exhibition of the Neue Künstlervereinigung in Munich. But it was too early for him to feel any relevance to his own work. Marc wanted to express the conviction that animals are more spiritual and beautiful than humans, which meant trying to convey in his own paintings an animal's view both of itself and of the world it inhabits. At first (1910–12), Marc attempted to express this through a symbolical use of color and a distinctive rhythm. However, in the late

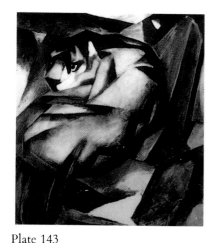

Plate 143

Franz Marc
The Tiger, 1912
Oil, 42⁷/₈ × 39 in.

Städtische Galerie im
Lenbachhaus, Munich

Pl. 143

Pl. 144

Plate 144

Franz Marc
Stables, 1913–14
Oil, 29¹/₈ × 62¹/₄ in.

No. 204

spring of 1912, Klee returned to Munich after a short trip
to Paris, where he had visited and talked with Delaunay
and Le Fauconnier and had seen many Cubist paintings by
Picasso in the Kahnweiler Gallery. In the fall of the same
year, Marc and Macke followed Klee to Paris, and
shortly afterwards Marc started to use color in an Orphist
manner, allied with a linear spatial structure deriving from
Cubism, to evoke the nature of some animal and unite
it with its surroundings. He began in *The Tiger* (1912) by
faceting the animal's body to express, by articulation,
the animality, fierceness and potential speed of a beast
of prey. After this, in paintings such as *Stables* (1913),
Marc employed transparent planes of color and a linking
rhythm to recreate an experience of reality. He did not,
therefore, have recourse to Cubist methods to make
reality more solid and tangible but to contribute to an
all-enveloping effect of space, which enhanced the pictorial
sense of mystery. Subsequently, Marc borrowed certain
Futurist and even Rayonnist devices to achieve more
dramatic effects before he finally adopted a symbolical,
non-figurative idiom in 1915.

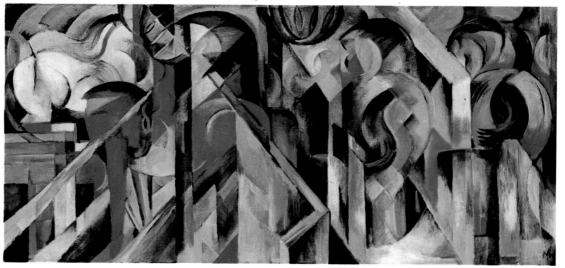

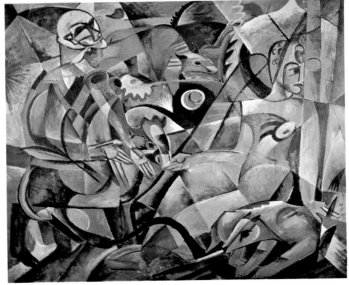

Plate 145

Heinrich Campendonk
Harlequin and Columbine, 1913
Oil, 64¹/₂ × 78 in.

No. 49

Heinrich Campendonk was the closest follower of Marc in his use of a Cubist-style structure, but his naïve imagery; unlike Marc's, derived from folk-art, as in *Harlequin and Columbine* (1913), where courtship is going on in a woodland glade with much fondling of animals. True Cubism played no part in the paintings of Macke and Klee, yet in 1914 both artists painted works (mostly watercolors)

Plate 146

Paul Klee
Red and White Domes, 1914
Watercolor, 5³/₄ × 5³/₈ in.

No. 149

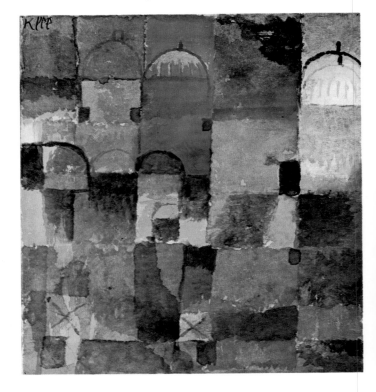

★ Klee published a German translation of Delaunay's essay *On Light* in the periodical *Der Sturm* in January 1913.

Pl. 146

Pl. 147

in which they used rectangular, over-lapping, transparent planes of color, derived from Orphism,★ to establish a luminous spatial structure and overall design (*Red and White Domes*, 1914). Klee, however, went further in his oil painting *Homage to Picasso* (1914), a respectful and uniquely personal tribute to one of the creators of Cubism. He chose an oval canvas, which carried Cubist associations, and made great play with textural variations and directed beams of light, as Picasso had done in 1911–12. Yet Klee omitted the realistic content of a Cubist picture and produced a composition of inclined and interlocking rectangular planes, which evoke an experience of space and light through their tonal relationships, but which unfortunately suggest a parody of a painting by Delaunay.

Plate 147

Paul Klee
Homage to Picasso, 1914
Oil, $13^3/_4 \times 11^1/_2$ in. (irregular oval)

No. 148

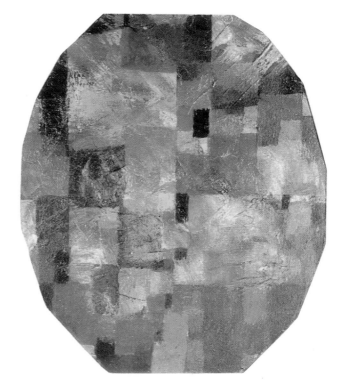

* Frantisek Kupka, who was ten years older, had left Prague and settled in Paris in 1895. In 1911–12 he was living in Puteaux and closely in touch with Villon and Duchamp, but Kupka's own painting was non-figurative and owed nothing either to Cubism or to Orphism. He played no part in the development of the modern movement inside Czechoslovakia, although Kupka helped his compatriots to see the latest French painting when they visited Paris.

150

Plate 148

Vincenc Beneš
Tram Station, 1911
Oil, 28 × 22⁵/₈ in.

No. 5

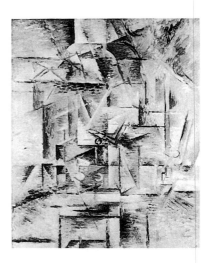

In Czechoslovakia : Filla, Kubišta, Procházka, Beneš, Gutfreund and Čapek

Plate 149

Emil Filla
Salome, 1912
Oil, 54 × 31¹/₄ in.

No. 89

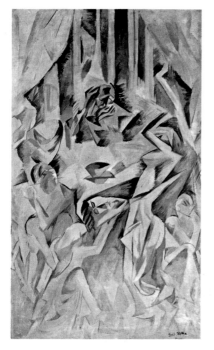

Czechoslovakia produced a small but very active group of *avant-garde* young artists*—notably Emil Filla, Bohumil Kubišta, Antonín Procházka, and the sculptor Otto Gutfreund—who responded positively to the language of Cubism and from 1911 on adapted it creatively to their own purposes. Situated geographically in the center of Europe, with Russia and Germany to the north, Italy to the south and France and Austria lying west and east, Czechoslovakia (or Bohemia as it then was) was open to several currents of artistic influence. Like the artists of most other European countries, Czech artists at the turn of the century were equally involved with open-air painting, symbolism and *art nouveau*. However, in 1905 the young progressives in Prague acquired new ideas of style and subject-matter after seeing an exhibition of works by Edvard Munch at the Mánes Union of Artists (similar to the Salon d'Automne in Paris). This was followed in 1907 by a showing of French Impressionist and post-Impressionist painting, which opened their eyes still further to the expressive possibilities of color and form. Then, in the winter of 1907-8, Filla, Kubišta and Procházka joined with some other progressive artists to form a group (The Eight) devoted to creating a modern Czech art on the basis of their recent stylistic discoveries.

In 1909 The Eight dissolved and merged with Mánes, after which Filla and Kubišta visited Paris, where Gutfreund (who returned to Prague in the summer of 1910) was already

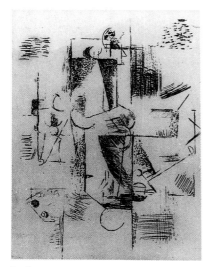

Plate 150

Emil Filla
Female Figure, 1913
Drypoint, 17¹/₈ × 14 in.

No. 93

★ The group also included architects, writers and art historians; it published two numbers of a review in 1911–13 which reflects their admirations and activities. Kubišta remained outside the group.

★ Works by Soffici were included in the group's 1913 exhibition, the first occasion on which Futurist paintings were shown in Prague.

★ The same French artists were represented in 1914 as in 1913. For the 1913 exhibition, Kahnweiler lent 31 items.

★ Kramář, who bought from Kahnweiler, lived partially in Paris. After 1914 he no longer bought for himself, but in 1919 he started buying modern French art again for a Society whose collections subsequently became the nucleus of the present Národní Galerie in Prague. Kramář was the author of an interesting book on Cubism (Prague, 1921).

working under Bourdelle. In 1910, strengthened by its new recruits, the Mánes Union showed a selection of works by Parisian artists from the Salon des Indépendants, which included many Fauve paintings but no examples of Cubism. However, in 1911, Filla and Procházka broke away from Mánes, which they regarded as too conservative, and formed the *Group of Avant-Garde Artists* (*Skupina výtvarných umělců*) with Vincenc Beneš, Josef Čapek, Gutfreund, Václav Špála, and a few others.★ The stylistic conceptions of this new group embraced their national cultural heritage, German Expressionism and Cubism, with some slight influence from Futurism in 1913.★ They were closely in touch with the Brücke artists, exhibited in several towns in Germany, and in 1913 had a group showing at the Sturm gallery in Berlin, where they encountered works by the Blaue Reiter and Futurist artists. Thus the *Avant-Garde* Czech artists repeatedly saw various forms of modern art. Also the Group sponsored three exhibitions—in the autumn of 1912, May 1913, and March 1914★—at which they showed, alongside their own works, German Expressionist paintings, works by Derain and Friesz (1912 only), and in 1913–14 many Cubist works by Braque, Picasso and Gris. Moreover, in Prague itself, they had access to a remarkable private collection of Cubist paintings (Braque, Picasso, Derain) which was being assembled by one of their well-wishers, the art historian Dr. Vincenc Kramář,★ who had begun by buying Picasso's bronze *Woman's Head* in the winter of 1910–11. It is therefore significant that while these young Czech artists borrowed formal and structural elements from true Cubism, they remained unaffected both by Orphism and by the experiments of other artists of the Cubist School in Paris, and none of them followed Kupka into non-figurative art.

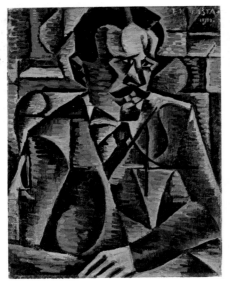

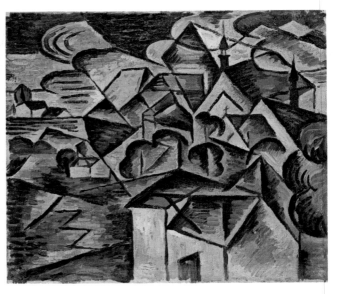

Plate 151

Bohumil Kubišta
Portrait, 1911
Oil, 26 × 20¹/₂ in.

No. 150

Kubišta was already writing from Paris to a friend in 1910 that, in his opinion, Braque and Picasso would have 'a great influence' on the development of modern art, because their work showed that 'color is only a relative consideration in painting.' This remark is significant because, at that time, the painting of the young Czechs was characterized by an expressionist use of color. After 1911, however, they reduced the intensity of their colors and concentrated more on formal discipline, though they never relinquished their concern with emotional expressivity. Thus the *Avant-Garde* Czech artists were not inclined to imitate true Cubism: they were not concerned with re-creating in all its fullness the solid tangible reality of a still life or a mere seated figure. They wanted their subjects to have a higher symbolic significance, to represent moments of spiritual intensity in the life of man, to express deep inner feelings and a sense of national awareness (*Views of Old Prague, St. Sebastian, Anxiety, Song of the Countryside*). Expressionism thus blended with Cubism in their works, Cubist analysis and fragmentation serving their need for expressive distortion and providing them with both a means of dramatization and a structural framework which held the composition together.

Pl. 153   Filla was the most constructive of the Czech Cubist painters and his *Bathers* (1912) shows that he had studied

Plate 152

Bohumil Kubišta
Landscape, 1911
Oil, 18¹/₈ × 21¹/₄ in.

No. 151

Plate 153

Emil Filla
Bathers, 1912
Oil, 49¹/₂ × 33 in.

Národní Galerie, Prague.

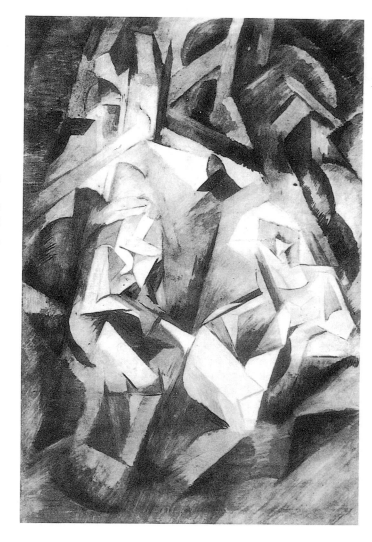

153

Plate 154

Antonin Procházka
Girl with a Peach, 1911
Oil, 13³/₄ × 11⁷/₈ in.

No. 293

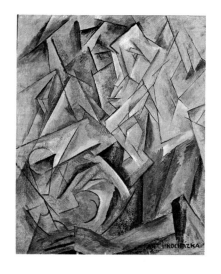

paintings by Braque and Picasso of 1909 intelligently. He attempted to keep the expressionist strain in check, and for twenty years Filla continued to follow in the steps of Picasso through the developments of late Cubism. Kubišta experimented with an analytical approach in 1911, and by 1913 had evolved a clear, personal form of Cubism before his urge for dramatic effects led him to Futurism in the next year. Procházka, Beneš, Čapek, and Špála were more eclectic artists who made use briefly of a Cubist approach to form before ending in formalization. The second most important Czech Cubist was the sculptor Gutfreund, who began to use a Cubist planar structure in 1911, and went on to make a significant contribution to Cubist sculpture between 1912 and 1919.

154

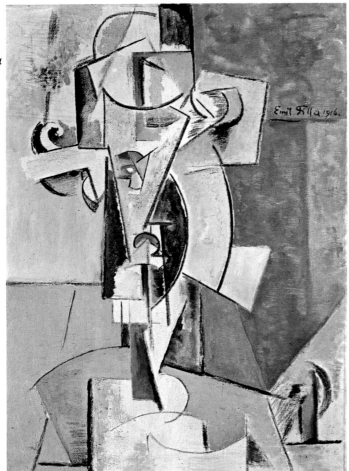

Plate 155

Emil Filla
Man's Head with Hat, 1916
Oil, 28³/₈ × 20¹/₄ in.

No. 90

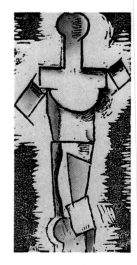

Plate 156

Joseph Čapek
Cubist Figure, 1913
Linoleum, 8³/₁₆ × 4 in.

No. 50

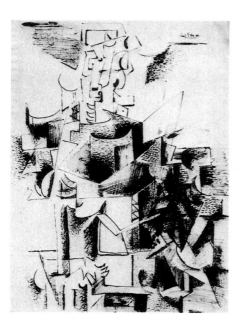

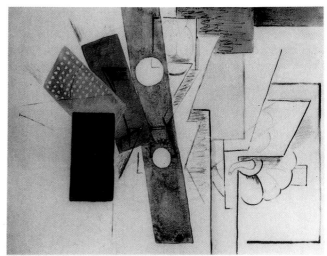

Plate 157

Emil Filla
Figure, 1921
Ink, 24⁷/₈ × 18¹/₂ in.

No. 92

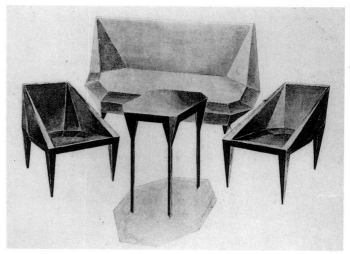

Plate 159

Vlatislav Hofman
Design for a Suite of Furniture, 1911
Pencil drawing
Reproduced from *Umělecký Měsičnik*, 1911–12

◀ Plate 158

Emil Filla
Still Life with Pears, 1915
Watercolor, $10^5/_8 \times 23^5/_8$ in.

No. 91

Pl. 159

In May 1914, the Mánes Union at last presented a show of works by artists of the School of Paris, selected by Alexandre Mercereau, which included Delaunay, Villon, de La Fresnaye, Friesz, Gleizes, Metzinger, Lhote, Marcoussis, Mondrian, Rivera and Duchamp-Villon. This was the first time that such a wide survey of the Cubists of the School of Paris had been seen in Prague. But it was widely remarked on that Braque, Picasso and Gris, who had been shown by the *Avant-Garde Group*, were missing. By this time both Filla and Gutfreund were back in Paris, where the declaration of war overtook them. After this the Group split up, and in the postwar years only Filla continued to work in a Cubist idiom.

A curious and interesting side-effect of the great interest for Cubism in Czechoslovakia is the stylistic influence it had between 1911 and 1913 on the design of furniture, household objects, ornamentation and the surface animation of architecture. This took the form of angularities, faceting and stylized geometrical shapes and was sufficiently widespread to suggest the possibility that a Cubist-style house might have resulted. The designers concerned—Vlatislav Hofman, Pavel Janák and Josef Gočár—were all members of the *Avant-Garde Group*.

In Russia : Gontcharova, Larionov, Malevich, Tatlin, Popova and Udaltsova

Between 1898, when the first number of the review *The World of Art (Mir Iskusstva)* edited by Diaghilew appeared, and 1914, when (in contrast to the break-up which occurred everywhere else) the modern art movement in Russia gained new strength following the return from Paris and Munich on the outbreak of war of some progressive young artists who had been working abroad, St. Petersburg and Moscow were constantly and quickly aware of any new style or development that occurred in Paris, Munich, Milan or Vienna. *The World of Art*, published by a group of friends in St. Petersburg, presented the Impressionists, the Symbolists and *art nouveau*, and in its last number (1904) the post-Impressionists. It was succeeded between the spring of 1908 and December 1909 —Moscow had by then replaced St. Petersburg as the artistic center—by a new review, *The Golden Fleece*, which was less aesthetically and more modern-minded, supported the *Blue Rose* group of young Russian artists, and was financed by a rich art-collecting merchant Nicolai Riabouchinsky. This review sponsored three memorable Franco-Russian exhibitions in Moscow, where not only Cézanne, Gauguin, Van Gogh, the Nabis and the Neo-Impressionists were represented, but also on a generous scale Matisse, the Fauves, Le Fauconnier and Braque (his 1908 *Nude* was shown in 1909). Futurism was known about immediately after its launching because the Manifestos were published in Russian, while the *avant-garde* Russian artists (always a small group) encountered Expressionist paintings of the Munich school (including Kandinsky) at an International Salon in Odessa in 1910.* Next, a new group, the *Jack of Diamonds*, which was formed in Moscow by some young 'Cézannists' (Falk and Lentulov) with Larionov and Gontcharova, held four exhibitions between December 1910 and the spring of 1913 at which

* This Salon was also shown in Kiev and St. Petersburg. The brothers Burliuk were responsible for thus bringing Moscow into touch with Munich.

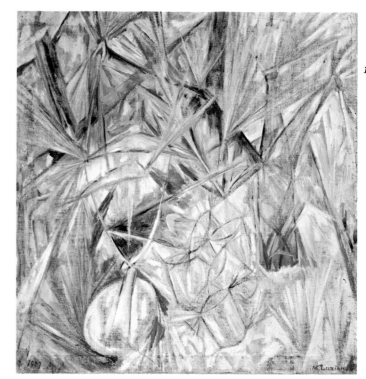

Plate 160

Michel Larionov
Glasses, 1911–12 (?)
Oil, 41 × 38¹/₄ in.

No. 156

* Braque's work, like that of Gris and Léger was passed up by Russian collectors.

works by Gleizes, Metzinger, Le Fauconnier, Lhote, and Léger were shown, as well as artists of the Brücke and Blaue Reiter. And finally, the Russians could always visit two outstanding and constantly growing private collections of modern French painting in Moscow belonging to the merchants Ivan Morosov and Sergei Shchukin. By 1914, Morosov had already acquired over one hundred paintings by the Impressionists, Cézanne, Gauguin, the Nabis and Matisse, while Shchukin owned in addition to Cézanne and Van Gogh, some forty works by Matisse and even more by Picasso, most of the latter dating from after 1907.*

Since the seventeenth century, the Russian Tsars and aristocracy had continually amassed collections of western European art and had repeatedly called on the services of foreign artists, architects and artisans to set the tone for and give a lead to Russian taste. So the influx of modern foreign art into Russia between 1900 and 1914 was not abnormal. However, this time it did not pass unchallenged. For, since the end of the nineteenth century a distrust of foreign influence had begun to develop in creative circles in Russia, where there was now a will to nourish a purely Russian art from Russian sources. And this at last broke through in painting. The founding of the *Blue Rose* group in 1907 marked the beginning of a nationalistic trend in the work of Larionov and Gontcharova, who until then had painted in a sub-Impressionist style. All at once they began to work in a 'primitivizing' idiom inspired by icons, the ornamental motifs of Russian peasant embroidery and '*lubki*' (peasant broadsheets), and concentrated on scenes of Russian popular life, especially that of peasants, soldiers and sailors. In their technique of summary simplifications and large areas of bright color, with no recourse to modeling or scientific perspective, Larionov and Gontcharova still owed something to what they had learned from the Nabis and the Fauves, just as it is difficult not to ascribe some share of responsibility for their 'new primitivism' to Gauguin, Henri Rousseau and the 'negro' element in the work of Picasso. At the same time, however, Larionov and Gontcharova cultivated a disrespect for those pictorial niceties which they associated with 'Munich decadence' or the 'cheap Orientalism of the Paris School,' and this led to their breaking with the *Jack of Diamonds* group in 1912.

At this moment—March 1912—Larionov and Gontcharova organized an exhibition of their own in Moscow with two young disciples, Kasimir Malevich and Vladimir Tatlin, under the title *The Donkey's Tail*, in order to demonstrate the existence of an independent Russian school of modernism. Hitherto, no Cubist influence had been apparent in Russian painting. But in the winter of 1911–12 Larionov had invented a new personal idiom, Rayonnism, which the poet Mayakovsky was to classify as 'a Cubist interpretation of Impressionism.' Rayonnism was de-

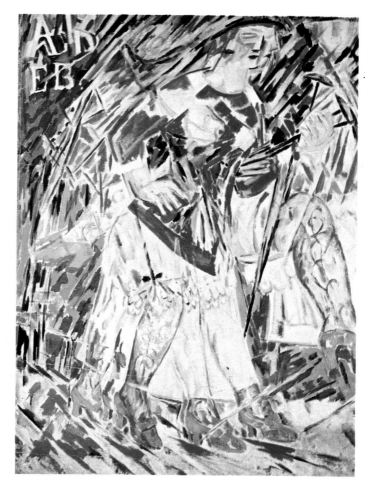

Plate 161

Michel Larionov
Woman Walking on the Boulevard,
1912
Oil, 45³/₄ × 33⁷/₈ in.

No. 157

scribed by Larionov himself as a purely Russian synthesis of Cubism, Futurism and Orphism in which he was 'concerned with spatial forms which are obtained through the crossing of reflected rays from various objects, and forms which are singled out by the artist. The ray is represented by a line of color. The painting is revealed as a skimmed impression, it is perceived out of time and in space.' In the first of his Rayonnist paintings, *Glasses* (1911–12?), as well as in *Woman Walking on the Boulevard* of roughly the same date, these various elements of the style are evident in the unfragmented bottle and glass, in the multiplication of the woman's moving limbs, in the busy network of criss-crossing lines and in the way color is applied. Some of Larionov's Rayonnist paintings, of which there are only a few, consist, however, simply of clashing, arrow-shaped planes of color with no visible subject. Gontcharova's Rayonnism, on the other hand, had more of a

Pl. *160*
Pl. *161*

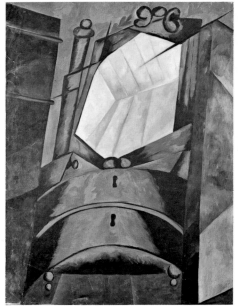

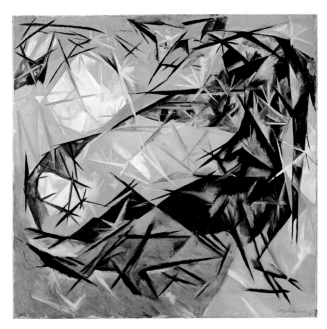

Plate 162

Nathalie Gontcharova
The Looking Glass, 1912
Oil, 35 × 26³/₈ in.

No. 106

Cubist background in its conception of form (*The Looking Glass*, 1912) and consisted at first of a network of lines of force and radiation emerging from a faceted form (*Cats*, 1911–12). Subsequently her conception moved nearer to Futurism (*The Cyclist*, 1912–13) and led to a mechanistic composition such as *The Machine's Engine* (1913). Yet all the while both of these artists were continuing to work on Russian themes in the 'new primitive' idiom, and when they left Russia in 1915 to work as stage-designers for the Diaghilew Ballet it was in the folk-art style that they were most successful.

Malevich, a less accomplished and creative artist than these two, began by imitating, rather coarsely, various French styles from Gauguin and the Nabis to Matisse. Then in 1911–12 Malevich came strongly under the influence of Gontcharova and took up peasant themes. 'Every work has a content,' he said at the time, 'expressed in primitive form and reveals a social concern.' Malevich's original 'primitive form' is exemplified by *The Woodcutter* (1911), a static composition in which he reduced the figure and the logs around him to elementary tubular forms—thus making them indistinguishable—and articulated a flattened pictorial space by giving different directions to the planes of the logs and employing contrasts of bright colors. Next,

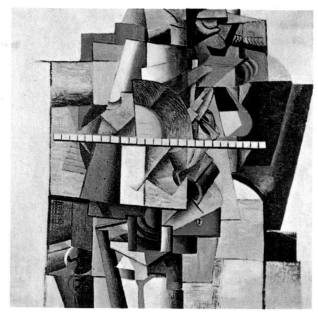

◀ Plate 163

Nathalie Gontcharova
Cats, 1911–12 (?)
Oil, 33¹/₂ × 33³/₄ in.

No. 105

Plate 164

Kasimir Malevich
Portrait of Matiushin, 1913
Oil, 41³/₄ × 42³/₈ in.

No. 202

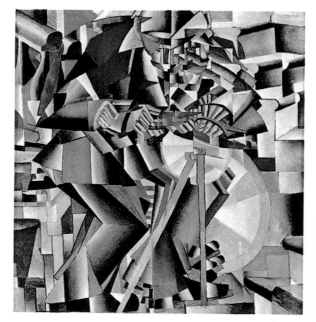

Plate 165

Kasimir Malevich
Scissors Grinder, 1912
Oil, 31³/₈ × 31³/₈ in.

No. 201

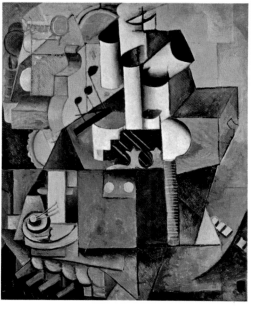

Plate 166

Kasimir Malevich
Musical Instruments, 1913
Oil, 32⁷/₈ × 27³/₈ in.

No. 203

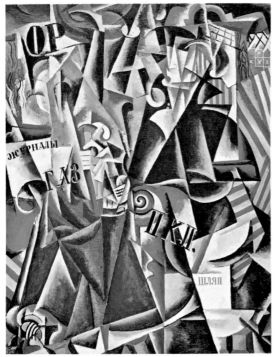
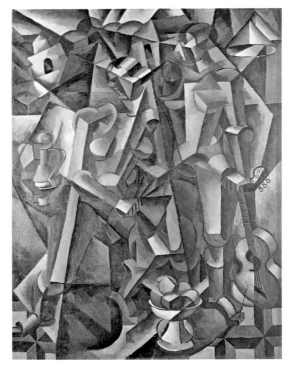

Plate 167

Liubov Popova
The Traveller, 1915
Oil, 56 × 41¹/₂ in.

No. 292

★ At this stage Malevich called his
work 'Cubo-Futurist.'

Pl. *164*

Pl. *166*

in *The Scissors-Grinder* (1912) he attempted to unite Cubist to Futurist means and suggest, by multiplication of the limbs, head and knife, violent and exhausting movement. Here Malevich tried to contain a figure in action within the spatial setting of a static, illogically disjointed, but would-be cubistically structured staircase,★ the whole composition being further animated by contrasts of bright, nondescriptive colors. Thirdly, after passing through a phase (1912–13) in which he owed something to Léger, Malevich arrived at a new style (*Portrait of M.V. Matiushin*, 1913) derived from the *papiers collés* and late Cubism of Picasso. In such paintings, planes, forms and identifiable fragments of objects are crudely piled up, with no regard for physical or spatial logic, in a manner which he himself referred to as 'Nonsense-Realism.' After this, in a 'desperate attempt to free art from the ballast of the objective world,' Malevich 'fled to the form of the square' and launched the non-figurative idiom which he called Suprematism.

Tatlin, the fourth artist of this group, was so impressed by the works of Picasso which he had seen in Shchukin's collection that, when he had earned enough money by playing the accordeon at an Exhibition of Russian Folk-Art

Liubov Popova
Two Figures, 1913
Oil, 63 × 48⁷/₈ in.

No. 291

in Berlin in the summer of 1913, he at once set out for Paris to visit him. In Picasso's studio, Tatlin saw and was impressed by a series of still lifes and guitars constructed in wood, metal and cardboard. But those constructions which he himself made in 1913–14 after his return to Moscow were purely non-representational.

Apart from this small *avant-garde* group, Russia produced two other interesting artists—Liubov Popova and Nadezhda Udaltsova—who used the language of Cubism creatively. These two painters left Moscow (where they had studied) for Paris in the fall of 1912, worked for a while under both Le Fauconnier and Metzinger and returned to Moscow in the summer of 1914. They were thus able to make direct contact with Parisian Cubism, and up till 1915 their painting reveals a comparable

Plate 169

Nadezhda Udaltsova
At the Piano, 1914
Oil, 42 × 35 in.

No. 308

Plate 170

Nadezhda Udaltsova
Violin, 1914
Oil, 20⁷/₈ × 16¹⁵/₁₆ in.

No. 309

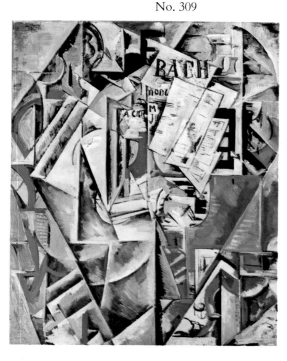

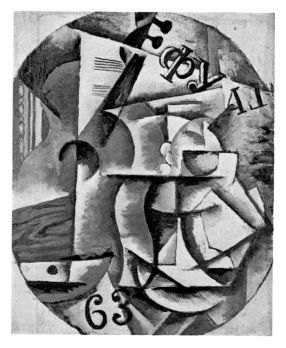

realism in the handling of representational forms and spatial structure to that which inspired Cubism proper. These two ladies, who were not affected by the folk-art movement, were at the start more accomplished artists than Malevich and Tatlin, but they too ended by adopting a non-figurative idiom.

In Italy : The Futurists

Italy was awakened suddenly to a new conception of what literature and art should attempt in the twentieth century when, on 20th February 1909, the poet Marinetti issued the First Futurist Manifesto. This was published in full in his own review *Poesia* in Milan, in *Le Figaro* in Paris, and simultaneously mailed to a large number of influential people. In bombastic language, Marinetti ordered the younger generation in Italy to defy tradition and the cult of the glorious Italian past and seek inspiration instead in the excitements of the contemporary world. 'We declare,' he wrote, 'that the world's splendor has been enriched by a new beauty: the beauty of speed . . . We shall sing of the great crowds excited by work, pleasure and rebellion; we shall sing of . . . the factories suspended from the clouds by the twisted strings of their smoke. . . . of broad-chested locomotives pawing at the rails like huge steel horses bridled with steel tubes; and of the gliding flight of aeroplanes . . .' Soon after the publication of the Manifesto, Marinetti was approached by three young painters—Carlo Carrà, Umberto Boccioni, and Luigi Russolo—who felt that artists too should take part in the movement. And a year later these three, with their friends Giacomo Balla★ and Gino Severini, launched first a Manifesto of the Futurist Painters (8th March, 1910) and next a Technical Manifesto of Futurist Painting (11th April.) In these later professional Manifestos they proclaimed them-

★ Boccioni and Severini had studied together under Balla in 1900–1.

selves 'the primitives of a new, completely transformed sensibility' and set forth an aesthetic in praise of speed, science, mechanization and universal dynamism, ideas which were to remain fundamental to their pictorial conceptions during the first active phase of the movement (1910–15). The Technical Manifesto showed a surprising awareness of modern scientific ideas in its references to the deformation and multiplication of images of moving things on the retina and to the vital principle of opposition between static and dynamic elements. It was also *avant-garde* in its insistence that traditional modes of pictorial representation were no longer valid when one could see and know that the 'sixteen people around you in a tram are successively one, ten, four, three. They stay still momentarily, but then they shift again, coming and going with the swaying and bouncing of the tram.' This was written a full year before Delaunay started working on the series of fragmented *Eiffel Towers* and almost two years before Duchamp painted his *Nude Descending*.

There was no lack of revolutionary-sounding ideas in all of this, but at the moment of launching their Manifestos the painters lacked the technical know-how to put them into practice. They were also in ignorance of modern developments outside of Italy.* True, Boccioni had been to Paris, but it was in 1902 and he had studied Impressionism. Severini had been living in Paris since 1906, but like his friends in Milan who had been initiated into Symbolism and Divisionism through Giovanni Segantini, Giuseppe Pellizza and Gaetano Previati, he himself had not advanced further. In 1909, no exhibition of French Impressionist or post-Impressionist painting* had been seen in Italy, and when Picasso was officially invited to send paintings to the Venice Biennale that summer, they

* Boccioni's claim in *Pittura scultura futuriste* of 1914 that they knew about Cubism in 1910 is certainly false. At any rate, there is no trace of Cubist influence on Futurist painting before the fall of 1911.

* Soffici's article on Cézanne in *La Voce* in 1908 broke wholly new ground for Italian readers.

Plate 171

Ardengo Soffici
*Decomposition of the Planes of a
Lamp*, 1912
Oil, 13³/₄ × 11³/₄ in.

No. 307

★ See A. Soffici, 'L'Esposizione di
Venezia 1909,' in *Scoperte e Massacri*,
Opere Vol. 1 (Florence, 1959), p. 382.
Picasso is referred to as 'a young
Spaniard who will be famous
tomorrow.'

★ Before arriving in Milan, Soffici
would have seen the Indépendants
of 1911 and discussed its Cubist
manifestation with Picasso, Apollinaire and Metzinger. Soffici's article
'Picasso e Braque' published in
La Voce in August 1911 was the first
discussion in Italian of Cubism.

were taken down a few days after the opening because
they were considered too aggressive.★

For over a year, the Futurists continued to work with
such pictorial means as they were familiar with, straining
the Divisionist technique of color and the Symbolist use
of linear rhythms to their expressive limits. Then in
May-June 1911, when the Futurists were already planning
to launch themselves on Paris with an exhibition, they
at last learned something at second-hand about Cubism.
Their informants were first Ardengo Soffici, a writer and
painter, who had lived in Paris in 1900–07, had known
Picasso, Apollinaire and their friends intimately for many
years, had recently been in Paris again and was probably
the only person in Italy who had a genuine understanding
of Cubism.★ The second informant was Severini, who
by then had become a friend of Picasso and Apollinaire
and brought with him magazine articles on and reproductions of Cubist paintings. These two men were
critical of the provincialism, outdated technique and
labored symbolism of Italian Futurist painting and urged

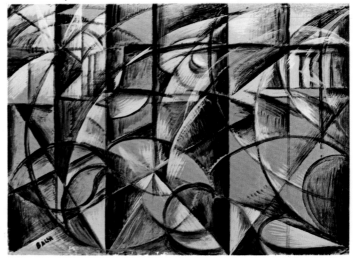

Plate 172

Giacomo Balla
Speed of an Automobile + Lights,
1913
Oil, 19¹/₂ × 27¹/₂ in.

No. 4

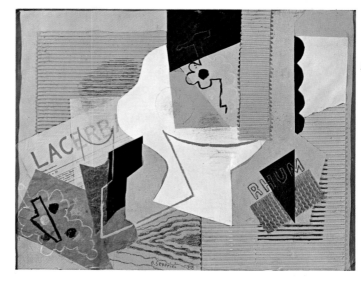

Plate 173

Gino Severini
Still Life with 'Lacerba,' 1913
Papier collé, 19⁵/₈ × 26 in.

No. 299

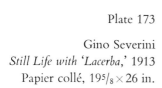

Plate 174

Gino Severini
Self-Portrait in Straw Hat, 1912
Charcoal, 21¹/₂ × 21⁹/₁₆ in.

No. 300

Marinetti to take Boccioni, Carrà and perhaps also Russolo with him to Paris so that they could look at the latest painting being done in France and discover 'the directions in which they ought to proceed' before exhibiting there in the spring of 1912. The party arrived in Paris in mid-October 1911, visited the Salon d'Automne where Metzinger's *Tea-Time*, Le Fauconnier's *Abundance*, Léger's *Three Figures*, Gleizes' *Women in a Kitchen* and Duchamp's *Portrait* were all exhibited, and, guided by Severini, did a round of artists' studios including those of Léger, Metzinger, Gleizes, Le Fauconnier and Picasso. It is only after this visit that Cubist influence permeated Futurist painting, for on their return to Milan the Futurists abandoned a number of pre-Paris works, reworked unfinished canvases and conceived new ones in a modified style which was strengthened by a Cubist type of spatial structure.

Futurism was the pictorial expression of a new under-standing and vision of reality, involving not so much a subject as everything connected with it. That is to say, the spectator and his state of mind, the sensations and emotions to which he was subject, the passage of time and a synthesis of light, space and motion. Each of the painters concerned interpreted the Futurist conception pictorially in his own way, so that Futurism never became a consistent style. Nor was it—nor did its interpreters think of

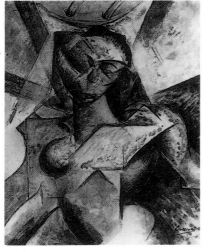

Plate 175

Umberto Boccioni
Figure Study, 1913
Ink and wash, 11¹/₂ × 9 in.

No. 13

it as—an offshoot of Cubism. On the contrary, after their visit to Paris the Futurists reproached Cubism with being tied to the past and felt even more convinced that Futurism was the most modern movement in the whole of Europe. Boccioni stated this clearly in his article 'The Plastic Principles of Futurism' published in *Lacerba* in March 1913: 'What we want to show is an object experienced in the dynamism of its becoming, that is to say the synthesis of the transformations that the object undergoes in its two fluctuations, relative and absolute. We want to create the style of movement. We do not want to observe, dissect, and transpose into images; we identify ourselves in the thing, which is profoundly different. That is to say, an object does not have for us an *a priori* form: we know simply the line which reveals the relationship between its weight (quantity) and its expansion (quality) ... It is our refusal to recognize an *a priori* reality which divides us sharply from Cubism.' Nevertheless, after their visit to Paris in 1911 and their second visit in February 1912 at the time of their exhibition at the Bernheim Gallery, Boccioni,

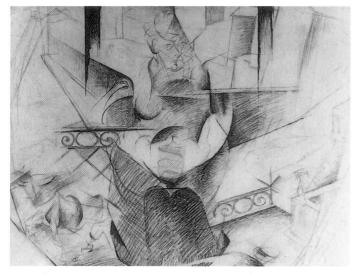

Plate 176

Umberto Boccioni
Study for 'Horizontal Volumes,' 1912
Pencil and ink, 17³/₄ × 23⁷/₈ in.

No. 12

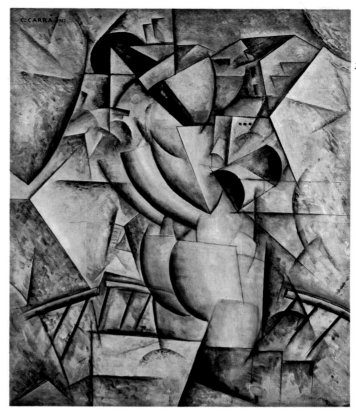

Plate 177

Carlo Carrà
Woman at Window (Simultaneity),
1912
Oil, 57⁷/₈ × 52³/₈ in.

No. 52

Plate 178

Gino Severini
Dancer, 1912–13
Crayon, 26 × 18⁷/₈ in.

No. 301

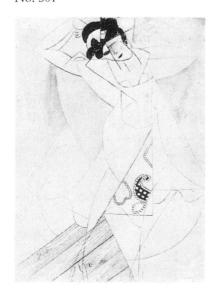

Carrà and their friends did take over certain elements from
Cubism and from Delaunay—transparent planes, disjointed perspectives, linear scaffolding—to clarify their
spatial organization and stabilize their compositions
(Carrà, *Woman with a Glass of Absinthe* (1911); *Portrait of
Marinetti* (1911, reworked 1913); Boccioni, *Elasticity*
(1912); *The Ungraceful* (1913)). Also their use of lettering
and numbers derived from Cubism, while the 'lines of
force' which they invented to represent directional movement were arrived at through a synthesis of early Cubist
analysis of form and their own emotionally expressive
rhythms derived from Symbolist painting.

The Cubist approach to painting only interested the
Futurists in as far as it represented an antithesis to the
impressionist approach which they had inherited. That
is to say, the Impressionists had captured fleeting images
of reality, but while they delighted in the play of light and
color they had allowed the material element to become
insubstantial. Braque and Picasso, on the other hand,

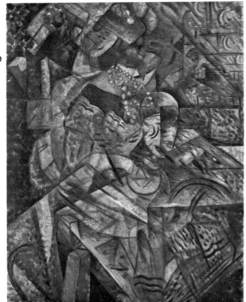

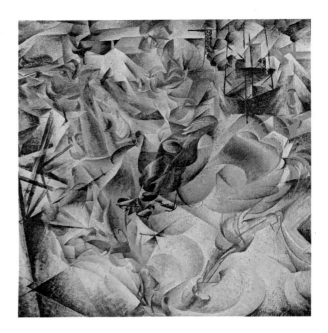

Plate 179

Carlo Carrà
Woman with Glass of Absinthe, 1911
Oil, $26^5/_8 \times 20^5/_8$ in.

No. 51

Plate 181

Carlo Carrà
Boxer, 1913
Ink, $17^3/_8 \times 11$ in.

No. 55

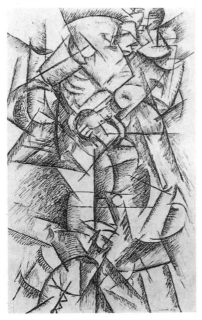

had restored the conception of volume and mass, but had painted a world at rest. 'Once one carves up something which is indivisible,' said Boccioni, 'and starts inventorying its component parts, one kills the life of that thing.' Therefore, the Futurists felt that Cubist painting lacked that vibration and sense of flux which they regarded as inseparable from any truly modern experience of reality. Thus Futurism was at heart a synthesis of Impressionism and ultra-modernity with a dash of Cubism thrown in. But experience was to teach the Futurists a lot about the technical limitations of pictorial representation. So between 1912 and 1915 one finds them experimenting with a range of idioms which at one moment border on Cubist analysis of forms, at another (especially in the work of Carrà) on *papiers collés* and late Cubism, while they also practiced a non-figurative idiom based on abstract rhythmic forms with a symbolic significance. Throughout, however, the Futurists continued to animate their paintings with a Divisionist use of color.

It is in the work of Soffici—never a full member of the Futurist group and always close to Picasso—that one finds the nearest equivalent in Italian painting to true Cubism (*Lines and Volumes of a Figure*, 1912). The painting of Severini too shows a marked Cubist influence, especially

◀ Plate 180

Umberto Boccioni
Elasticity, 1912
Oil, 39³/₈ × 39³/₈ in.

No. 6

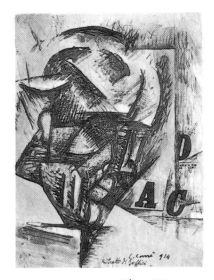

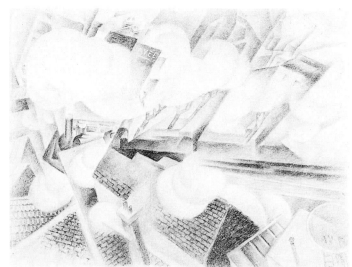

Plate 182

Carlo Carrà
Portrait of Soffici, 1914
Ink and collage, 8¹/₄ × 5⁷/₈ in.

No. 56

Plate 183

Gino Severini
The Train in the City, 1914
Charcoal, 19⁵/₈ × 25¹/₂ in.

No. 302

Plate 184

Carlo Carrà
Standing Figure (Idol), 1914
Pencil, 44⁷/₈ × 18¹/₂ in.

No. 57

Plate 185

Mario Sironi
Self Portrait, 1913
Oil, 20¹/₄ × 19¹/₄ in.

No. 305

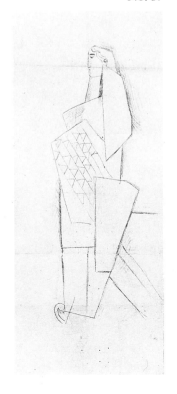

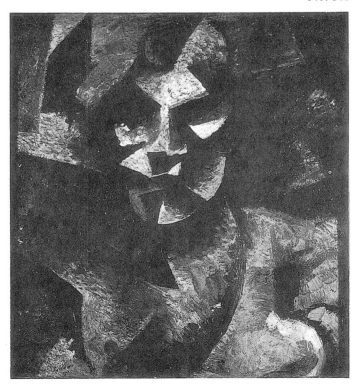

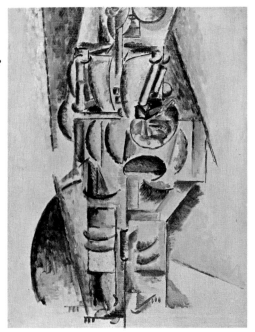

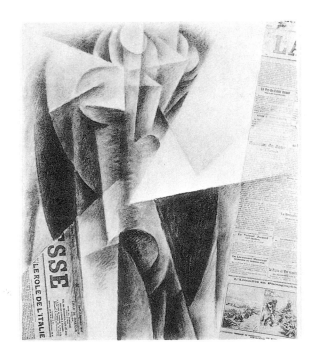

Plate 186

Ardengo Soffici
Lines and Volumes of a Figure, 1912
Oil, 13³/₄ × 11³/₄ in.

No. 306

Plate 188

Gino Severini
Seated Woman, 1914
Watercolor, 16 × 13¹/₂ in.

No. 304

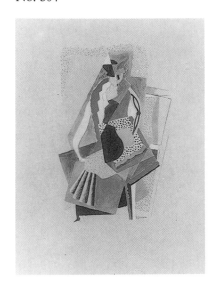

from 1912 on, though he gave it a somewhat decorative interpretation before developing a stylized late Cubist idiom in 1915–16 (*Still Life*, 1917). Sironi too, who joined the Futurist group in 1913, flirted for a moment with a cubistic handling of form. On the other hand, during the last two years of his life Boccioni worked backwards away from the bustle of Futurism through a subtly colored, analytically composed type of early Cubism, to the calm of a richly colored late Cézannesque idiom.

Futurism had repercussions internationally because Marinetti and the artists of the group traveled extensively and showed their works in many cities, but also because its cult of ultra-modernism in art fitted the mood of the time. However, it is important to emphasize that when Léger and Delaunay used the words 'dynamism' and 'simultaneity' in connection with their own pictorial conceptions, they meant something wholly different from the Futurists. The French artists relied in their paintings on static contrasts of form and color, which meant that they achieved their purposes by purely plastic means. But, to the Futurists, 'dynamism' and 'simultaneity' lay in the forcefulness and movement inherent in the subject itself,

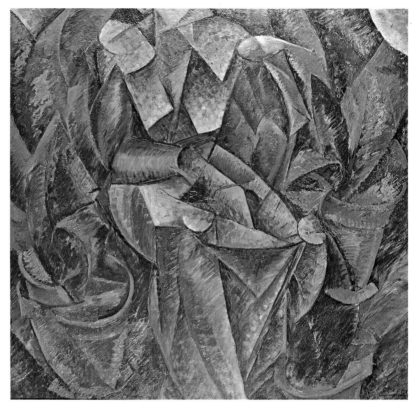

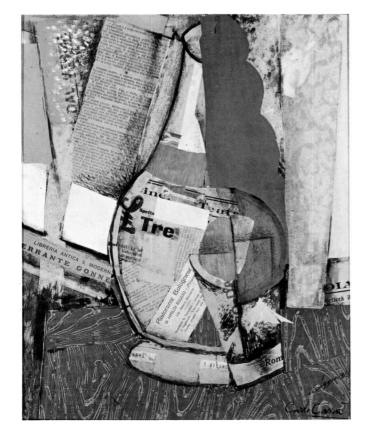

◀ Plate 187

Gino Severini
*Bottle, Vase and Newspaper
on Table*, 1914
Charcoal and collage,
$22^1/_8 \times 18^5/_8$ in.

No. 303

Plate 189

Umberto Boccioni
Spiral Composition, 1913
Oil, $37^3/_8 \times 37^3/_8$ in.

No. 7

Plate 190

Carlo Carrà
Bottle of Wine, 1914
Papier collé, $16 \times 13^1/_2$ in.

No. 53

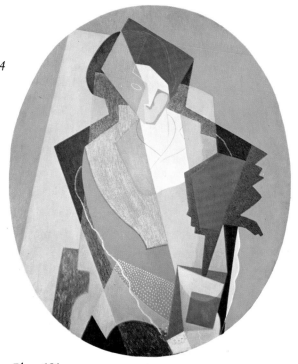

Plate 191

Gino Severini
Seated Woman, 1916
Oil, 39³/₈×31⁷/₈ in. (Oval)

No. 297

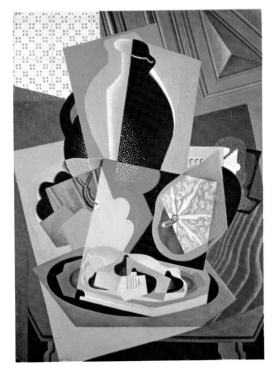

Plate 192

Gino Severini
Still Life with Pumpkin, 1917
Oil and collage, 36¹/₄×25⁵/₈ in.

No. 298

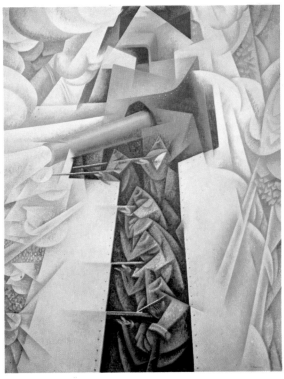

Plate 193

Gino Severini
Armored Train in Action, 1915
Oil, 46×34¹/₂ in.

No. 296

in its extension into time and space, and in the expressive means by which the spectator was made to feel himself situated in the middle of it all. We can therefore say that while Futurism borrowed some stylistic elements from Cubism to help in the solution of its own expressive problems, it represented a fundamentally anti-Cubist attitude and contributed nothing to the development of Cubism as a style.

American Artists in New York and Paris: Weber, Marin, Stella, MacDonald-Wright, Russell and Bruce

If Cubist painting was seen in America before 1914 it was due to the determination of certain liberal, progressive artists, some of whom had lived and worked in Paris during the first decade of the century, while others knew about the movement without leaving America. Together they sponsored the famous Armory Show which opened in New York in February 1913. The original idea behind this exhibition was that of a demonstration against the conventional art favoured by the National Academy of Design and other such Salons in order to stimulate awareness of a new modernism which was then developing in America. But as preparations for the show advanced, the conservatives on the Organizing Committee lost out to a more radical group of artists (Arthur B. Davies and Walt Kuhn in particular) who were determined to make it an international survey of modernism and called in Walter Pach, an expatriate critic and painter, to act as their European guide and ensure full coverage. The International Section was dominated by works of the French School, all the great nineteenth century artists being represented, while the moderns included the Nabis, the Fauves and the following Cubists: Braque, Léger, Picasso, Delaunay, Gleizes, Duchamp, de La Fresnaye, Villon, Picabia, and Duchamp-Villon. Expressionism was represented by Munch, Kandinsky, Kirchner and Lehmbruck; but the Russians, the Czechs, and Mondrian were omitted, while the Futurists refused to participate because they were not allowed to exhibit as a group apart.*

The Armory Show roused the art-conscious public of America and greatly affected subsequent stylistic developments in modern American art. In 1913 American painters still mostly favoured social realism in their choice of subjects and worked with a palette of strong colors. But the Armory Show revealed that several young Americans who had gone to Europe were currently working, either in New York or Paris, in a style which owed something to Cubism, something to Delaunay and also something to Futurism. The most interesting of these was Max Weber, who had arrived in Paris in 1905, had known and admired the work of Henri Rousseau, had worked briefly under Matisse, and had seen early Cubist works by Picasso before returning to New York in January 1909. In the winter of 1910–11 Weber, who by then had become interested in 'primitive' styles, painted *Composition with Three Figures* in which the formal simplifications and elementary faceting recall similar compositions by Picasso of 1908–9. But once Weber had left Paris, he was out of touch with the later evolution of Cubism,* so that in the following three years it was the influences of Rousseau and Matisse which increasingly determined his style.

Pl. 195
Pl. 197

* Except of course through reproductions, and through the large exhibition of drawings by Picasso organized by Stieglitz and Steichen at '291' in April 1911.

Meanwhile, John Marin, a romantic scenic artist in the Whistlerian tradition, had returned to New York in 1910 after spending five years in Europe, and so in 1912 had Joseph Stella. It was the dealer Alfred Stieglitz who introduced Marin after his return to contemporary French art by showing him late watercolors by Cézanne and

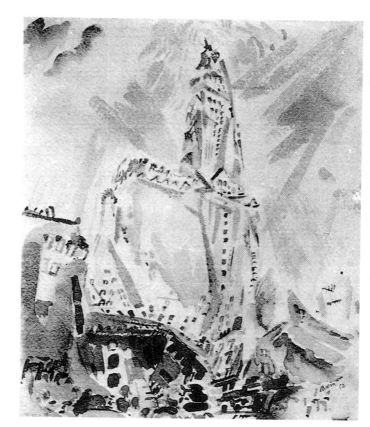

Plate 194

John Marin
The Woolworth Building, no. 31, 1912
Watercolor, 18⁷/₈ × 15¹/₄ in.

The National Gallery of Art,
Washington, D.C.

Pl. 194

★ *American Art Since 1900* (1967), p. 87; see also p. 85: 'For the majority of Americans who called themselves Cubists, Cubism meant little more than sharp lines and acute angles. Cubism was seen, not as a new attitude of mind, but in terms of its surface effects.'

early Cubist drawings by Picasso. Under these influences, Marin evolved a graphic idiom incorporating faceting and formal fragmentation to express his personal emotions on being faced with 'the electric vitality of New York and the vibrant light and air of the Maine coast' (Lloyd Goodrich). Marin's painting cannot be described as Cubist, although he used Cubist devices in a mild way. Generically it is more affiliated by its concern with dynamic movement and flux in nature, as well as by its inherent expressionism, with the art of Delaunay and the Futurists (e.g. *The Woolworth Building*, 1912). 'Significantly,' writes Barbara Rose, 'the most intellectual phase of Cubism, its formative analytical period, made little discernible impression on American artists. There is almost no evidence that the analytical works of Braque and Picasso that were shown at the Armory Show were understood or imitated by American artists.'★ American artists, it seems, reacted vividly and emotionally to reality as they experienced it and were not interested in being able to observe, dissect and transform its material aspects into static images. For

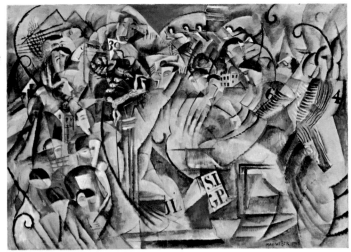

Plate 195

Max Weber
Athletic Contest, 1915
Oil, 40 × 60 in.

No. 319

the generation of 1912—especially for those artists recently returned from Europe—the stunning spectacle of the engineering and constructional feats which marked the emergence of a new world in New York appeared to be 'a concrete manifestation of the spirit of explosive growth, vitality and romantic hope of America' (Sam Hunter), and this sort of vision seemed to demand expression in Futurist terms. Stella had learned about Futurism at first-hand in Paris and Italy in 1911–12, so he was already equipped with the means to realize *Battle of Light, Coney Island* (1914) and *Brooklyn Bridge* (1917–18). Again, although Max Weber had continued to use certain Cubist formal devices since 1911, he too used near-Futurist methods in later works such as *Grand Central Terminal* (1915), *Rush Hour, New York* (1915) and *Athletic Contest* (1915) to express, in more abstract than representational terms, the bustle, garishness, speed and excitement of New York city life.

Pl. 197
Pl. 195

This flirtation with Cubism and Futurism in America itself was finished by 1918, though in Germany Feininger continued to work in a Cubist idiom for several more years. But in Paris a group of expatriate American artists— Morgan Russell and Stanton MacDonald-Wright, also Patrick Bruce—who had settled there in 1907 had evolved, out of the color theories of Chevreul and von Helmholtz and the recent painting of Delaunay and Kupka, a purely abstract colorist idiom akin to Orphism which they called Synchromism. The great difference was, however, that

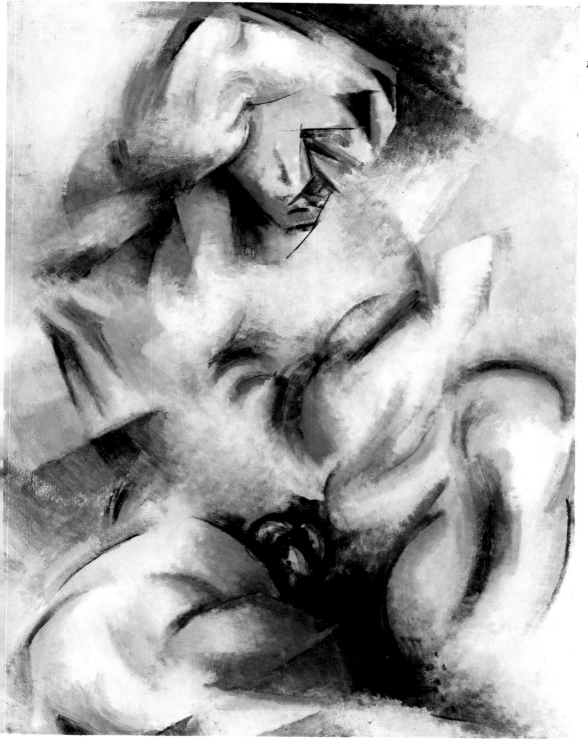

Plate 196

Stanton MacDonald-Wright, *Synchromy in Purple*, 1917 No. 200
Oil, 36 × 28 in.

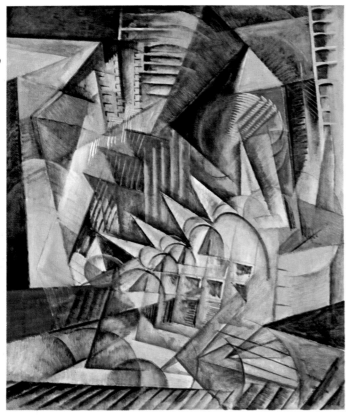

Plate 197

Max Weber
Rush Hour, New York, 1915
Oil, 36 × 30 in.

No. 320

where Delaunay used 'simultaneous' contrasts of color
to evoke light and give form to space, the Synchromists
either used the visual illusion created by juxtaposed colors
advancing and retreating to evoke an undefined, half-
imaginary form in space, or applied bands of color
systematically in order to set up a polyphonic rhythm. In
both cases their idiom was non-figurative. Morgan
Russell's work was seen for the first time in America at
Pl. 196 the Armory Show, and the Synchromists exhibited as a
group in New York in March 1914. By 1919 they had
abandoned Synchromism to become banal figurative
artists.

In England: The Vorticists
Until well after 1912, art in England followed a sub-
Impressionist course unaffected by European stylistic
developments. The first Post-Impressionist Exhibition
organized by Roger Fry in November 1910, at which the
most 'advanced' painting shown was Picasso's early Cubist
Portrait of Clovis Sagot (1909), shocked the public but had

no effect on English art, while the second, held in October 1912, went further and included some representative Cubist works by Braque and Picasso but was no less negative in its effect. No exhibition devoted exclusively to Cubist painting was seen in London before 1914: indeed, at a third showing of modern painting in the autumn of 1913, which included a large group of Italian Futurist works, there was one Cubist and one Orphist painting by Delaunay, while Cubist paintings by Picasso were only shown in photographs. England was, however, subjected to a full experience of Futurism, beginning with a lecture on it by Marinetti at the Lyceum Club in 1910, followed by a Futurist Exhibition at the Sackville Gallery in 1912, an exhibition of Futurist works by Severini at the Marlborough Gallery in April 1913, and a second Futurist Exhibition at the Doré Galleries in April 1914.

Not surprisingly, therefore, the first modern painting which was produced in England between 1913 and 1915 was strongly influenced by Futurist conceptions, both in its reliance on justificatory Manifestos and its concern with modernism and the power of machines. Wyndham Lewis, a theorist, propagandist and painter, was the moving spirit of a group of young artists—including Henri Gaudier-Brzeska, Edward Wadsworth, David Bomberg, William Roberts and some lesser figures—who in March 1914 formed The Rebel Art Center. It was the American poet Ezra Pound, another spokesman for the group, who applied the name Vorticism to the form of art which they invented. Like the Futurists in Italy, these English artists were in revolt against an artistic outlook whose values were sentimental and which had become smug through lack of a modernist challenge. Through a manifesto-periodical entitled *Blast* the group noisily proclaimed their likes, dislikes and aims. 'My object is the construction of Pure Form,' wrote Bomberg in 1914. 'I reject everything in painting that is not Pure Form.' To which in 1915 Wyndham Lewis added: 'A machine is in a greater or lesser degree a living thing. Its lines and masses imply force and action.' Thus unlike Futurism, which was an art of movement, Vorticism was static, adopted a machine aesthetic of 'bareness and hardness' and produced compositions with non-imitative forms in which emphatic linear movements and strong oppositions of dark and light colors were used to express the abstract concepts of force and energy. Rigid and formalist though it was, Vorticism had vitality, but it was short-lived because, before it could get going, the group was disrupted when the artists were mobilized.

The Vorticist group held one collective exhibition at the Doré Galleries in June 1915, when Lewis formulated its character in the Preface to the Catalogue as follows:

By Vorticism we mean:—

a.   Activity as opposed to the tasteful passivity of Picasso.

b.   Significance as opposed to the dull and anecdotal character to which the Naturalist is condemned.

c.   Essential movement and Activity (such as the energy of a mind) as opposed to the imitative cinematography, the fuss and hysterics of the Futurists.

This situates the intentions of the Vorticists as being equally opposed both to Cubism and to Futurism, though they derived much of their vocabulary from the latter. By 1916 Vorticism was dead.

Late Cubism:
1914–1921

4

**Braque and Picasso:
Pasted Papers and Paintings,
Summer 1912—Summer 1914**

By the summer of 1912, as we saw, Braque and Picasso had made of Cubism a language in which they were not only able to re-create forms, volume and space in a new way, but which they were at last beginning to enliven with small passages of color and textural variations. Thus true Cubist paintings had become more tactile and descriptive and acquired a new surface realism. Braque and Picasso had never intended their paintings to be imitations of any existing reality. Now they wanted them to have a still more independent status, that is to say they wanted them not only to be conceptual re-creations of reality but also to be in themselves additions to that reality. So they began to talk of a picture as a *tableau-objet*, a picture-object which was related to but co-equal with everything around it. Pictures regarded in this way obviously needed to be enlivened with color.

Braque took the first decisive step in this direction, for he perceived certain implications resulting from the *collage* of American cloth which Picasso had introduced into his *Still Life with a Caned Chair* at the end of May 1912. If an object could be convincingly represented in a painting by some ready-made element which was a literal, colored equivalent of itself, Braque reasoned, it should be possible to treat color as a free element in the composition. Thus line and color could serve separate functions, the role of line being to re-create forms and space, as well as to integrate the planes of color and the 'real' elements into the pictorial structure. Braque first put his ideas to the test in September 1912 at Sorgues, near Avignon, where he and Picasso were spending the summer. Picasso had returned to Paris for a short while, and Braque was considering how to achieve his purpose, when he observed in a shop-window a roll of wallpaper printed to resemble

Plate 198

Georges Braque
Man with a Pipe, 1912
Papier collé, 24³/₈ × 19¹/₄ in.

No. 37

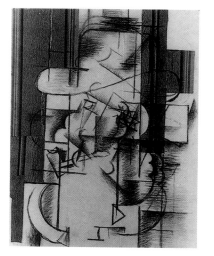

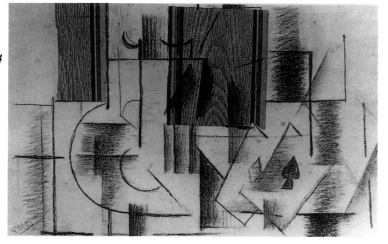

Plate 199

Georges Braque
Glass and Playing Card, 1912
Papier collé, 11⅝ × 18⅛ in.

No. 36

Plate 200

Georges Braque
Still Life on a Table, 1913
Papier collé, 18½ × 24¾ in.

No. 39

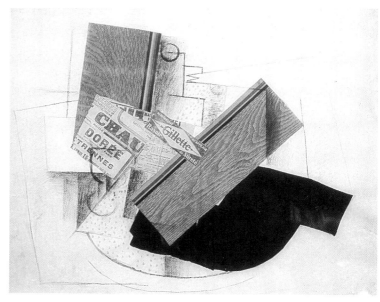

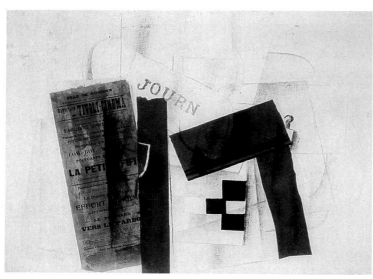

Plate 201

Georges Braque
The Program, 1913
Papier collé,
28¾ × 36⅜ in.

No. 40

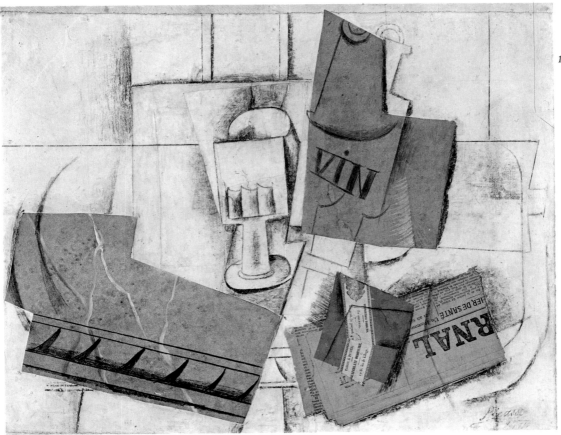

Plate 202   Pablo Picasso, *Still Life with Newspaper*, 1914   No. 261
Papier collé, 25⅝ × 19¾ in.

oak-paneling. He cut three strips of this and arranged them to form the colored basis of a composition. Then he gave them pictorial meaning by drawing over and into them the planes, volumes and representational details of a still life with a fruit-dish and glass on a table. In the process, the three strips of wall-paper came to represent a background plane of paneling and in the foreground a drawer in a wooden table.

Pls. 198, 199   Such was the first *papier collé*, and it is very similar in style to Braque's *Man with a Pipe* (1912). However, even Braque must have been surprised by the break-through resulting from his new technique because, from then on until the summer of 1914, both he and Picasso, whose first *papiers collés* date from a few weeks later, continued to use it with increasing boldness and invention (Braque,

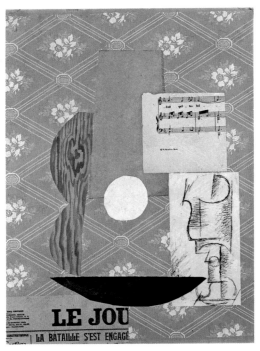

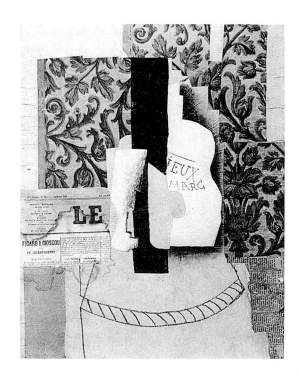

Plate 203

Pablo Picasso
Guitar and Glass, 1913
Papier collé, 18⁷/₈ × 14³/₈ in.

No. 260

Plate 205

Pablo Picasso
Bottle and Glass on Table, 1912–13
Charcoal and collage, 24⁵/₈ × 18⁵/₈ in.

No. 258

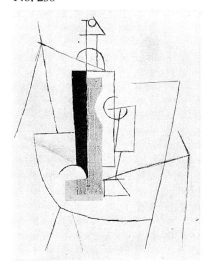

Still Life on a Table, The Program; Picasso, *Bottle and Glass*). The two artists tried out this technique at once to see how it would work with figures, and then moved on to a succession of still lifes in which bits of newspaper, cigarette packs, boxes of matches and wall paper of many different designs, colored fruits, visiting cards and shaped papers representing musical instruments took their place. Also this medium proved to be, for Braque and Picasso, the start of the use of a range of bright and subtly varied colors (Picasso, *Still Life with Newspaper*). Both Braque and Picasso saw and came to relish too the paradoxical new relationship between 'true' and 'false' which this technique enabled them to create. For, the various kinds of paper which they pasted together were (like the original piece of American cloth) literally more 'real,' since they were fragments of the real world, than the objects whose reality was created by drawing or painting and with which they shared an intimate pictorial relationship on equal terms. Yet in another sense most of the pieces of pasted paper were as false as the drawn or painted objects, because they purported to be the wood of a table or a violin, or a cloth or a glass, whereas they were really only pieces of paper. Thus Braque and Picasso

Plate 204

Pablo Picasso
Bottle and Glass, 1912
Papier collé, 24³/₈ × 18⁷/₈ in.

No. 257

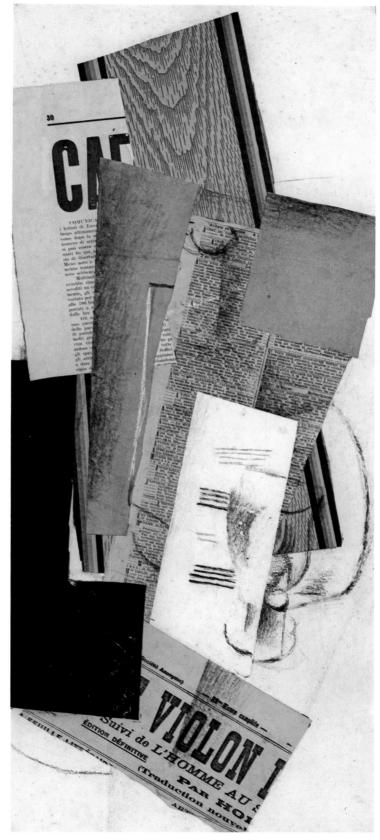

Plate 206

Georges Braque
Glass, Carafe and Newspaper,
1913
Papier collé, 24⁵/₈ × 11¹/₄ in.

No. 38

were in effect obliging real fragments of a non-pictorial world to play unreal roles in a pictorial world of their own creation.

The technique of *papiers collés* assumed a growing importance for both artists firstly because it enabled them to inject a new kind of realism into their art, but secondly because it was yet another defiance of the cult of *belle peinture* and of the belief that fine art was inseparable from a use of fine materials. Moreover this technique was an ironic comment, like the *trompe-l'œil* rendering of a nail in early Cubist paintings, on the conventional notion that reality could only be properly rendered through eye-fooling images created by the hand of a highly skilled artist. By establishing that reality could be pictorially re-created with only the humblest materials, the technique of *papiers collés* reinforced the idea of the *tableau-objet*. It also transformed the ideas of Braque and Picasso as to the relationship between color and form. More importantly, it led them to the conclusion that they could create their own pictorial reality by building up towards it through a synthesis of different elements. Thus in the winter of 1912–13 a fundamental change came about in the pictorial methods of the true Cubists. Whereas previously Braque and Picasso had analyzed and dissected the appearance of objects to discover a set of forms which would add up to their totality and provide the formal elements of a composition, now they found that they could begin by composing with purely pictorial elements (shaped forms, planes of color) and gradually endow them with an objective significance.

This discovery marked the parting of the ways, however, between Braque and Picasso, because by this

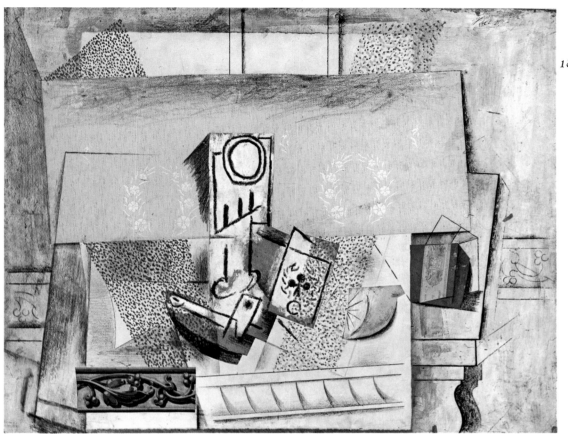

Plate 207

Pablo Picasso
Glass, Pipe and Lemon, 1914
Papier collé, 19³/₄ × 25¹/₂ in.

No. 262

Pl. 205

Pls. 207, 208

time their individual personalities had matured to the point where each was ready to exploit the possibilities of a new technique in his own manner. Braque's work in *papiers collés*, for instance, never shows the degree of freedom and fantasy that one finds in the work of Picasso, and he was more restrained in his use of color. Unlike Picasso and Gris, Braque never used *papiers collés* in conjunction with oil paint but only with drawing. For Braque, either the pasted papers represented themselves or they were planes of color around and into which he organized his composition. Braque's work was always more sober than that of Picasso, so that one never finds in it those deliberately selected news items, topical references or punning witticisms that Gris, as well as Picasso, delighted in. Moreover, Braque never made an entire and somewhat elaborate composition in *papiers collés* as Picasso did in *Glass, Pipe and Lemon* (1914) or Gris in *Guitar, Glasses and Bottle* (1914). However, when both artists began to translate their experiences with *papiers collés* into terms of

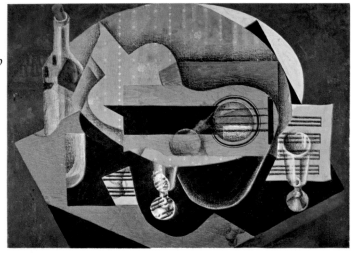

Plate 210 ▶

Georges Braque
Violin (Valse), 1913
Oil, 28³/₈ × 21¹/₄ in.

No. 32

Plate 208

Juan Gris
Guitar, Glasses and Bottle, 1914
Papier collé, 23⁵/₈ × 31⁷/₈ in.

No. 128

oil paint, the same clarification of structure and simplifications of form were apparent in the work of each, which
was a marked contrast with the elaborately informative
paintings they had done during the summer of 1912. The
beginning of this new phase of achievement is illustrated

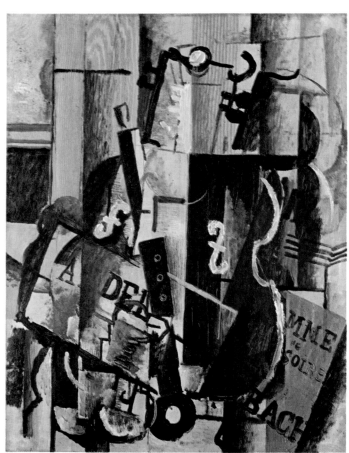

Plate 209

Georges Braque
Still Life with Clarinet and Violin,
1912–13
Oil, 21⁵/₈ × 16⁷/₈ in.

No. 30

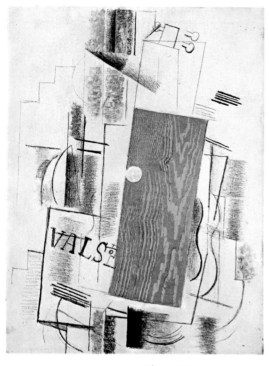

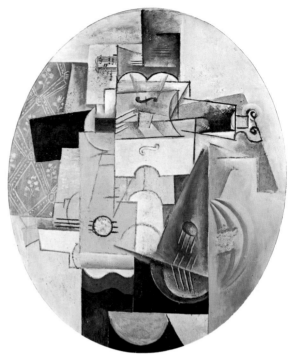

Plate 211

Pablo Picasso
Musical Instruments, 1913
Oil, 39³/₈ × 31⁷/₈ in. (Oval)

No. 243

Plate 212

Pablo Picasso
Glass and Bottle of Bass, 1913
Papier collé, 22⁷/₁₆ × 17³/₄ in.

No. 259

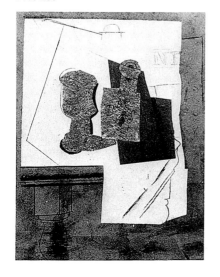

by such lucid and economical compositions as Braque's *Violin* (1913) or Picasso's *Seated Woman with a Guitar* (1913) and *Glass and Bottle of Bass* (1913). From then on, however, their whole effort was directed towards enriching and humanizing the new 'synthetic' Cubist idiom which they had evolved.

Some writers have missed the point of *papiers collés* and have maintained that they were no more than a device for laying-in the composition of a painting. They were nothing of the sort: *papiers collés* were always intended to exist as works of art in their own right, but in addition they turned out to be the source of major stylistic inventions. It was only when Braque and Picasso understood more fully the significance of their discovery that they began to transpose *papiers collés* into terms of oil paint, and this resulted in the synthetic methods of late Cubism and the further discovery that pasting and painting could be effectively combined in one picture.

An important stylistic outcome of *papiers collés* was that the pictorial space in late Cubist paintings became still more flattened and that they therefore became more surface-

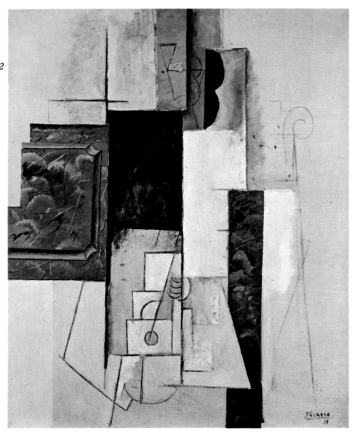

Plate 213

Pablo Picasso
Seated Woman with Guitar, 1913
Oil, 39³/₈ × 32 in.

No. 242

Pls. 214, 216, 217, 244

elaborated. For the synthetic elements out of which the structure was built up were paper-thin planes, superimposed, not transparent, and with defined edges. Braque and Picasso knew they could distinguish these from one another with color, textural variations and over-drawing,

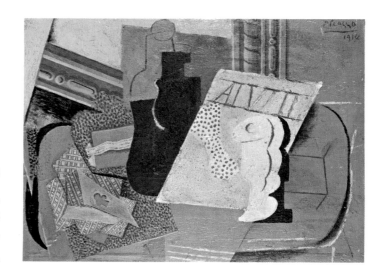

Plate 214

Pablo Picasso
Playing Cards, Bottle and Glass, 1914
Oil, 14¹/₂ × 19³/₄ in.

No. 244

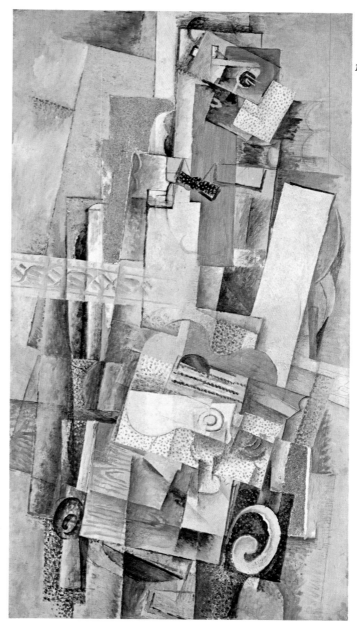

193

Plate 215

Georges Braque
The Guitar Player, 1913–14
Oil, 51¹/₄ × 28³/₄ in.

No. 31

which gave them representational significance. There remained, however, the problem of detaching them from each
other so as to evoke volume, and this problem Braque and
Picasso solved with light. Color now being separated
from form as an element in the painting, the two artists
could direct light how they liked without fear of formal or
tonal modifications. So they used light, and its concomitant
shadow, to differentiate between the planes and situate
volumes in space, as is evident on the left side of Braque's
Pl. 215   great synthetic figure painting *The Guitar Player* (1913).

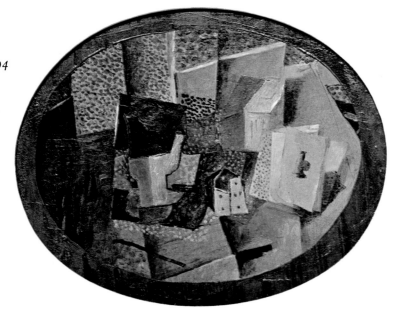

Plate 216

Georges Braque
Still Life with Ace of Clubs, 1914
Oil, 14$^1/_2$ × 21 in. (Oval)

No. 33

The color structure of synthetic Cubist paintings thus came to be organized in two ways: local color used descriptively and monochromatic shading used to create form. Color and light could thus function pictorially as independent elements in the same way as color and form.

At this stage, Picasso also experimented in a few paintings with a sort of relief technique. That is to say, he used sand mixed with paint to build up around certain objects an area of heavy impasto so as to create a false three-dimensional effect on the surface of the canvas. This worked like a low-relief sculpture when the painting was exposed to the light of reality and set up a second play of shadows. Gradually therefore the synthetic idiom revealed itself capable of infinite extension. So we find both Braque and Picasso making great efforts in 1913–14 to modify the severity of their synthetic structures and enrich their paintings with more and stronger colors and more naturalistic details. One means they greatly favoured was the dotting technique of pointillism, which they employed to enliven surfaces, to evoke a play of light, to counteract the monotony of planes of one color and to create a decorative effect (Braque, *The Guitar Player*; Picasso, *Fruit-Dish,* *Bottle and Guitar*). It is this element which has given rise to the meaningless classification of late Cubism as 'rococo.'

Pl. 218

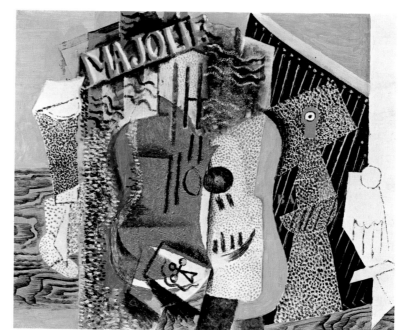

Plate 217

Pablo Picasso
Ma Jolie, 1914
Oil, 18¹/₂ × 21⁵/₈ in.

No. 246

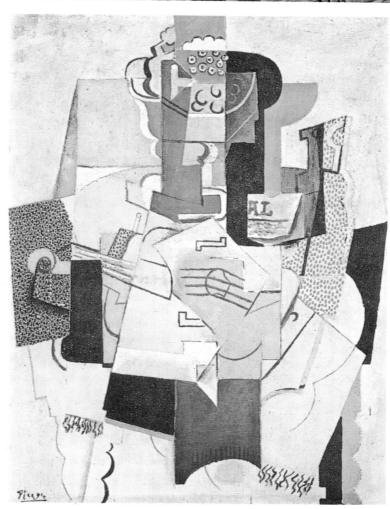

Plate 218

Pablo Picasso
Fruit-Dish, Bottle and Guitar,
1914
Oil, 36¹/₄ × 28³/₄ in.

No. 245

Juan Gris : Paintings and Pasted Papers, 1912–14

The third of the true Cubist painters, Juan Gris, was six years younger than Braque and Picasso. He arrived in Paris from Madrid in 1906 at the age of nineteen and settled in the same building in Montmartre as his compatriot and friend Picasso. Gris played no part in the evolution of Cubism during the following five years because he was earning his living as a humorous draughtsman and completing on his own his formation as a painter. Nevertheless he was able to follow Picasso's development closely and when, at the end of 1911, he first allowed friends to see some of his pictures,★ they found that this intensely serious young man had been finding his own way towards Cubism by a reappraisal of its origins in the work of Cézanne. Admittedly he was not imitating Cézanne, but the broken contours, the sense of volume, the varying perspectives and the definition of planes were there, although unlike Cézanne Gris gave his forms strong outlines. *Bottle of Wine and Water Jar* (1911) is the equivalent in Gris' work of early Cubist works of 1908–09 by Braque and Picasso.

★ Gris' first exhibition was a showing of 15 works at Clovis Sagot's gallery in Montmartre in January 1912.

Plate 219

Juan Gris
Place Ravignan, 1911   *Pl. 220*
Pencil, 17¹/₈ × 12 in.

No. 132

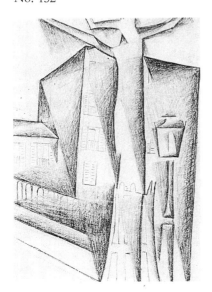

It was characteristic of Gris that, when he began to paint seriously, he did not try to imitate the appearance of his friends' latest paintings but sought first to understand, through personal experience, how they had arrived at their conceptions of form and of spatial structure. Gris was a less intuitive and empirical artist than Braque or Picasso. He had been trained in the methods of science and engineering, was of an intellectual turn of mind, and was ready to use mathematical calculations to make his version of Cubism more rational. This is evident in a number of early drawings where the angles and intersections of lines and forms have been calculated with a protractor and compass, thereby pro-

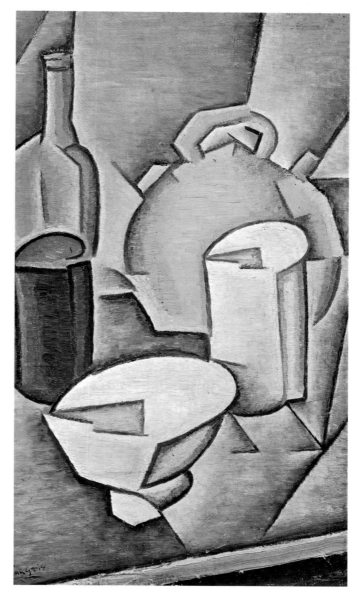

Plate 220

Juan Gris
Bottle of Wine and Water Jar, 1911
Oil, 21³/₄ × 13 in.

No. 107

★ Between themselves, Braque and
Picasso referred to Gris on this
account as '*la fille soumise*' (subjugated
daughter), an expression with a
double entente since it also means
'registered prostitute.'

ducing a somewhat schematic effect (*Flowers in a Vase*, 1912).
Yet even so Gris always tempered his science with the
workings of his personal sensibility,★ and the many
pentimenti and freely invented passages in his paintings are
evidence of his constant concern that the reality of natural
forms should not be subjected to 'monstrous' distortions
dictated by some pre-determined design. It was this
duality in his nature that saved Gris' Cubism from
becoming systematic, while his logical mind, original
vision and remarkable technical ability gave him the
strength to make a major creative contribution to the
development of Cubism.

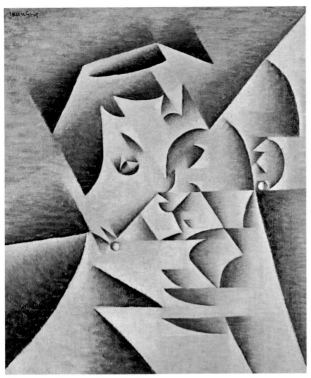

Plate 221

Juan Gris
The Artist's Mother, 1912
Oil, 21³/₄ × 18 in.

No. 109

* Exhibited at the Indépendants in March 1912.

Plate 222

Juan Gris
Flowers in a Vase, 1911–12
Charcoal, 17¹/₂ × 12 in.

No. 133

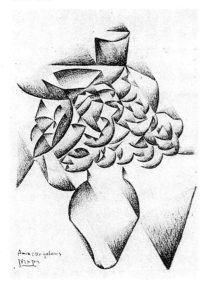

Once Gris had begun to paint seriously, he made rapid progress, and the portraits of his mother and of Picasso,* executed early in 1912, show him handling an analytical idiom with clarity and economy, especially in the combined profile and full-face views of the heads, in the way the figure is related to the space around it, and in the evocation of volume. But owing to Gris' aim to reconcile a logical presentation of things with a strict formal organization of his canvas, these paintings are more stylized than comparable early Cubist works by Braque and Picasso. Also Gris used light (from a single source) as an active factor for developing forms. Chiaroscuro effects are therefore very marked throughout his work and in a number of his early paintings Gris experimented with planes of light formalized as a succession of diagonal bands. Gris' objects have simple forms which are illuminated along their contours, these being broken into here and there by shadows. But Gris uses this contrast of light and shadow to flatten the pictorial space and fuse objects with the background (*Guitar and Flowers*). However, the concessions which Gris found himself obliged to make on account of the distorting effects of

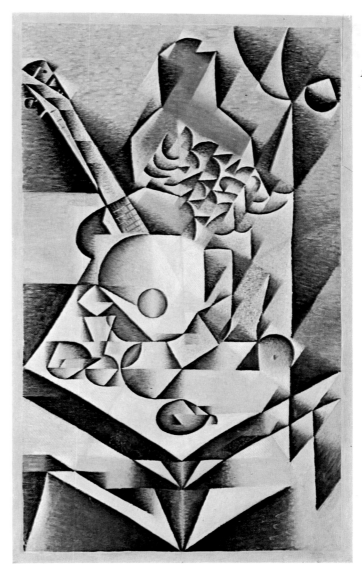

Plate 223

Juan Gris
Guitar and Flowers, 1912
Oil, 44$^1/_8$ × 27$^5/_8$

No. 110

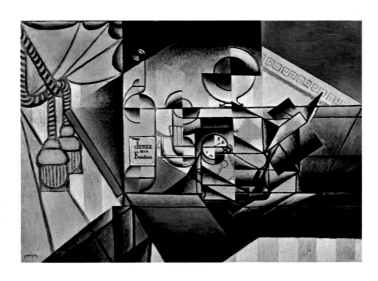

Plate 224

Juan Gris
Still Life with Bottle and Watch, 1912
Oil, 25$^3/_4$ × 36$^1/_4$ in.

No. 111

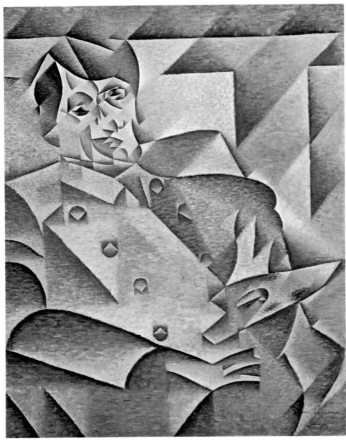

Plate 225

Juan Gris
Portrait of Picasso, 1912
Oil, 36⁷/₈ × 29¹/₄ in.

No. 108

Pl. 224

light displeased him, and in the paintings which followed, during the summer and fall of 1912 (*Bottle of Sherry and Watch*), he began to impose on his composition a firm over-all linear framework which served to make forms more explicit, to define spatial relationships and to make the composition static.★

★ Gris was closely in touch at this time with Gleizes, Metzinger, and Marcoussis, who were influenced by his methods. They all exhibited at the *Section d'Or*. It was Gris' capacity for reasoning and theory, for explaining Cubism, which appealed to these other artists.

Gris' linear framework of squares, triangles and cylinders—which he imposed over his subject like the leads in a stained-glass window—derived in part from his formal division of the canvas and in part also from the outlines of objects represented. Within the compartments of this framework, Gris included realistic details and separate aspects of whatever was represented. He thus assembled a total image out of static partial aspects and left the spectator to re-integrate the whole for himself by a visual-intellectual synthesis. This was a personal interpretation of the analytical procedure of early Cubism, and Gris went further than either Braque or Picasso in the number of views in section, plan and elevation which he managed to combine. This was yet another expression of his desire to respect reality in its entirety, and it is significant that Gris never passed over its solid tangible aspects to concentrate, as Braque and Picasso had done in 1910–11, on clarifying the planar and spatial structure of his Cubist compositions. Another feature in which Gris' painting differs from that of Braque and Picasso is that he never worked in a neutral palette. Color is present, although subdued, in the *Portrait of Picasso*, while by the spring of 1913 Gris was composing with areas of bright color, some of which were descriptive, others conditioned by tonal necessity, and still others chosen to complete a harmony.

Plate 226

Juan Gris
Playing Cards and Glass of Beer, 1913
Oil and collage, 20⅝ × 14⅜ in.

No. 112

Plate 227

Juan Gris
Landscape at Céret, 1913
Oil, 36¼ × 23⅝ in.

No. 113

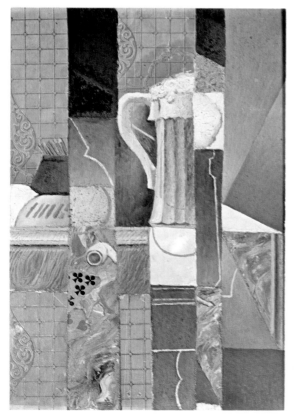

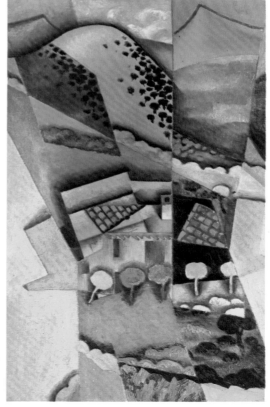

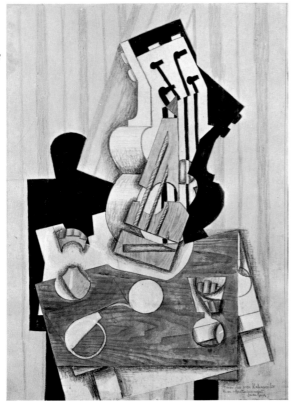
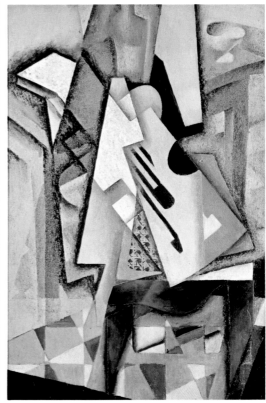

Plate 228

Juan Gris
Still Life with a Guitar, 1913
Watercolor, 25⅝ × 18¼ in.

No. 134

Plate 229

Juan Gris
Guitar on a Chair, 1913
Oil and collage, 39⅜ × 25⅝ in.

No. 114

By the spring of 1913, Gris had dispensed with his linear framework and had arrived at a new compositional device—deriving undoubtedly from the technique of *papiers collés*—namely a system of vertical, horizontal and triangular planes which overlap but are not transparent (*Playing Cards and Glass of Beer*; *Landscape at Céret*). These planes, which are differentiated from each other tonally, and often texturally as well, provide the spatial structure of the composition as they take their places in front of or behind others. On each of them Gris either represents, in its solidity, a single aspect of one or more objects, or else in outline some related aspect. These methods were purely personal and used only by Gris.

Already in September 1912, Gris—who was therefore not much behind Picasso and Braque—had begun to introduce *collage* into his oil paintings: a piece of mirror, 'because it could not be imitated,' into *The Washstand*, and a label into *Bottle of Sherry and Watch*. However, Gris never employed *papiers collés* simply in conjunction with drawing. Instead he used the technique right away, in

Pl. 224

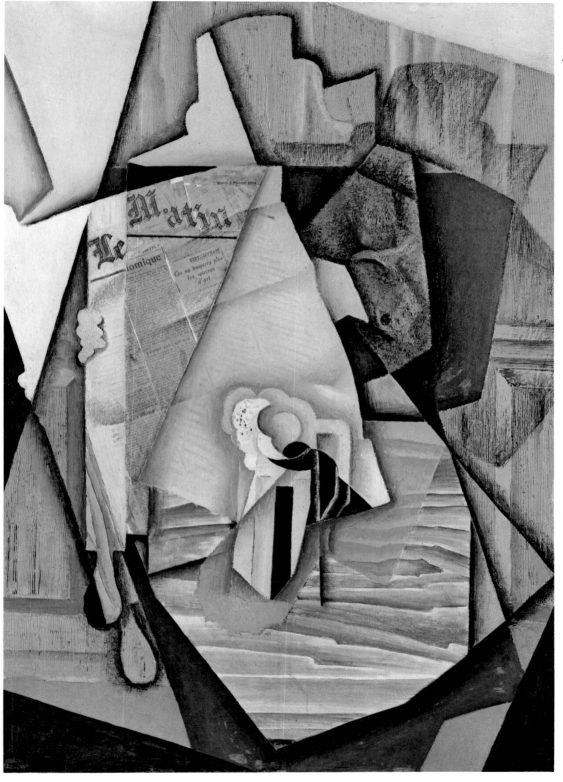

Plate 230   Juan Gris, *Figure Seated in a Cafe*, 1914   No. 115
Oil and collage, 39 × 28¼ in.

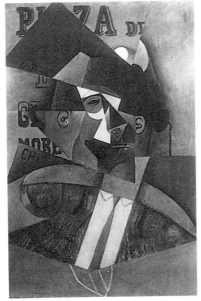

Plate 231

Juan Gris
The Bullfighter, 1913
Oil and collage, 36¼ × 23⅝ in.

Mrs. Mary Hemingway, New York.

Pl. 230

Plate 232

Juan Gris
Still Life with a Bunch of Grapes, 1914
Papier collé, 31⅞ × 23⅝ in.

No. 130

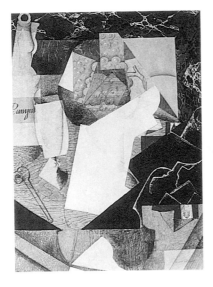

the summer of 1913, as a means of introducing literal, descriptive details into oil paintings (*Guitar on a Chair*)—part of an engraving, a page of a book, bottle labels, wall paper, playing-cards—with as much invention as in the works of Picasso. Nevertheless, though Gris made his painting subtler, richer and more informative by these means, his Cubist handling remained stiff by comparison with that of Braque and Picasso. It also differed significantly in that Gris often used repeated views in the form of a black negative image to assert the totality of objects, and also isometric views (which are a special form of scientific perspective) to complete his pictorial re-creations of them. Through all of this, Gris' ways of evoking volume were more forceful and dramatic than those of Braque and Picasso (*Man in a Café*, 1914). Also, because Gris treated the basic pictorial design as partially independent of the objective content of his painting, and did not restrict his color to descriptive purposes, he arrived at a use of *papiers collés* in 1914 which was significantly different from that of either Braque or Picasso. That is to say, Gris first established a composition with differently shaped, colored papers and then allowed them to suggest the objective content of the painting which he could finally realize (*Fruit-Dish and Carafe*). This he completed, as the image evolved, either by pasting in additional elements or by modifying the design. However, unlike Picasso, Gris avoided decorative elements, although he did incorporate little witticisms. Thus Gris' contribution to the use of *papiers collés* and to the development of the synthetic Cubist language was both important and personal.

Through his sincerity and originality, Gris achieved an independent position at the heart of Cubism. Like Braque

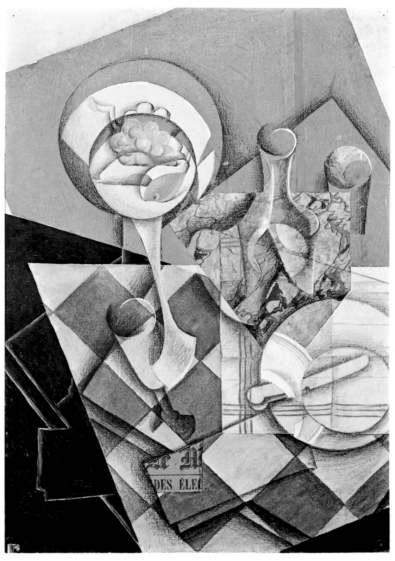

Plate 233

Juan Gris
Fruit-Dish and Carafe, 1914
Papier collé, 36¼ × 25½ in.

No. 129

and Picasso, he combined in his paintings of 1913–14 an analytical with a synthetic treatment of forms in his recreation of objects. But unlike them, Gris based his compositions on an arrangement of differently colored elements which he referred to as his 'flat, colored architecture.' And he adopted this procedure because, he said, he found it 'more natural to make subject "X" coincide with the picture that (he had) in mind than to make picture "X" coincide with a given subject.' That is to say, Gris began 'with an abstraction in order to arrive at a true fact,' a procedure which gives his early Cubist paintings a characteristic severity but also allowed him to indulge in an exceptional richness of color.

Cubism in Paris during the War Years

The declaration of war in August 1914 accomplished the break-up of a movement which by the end of 1913 had already begun to disintegrate from within. By that time it was clear to all that the artistic values of the nineteenth century had been toppled, that a new artistic tradition had been initiated and that the urge was widespread to produce a new type of art for the twentieth century. That this urge manifested itself in conceptions of which some were genial and fertile, while others were foolish and sterile, mattered little. An element of idealism was involved simultaneously with an element of competition among artists during the period 1907–14, and this had spurred even the weaker ones on to give briefly of their best before falling away. Cubism was at once the central event of the period, while its spiritual and material clarity made of it the most challenging stylistic conception. For good and for bad Cubism inspired a number of related movements, some leading to non-figuration, which was the absolute antithesis of Cubism.

Plate 234

Henri Matisse
Pink and Blue Head, 1914
Oil, 29³/₁₆ × 17³/₈ in.

Jean Matisse, Paris.

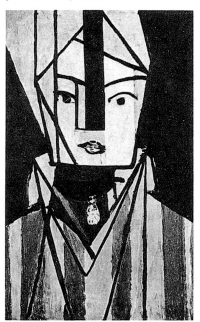

After 1913 no new painters took up Cubism and made a significant contribution to its development, because those who did tried to start from the appearance of late Cubism without understanding its basic premises. But it is interesting that Matisse, at the age of forty-five and already long established as the leading colorist of the Paris School, should have felt impelled to experiment briefly, in 1914–15, with the Cubist technique. Thus in his *Pink and Blue Head* (1914?) Matisse attempted with a planimetric linear structure, imposed over areas of flat luminous color, to give volume to a head in the way that Picasso and Gris had done in paintings of 1912. Then again in *Goldfish* (1914–15; coll. Schoenborn, New York) he introduced a Cubist-type linear grid to arti-

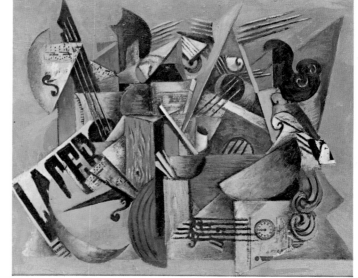

Plate 235

Serge Férat
Still Life with Violin, 1913
Oil with collage, 21¼ × 25⅝ in.

No. 88

★ The linear structure in both paintings is reminiscent of that sometimes used by Gris in 1912—13. Was Matisse's belated interest in Cubism aroused by Gris? Was he briefly influenced by Gris? The date of *Pink and Blue Head* is uncertain: it is usually catalogued as 1913?, but seems on stylistic grounds to be later. We do not know when Matisse met Gris: they had a great friend in common, Germaine Raynal, who was painted by Gris in the fall of 1912 and by Matisse in the winter 1913—14. At all events, Gris was on close terms with Matisse at Collioure in September 1914, when they talked painting 'relentlessly' (Gris, *Letters*) day after day.

culate a highly simplified and flattened spatial structure by suggesting intersections of different planes.★ But Matisse's flirtation with Cubist methods was neither deeply engaged nor of long duration. He had come to it too late to be able either to assimilate such a complex, revolutionary idiom or to reconcile its down-to-earth realism with his own opposing hedonistic aesthetic.

It was those not eligible or fit for military service, foreign artists and some sculptors, who carried on Cubism in Paris through the war years. But the most important work was done by Picasso, Gris, Henri Laurens, Jacques Lipchitz and, from 1917 onwards when he was demo-

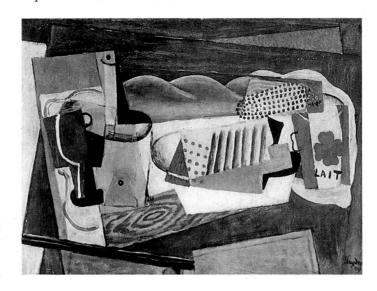

Plate 236

Henri Hayden
Still Life with a Bottle of Milk, 1917
Oil, 18 × 24½ in.

No. 146

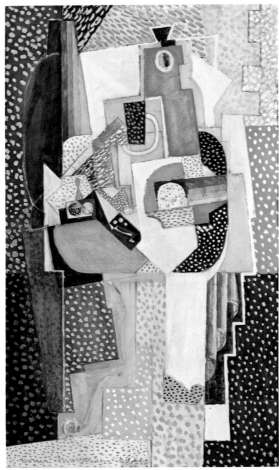

Plate 237

Louis Marcoussis
Still Life on a Table, 1921
Gouache, 20 × 12 in.

No. 207

Plate 238

Jean Metzinger
Still Life, 1917
Oil, 32 × 25⁵/₈ in.

No. 215

Plate 239

Albert Gleizes
Broadway, 1915
Oil, 38³/₄ × 30 in.

No. 100

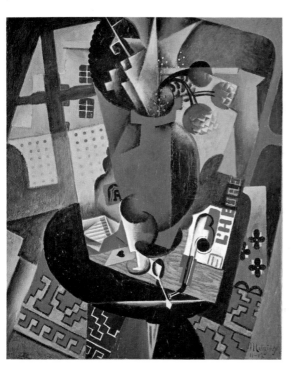

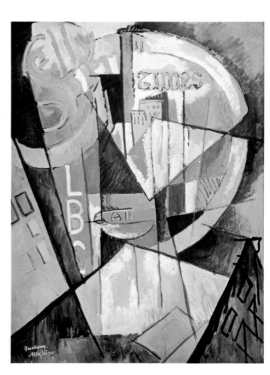

Plate 240

Diego Rivera
The Café Terrace, 1915
Oil, 23⁷/₈ × 19¹/₂ in.

No. 295

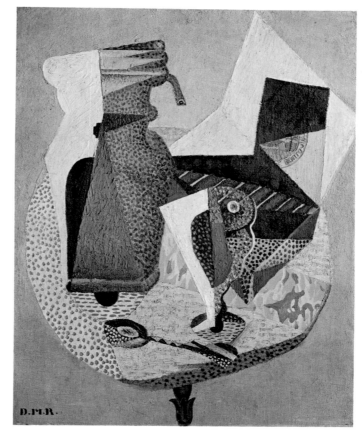

Plate 241

Louis Marcoussis
The Habitué, 1920
Oil, 63³/₈ × 38¹/₈ in.

Peggy Guggenheim Collection,
Venice.

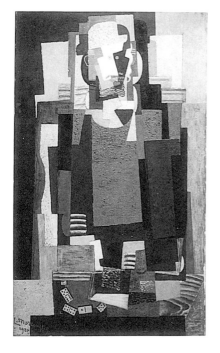

bilized, by Braque. Severini, who had moved nearer to Cubism in 1913–14, when he produced a charming series of *papiers collés* which were more decorative than profoundly creative, continued to work in a Cubist style in Paris until 1919. Apart from him, three other foreign artists were living in Paris at the time who also painted Cubist works: Serge Jastrebzoff-Férat, a Russian who was a close friend of Apollinaire and Picasso, and began to produce Cubist compositions in 1913; Diego Rivera, a Mexican artist who proved an adept follower of the true Cubists between 1914 and 1916; and Henri Hayden, a Polish artist, who became a friend of Metzinger and Gris and painted derivative Cubist-style still lifes between 1916 and 1920. Nearly all of those who came back from the front abandoned their pre-war Cubist style, Léger in particular adopting in 1917 a machine aesthetic. But Metzinger continued to work in a Cubist style between 1916 and 1919, while Marcoussis, whose pre-war output of Cubist paintings had been very small and uneven in quality, produced his major work: *The Habitué* in 1920.

Picasso : Painting 1914–21

By 1914–15 Picasso, then working on his own, felt sure enough of his control over the synthetic Cubist language to want to put its full representational possibilities to the test and establish a valid antithesis with regard to naturalism. So he began to make the forms of his objects correspond more nearly with everyday appearances and employed various devices to complete and enrich the synthetic Cubist language (*Vive la France; Still Life with Fruit*). As far as he could, Picasso kept the planes of his composition flat, as they had been in *papiers collés*, but gave it a boost of new vitality by employing stronger and more varied colors, by introducing ornamental *motifs* and by making lively textural variations (*Guitar, Bottle and Flute*). In other paintings, on the contrary, Picasso reacted against this tendency and re-emphasized the flatness, severity and almost abstract structural basis of synthetic Cubism (*Woman with a Guitar; Harlequin, 1915*). Picasso was making an effort in all of these ventures towards humanizing late Cubism, because he realized that

Pls. 242, 243

Pl. 244

Pl. 245, 246

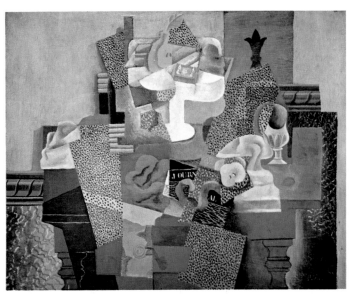

Plate 242

Pablo Picasso
Still Life with Fruit, 1915
Oil, 25 × 31¹/₂ in.

No. 248

Plate 244 ▶

Pablo Picasso
*Guitar, Bottle and Flute
on a Table*, 1915
Oil, 42 × 28 in.

No. 249

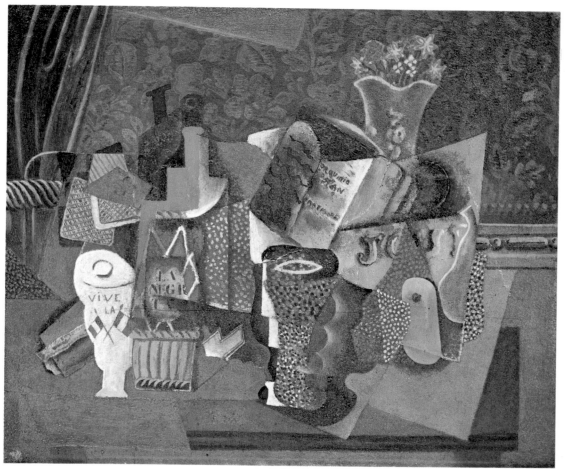

Plate 243   Pablo Picasso, *Vive la France*, 1914   No. 247
Oil, $20^1/_2 \times 25$ in.

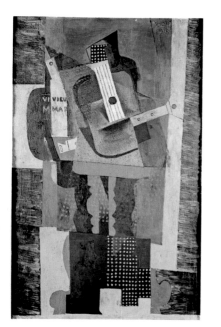

if he did not succeed his new idiom could not become a viable alternative to naturalism.

Picasso was hoping to find for himself a workable equation of values between Cubist reality, visual reality and the accepted pictorial reality created by the eye-fooling methods of naturalism. Now Picasso had not lost that inventive spirit which, in 1912–13, had inspired his experiment of introducing a 'real' element into a painting through *collage*. In 1915–16 this spirit re-asserted itself and prompted Picasso to attack reality simultaneously from two angles. Thus while continuing to work in a synthetic Cubist idiom, he again began to make naturalistic drawings of people and objects, and in some paintings one finds side by side a naturalistically drawn

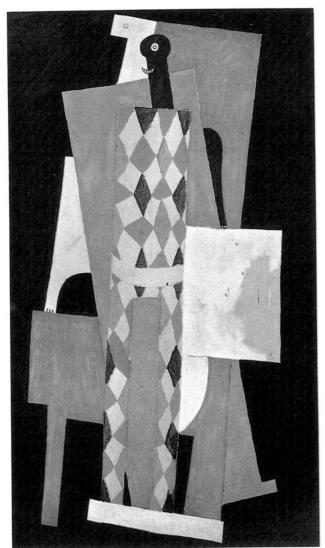

212

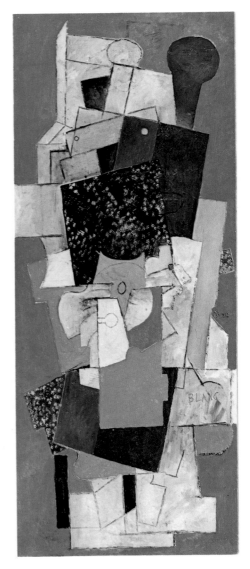

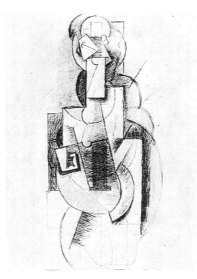

Plate 247

Pablo Picasso
Woman with Guitar,
1914
Pencil, 25 × 18³/₄ in.

No. 271

Plate 249 ▶

Pablo Picasso
Still Life with Clarinet and Guitar, 1915
Watercolor, 7¹/₂ × 6 in.

No. 273

◀ Plate 245

Pablo Picasso
Harlequin, 1915
Oil, 72^1/$_4$ × 41^3/$_8$ in.

No. 251

◀ Plate 246

Pablo Picasso
Woman with Guitar, 1915
Oil, 72^3/$_4$ × 29^1/$_2$ in.

No. 250

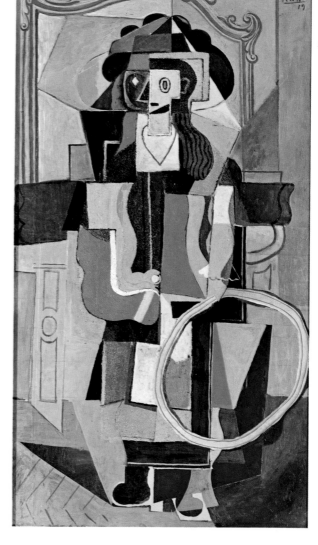

Plate 248

Pablo Picasso
Girl with a Hoop, 1919
Oil, 31^1/$_8$ × 16^3/$_4$ in.

No. 254

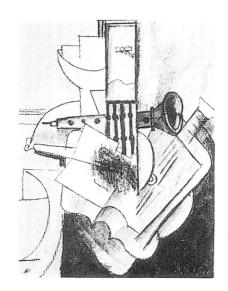

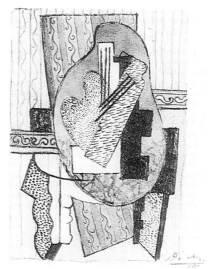

Plate 250

Pablo Picasso
Still Life with Guitar, 1915
Watercolor, 5^3/$_4$ × 4^3/$_4$ in.

No. 272

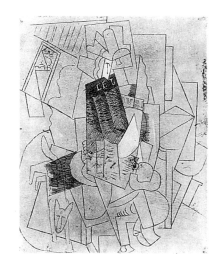

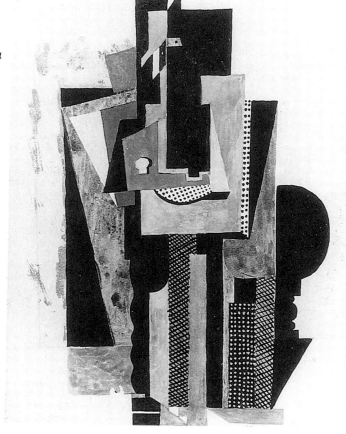

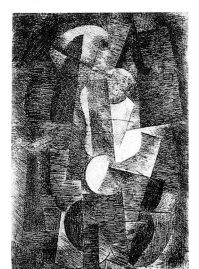

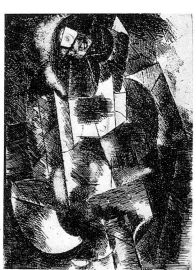

Plate 251

Pablo Picasso
Man Seated at Table, 1916
Gouache, $10^3/_4 \times 8^3/_4$ in.

No. 274

Plate 253

Pablo Picasso
Man with a Guitar, 1915
Engraving, $6^1/_{16} \times 4^9/_{16}$ in.

No. 285

Plates 254, 255

Pablo Picasso
Max JACOB:
Le Siège de Jérusalem, 1913
Drypoints, Plate I $6^3/_{16} \times 4^9/_{16}$ in.
Plate III $6^5/_{16} \times 4^5/_{16}$ in.

No. 287

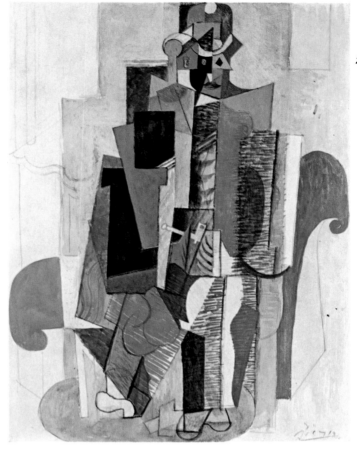

◀ Plate 252

Pablo Picasso
Man with a Dog, 1914
Etching, $10^7/_8 \times 8^5/_8$ in.

No. 283

Plate 256

Pablo Picasso
Man with Pipe Seated in Armchair,
1916
Gouache, $13 \times 10^3/_{16}$ in.

No. 275

Plate 257

Pablo Picasso
Bottle, Playing Card and Pipe on
Table, 1919
Oil, $19^3/_4 \times 24$ in.

No. 253

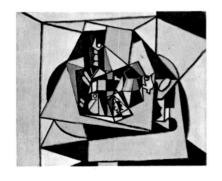

object, another re-created in analytical terms and a third created by a synthetic procedure. This abrupt return to naturalism was interpreted by many people as a renunciation of Cubism, an admission of defeat. But Picasso is no purist, no respecter of conventions, least of all of those which he might be creating for himself in his own work. He already knew where the limitations of the naturalistic approach lay; now he was trying to find out those of Cubism, as Gris was to do after him. This brought Picasso to the realization that the naturalistic approach to reality with its inevitable illusionism was, in its way, no less valid than that of Cubism, and that they should be regarded as complementary to each other. This double-play—which Picasso put to a living test in his designs for the ballet *Parade* (1916–17)—has prevailed in his art ever since, and it reflects a conviction, which is certainly Cubist in spirit, that the painter cannot fully express what he sees and knows about reality if he

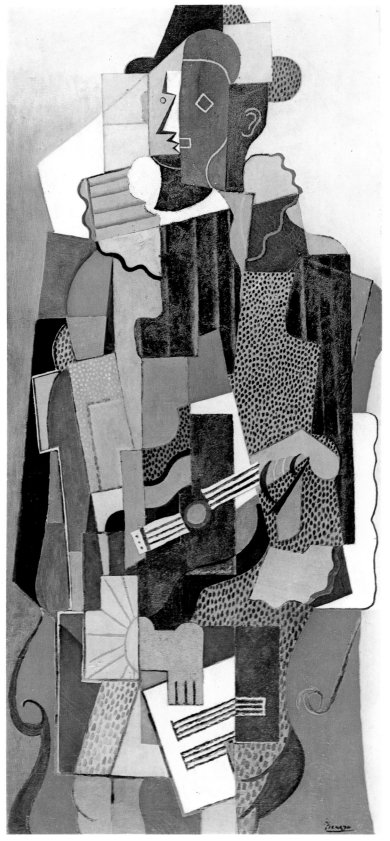

Plate 258

Pablo Picasso
Harlequin, 1918
Oil, $58 \times 26^{1}/_{2}$ in.

No. 252

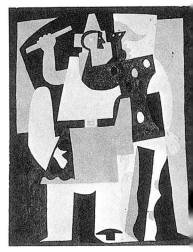

Plate 259

Pablo Picasso
Pierrot and Harlequin, 1920
Gouache, $10^{1}/_{2} \times 8^{1}/_{4}$ in.

No. 277

Plate 261 ▶

Pablo Picasso
*Guitar and Music
Score on a Table*,
1920
Gouache, $10^{1}/_{2} \times 8$ in.

No. 278

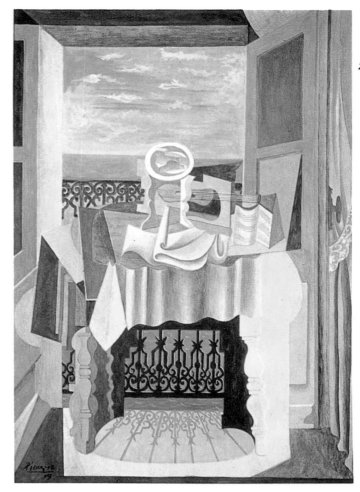

Plate 260

Pablo Picasso

Open Window at St. Raphael, 1919

Gouache, 13³/₄ × 9³/₄ in.

No. 276

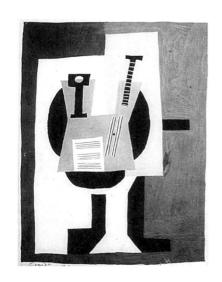

re-creates it only in a single manner. Thus Picasso alternated between two pictorial approaches to reality in order to find something more, because experience had taught him that a whole is made up of the sum of its facets. And the outcome of these various experiences is revealed in the elaboration and new monumentality of two such impressive late Cubist figure paintings as *Harlequin* (1918) and *Girl with a Hoop*. Moreover, at this stage Picasso turned his attention to the problem (which Gris had dealt with five years earlier) of marrying, in synthetic Cubist terms, the confined internal space of a room with the external space beyond an open window (*Still Life on a Table in Front of an Open Window*, 1920).

But the synthetic Cubist procedure reached one of its fullest and most successful attainments in two great

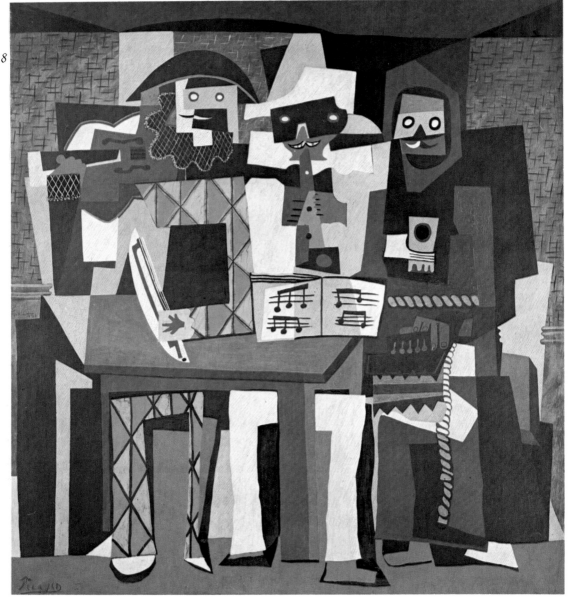

Plate 262

Pablo Picasso, *Three Masked Musicians*, 1921   No. 256
Oil, 80 × 74 in.

★ Hayden's painting of a similar subject, exhibited at the Indépendants in the spring of 1920, a lifeless confused work, gives the measure of the difference between an un-inspired Cubist imitator and one of the creators of the style.

figure compositions which Picasso painted at Fontainebleau in the summer of 1921, the two versions, so alike and yet so different, of *Three Masked Musicians*.★ Here, formal clarity, simplicity, monumentality, richness of color and a subtly varied but never excessive use of ornamental passages combine with humor, gaiety and vivid charac-terization to re-create three familiar personages of the Commedia dell'Arte, which Picasso had already made his own in a number of earlier works.

Braque : Painting 1917–21

Braque's close partnership with Picasso was brought to a sudden end when he was recalled to his regiment at the outbreak of war. Thus the continuity of Braque's pictorial evolution, unlike that of Picasso, was interrupted for three years. When he was able to paint again, after recovering from a serious headwound, he had to find his way alone, and not unnaturally this took time. But eventually Braque's individual personality, which had already been manifest in his paintings of 1913–14, emerged fully in a glorious series of paintings done between the summer of 1917 and 1921. After some new experiments with *papiers collés* on a much bolder scale, and painting a large full-length figure (*The Guitar-Player*, 1917–18) in a stiff, greatly elaborated synthetic Cubist idiom, Braque found a freer and more masterly way of handling form and space in late Cubist paintings such as

Pls. 263, 264   *The Guitar* (1918) and *Still Life with Musical Instruments* (1918). Braque was not attempting to carry on from the point where he had left off, nor did he, unlike Picasso, re-examine the values of naturalism. Braque simply modified his earlier synthetic Cubist idiom to suit his

Plate 263

Georges Braque
Still Life with Musical Instruments, 1918
Oil, 35 × 25 in.

No. 35

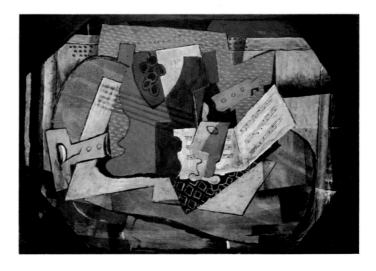

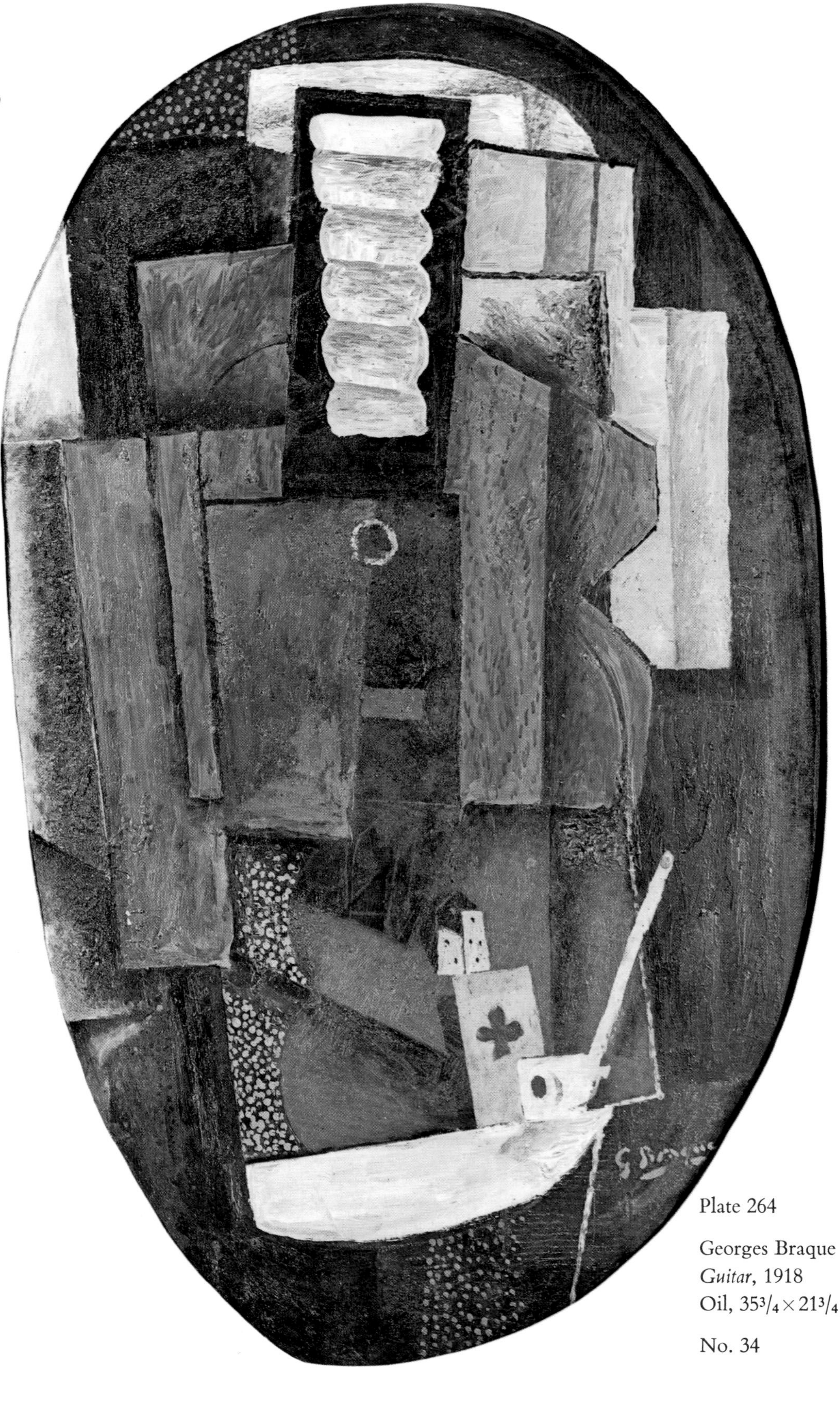

Plate 264

Georges Braque
Guitar, 1918
Oil, 35³/₄ × 21³/₄ in. (Oval)

No. 34

new vision of a more sensuous reality and began to work with bolder, looser, more tactile (though nonetheless flattened) forms, more resonant colors and subtler variations of texture. Where Braque had been primarily concerned before 1914 with solving problems of form and space in a rational manner and had only begun during the last few months before his mobilization to allow decorative and sensuous values to play an active part in his painting, between 1918 and 1921 these became major considerations. Like Picasso, Braque too was trying to humanize and enrich his late Cubist style,* though by very different and wholly personal means. His work at this time is characterized by its serenity, smoothness, suavity and resonance; his forms are more freely invented, and have an appealing pliability, but they are still Cubist in conception although they correspond more nearly than before with natural appearances. In short, Braque was trying in these late Cubist paintings to arouse in the spectator not so much a visual or intellectual as a tactile experience of reality and space. This was Braque's personal contribution to the expressive range of late Cubism, and he continued to elaborate it in a succession of luscious, sonorous, lyrical still lifes during the next ten years.

* The figure appears rarely as a subject in the work of Braque, even between 1908 and 1914; in the immediate post-war he again concentrated on still life which, as in the work of Chardin, became a symbol of human delights and activities. Braque executed no figure subject between 1918 and 1922.

Juan Gris: Painting 1915–21

In 1915, with the experience of *papiers collés* behind him, Gris first attempted to enlarge the expressive possibilities of his painting and then to make it more concrete. In a letter of March 1915, he remarked that he had given up 'those inventories of objects' which he had now come to think of as 'boring,' and was aiming at a much greater unity in his composition. This did not prevent Gris, however, from undertaking still life compositions with more objects

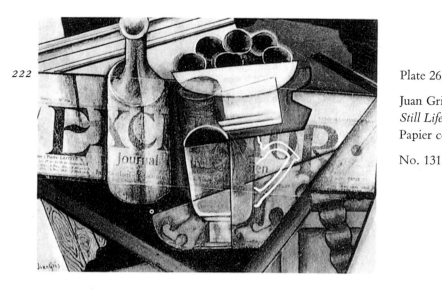

Plate 265

Juan Gris
Still Life with Grapes, 1915
Papier collé, 10 × 13 in.

No. 131

Plate 268 ▶

Juan Gris
Breakfast, 1915
Oil, 36¹/₄ × 28³/₄ in.

No. 118

Plate 266

Juan Gris
Coffee-Grinder and Glass, 1915
Oil, 15 × 11³/₄ in.

No. 117

than before, because he enjoyed the challenge to his inventiveness and sense of logic of the need not only to re-create their forms and volumes but also to establish the complex spatial relationships between them. This Gris managed by an intelligent combination of fragmentation, literalism, drawing and changes of view-point helped by chiaroscuro to bring out volumes. So conscious was he that he had made progress, however, that Gris was writing of his

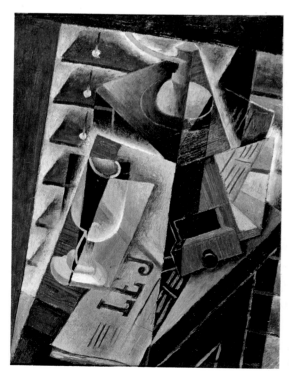

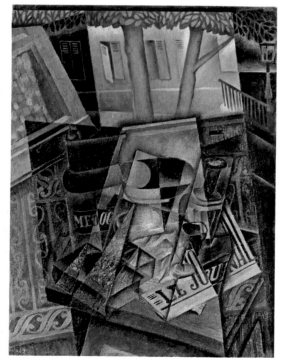

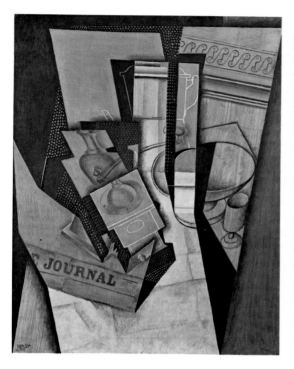

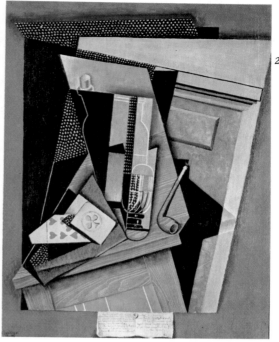

Plate 269

Juan Gris
Still Life with Poem, 1915
Oil, 31³/₄ × 25¹/₂ in.

No. 119

◀ Plate 267

Juan Gris
*Still Life in Front of an Open
Window: Place Ravignan*, 1915
Oil, 45⁷/₈ × 35¹/₈ in.

No. 116

★ In 1910–11, Picasso and Braque
had painted one or two views from
their studio windows in Montmartre
and Céret, and in 1915 Picasso
painted a *Still Life on a Table in a
Landscape* (Basel Museum). But only
external space was involved in all
of these paintings.

work, in June, as being 'less dry and more plastic.' At
that time he ventured on a major innovation.★ In the
composition *Still Life in Front of an Open Window* (*The
Place Ravignan*), Gris had to create a smooth transition
from an interior space to an exterior space, which
meant solving problems of natural light and recession.
These Gris handled not merely cleverly but inventively,
and without recourse to scientific perspective. He
based his composition on layers of tonally differentiated,
transparent planes, placed one over the other at different
angles, and on a contrast in scale between objects on the
background plane and those in the foreground. Gris
thus created a movement forward from the pale blue
background plane of the house to the front edge of the
table, where he introduced warmer tonalities. And he
emphasized this movement, which was bound up with
separating the two areas of space, by diagonals running
in from the side of the canvas to create a narrow window-
opening, in front of which he introduced, to mark the
division, a plane of darker color.

Next, throughout the summer of 1915, Gris turned his
attention to developing the 'sensitive and sensuous'

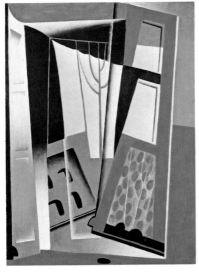

Plate 270

Juan Gris
Open Window, 1917
Oil, 39³/₈ × 28⁵/₈ in.

No. 124

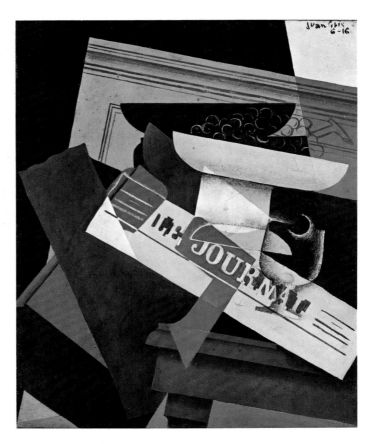

* Perhaps this new preoccupation was an outcome of his conversations with Matisse in the previous summer.

Plate 272
Juan Gris
Siphon and Glass, 1916
Gouache, 17³/₄ × 13³/₄ in.
No. 135

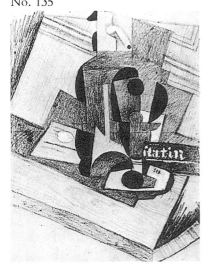

aspects* of painting, which he felt he had until that moment disregarded. First he experimented in some small and simple still lifes with textural variations and ornamental *motifs*. But this phase was of short duration because, during the fall and winter of 1915–16, Gris allowed his paintings to become more 'concrete and concise' again (letter of December 1915) as he clarified, purified and made them more legible. Gris reduced the number of objects represented, used fewer simultaneous aspects, relied for his spatial effect on a bolder and more economical planar structure and used pointillistic dotting to ventilate the composition and create an ornamental effect (*The Breakfast*; *Still Life with a Poem*). At the same time Gris adopted conceptual rather than visual forms, to which he had inclined hitherto, so that he re-created objects in more generalized terms (*The Grapes*, 1916). That is to say, objects lost their individuality but became more unified. Simultaneously Gris cut down the range of colors in his set of basic forms, but enriched them in another sense by introducing a

◀ Plate 271

Juan Gris
Grapes, 1916
Oil, 21³/₄ × 18¹/₂ in.

No. 121

Plate 273

Juan Gris
Fruit-Dish on a Table, 1916
Oil, 19³/₄ × 24 in.

No. 120

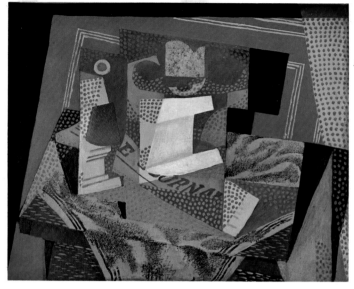

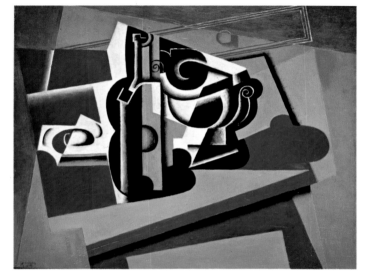

Plate 274

Juan Gris
Still Life, 1917
Oil, 29 × 36 in.

No. 123

Plate 276

Juan Gris
*Siphon, Checker-board and
Glass*, 1917
Charcoal, 18¹/₂ × 12¹/₄ in.

No. 137

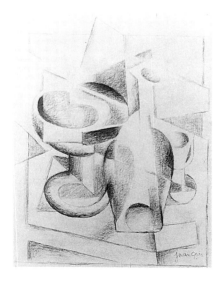

Plate 275

Juan Gris
Still Life, 1917
Pencil, 24³/₈ × 18⁷/₈ in.

No. 136

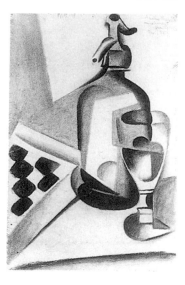

Pl. 274

Pl. 278

play of formal metaphors and correspondences between them (*Still Life with Bottle and Dish*, 1917). His outstanding achievement in this phase, and one of his greatest Cubist works, is the formally simple, serene, and monumental *Portrait of Josette*.

But other influences were also at work in Gris' painting at this time. He began, like Picasso, to make naturalistic drawings of objects, and also some portraits. He looked back from his new stand-point at the work of Cézanne, whence he had begun, and in 1918 re-interpreted a *Portrait of Mme. Cézanne*★ in the flattened terms of a late synthetic

★ Venturi No. 572, of *c.* 1886, now in The Art Institute of Chicago. Presumably Gris only knew the painting from a reproduction.

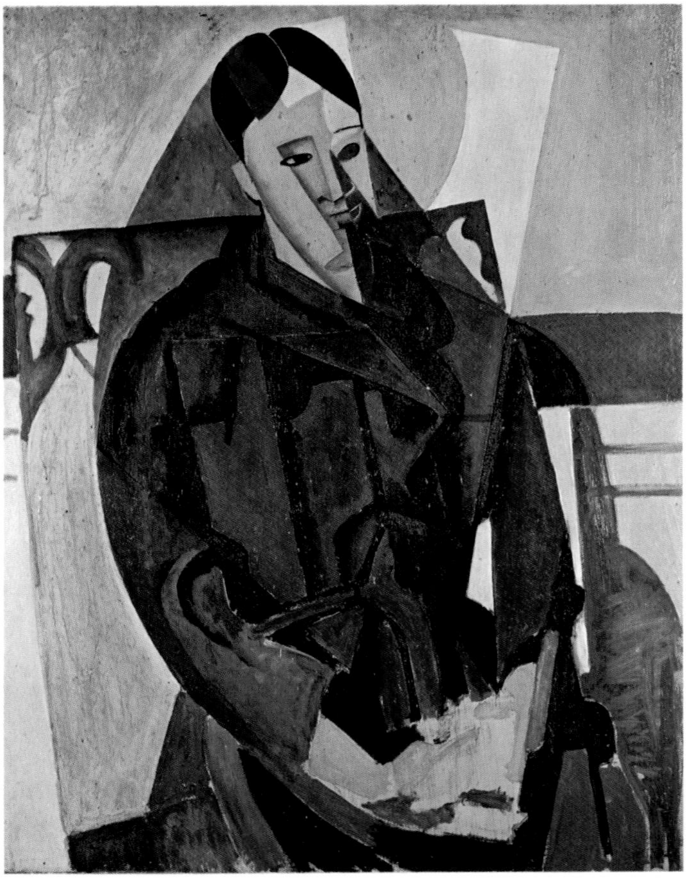

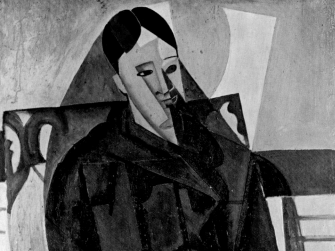

Plate 277

Juan Gris
Madame Cézanne (After a painting by Cézanne), 1918
Oil, 35⁷/₈ × 28³/₈ in.

No. 127

Plate 278 ►

Juan Gris
Portrait of Josette, 1916
Oil, 45¹/₂ × 28¹/₂ in.

No. 122

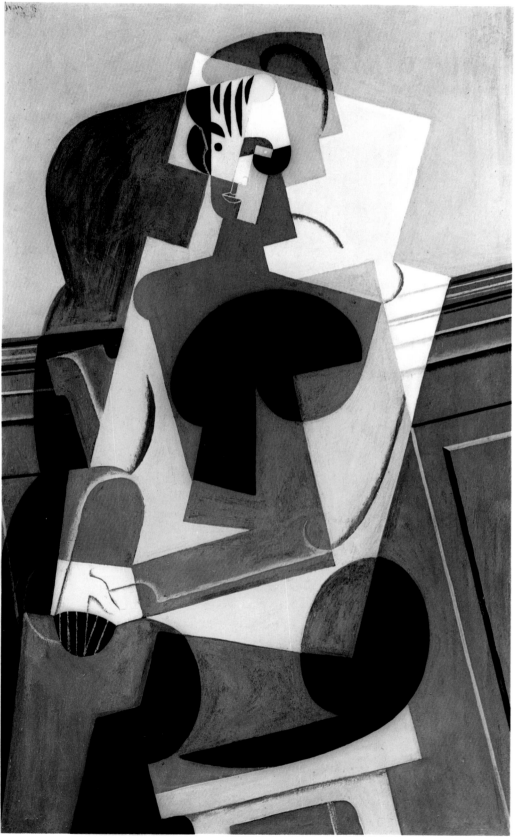

Cubist idiom. Gris also came under the influence of two sculptor friends, Lipchitz and Laurens, and painted a number of still lifes in imitation of their painted Cubist

Pl. 279 bas-reliefs (*Still Life with Guitar*, 1917). Then in 1917–18, as a reaction against the austerity of his work in 1916, Gris experimented again with more complex compositions, painted in brighter colors and enriched with a variety of ornamental patterning. The impressive, animated

Pl. 280 *Harlequin with a Guitar* (1917), which makes an interesting
Pl. 258 contrast with the more statuesque *Harlequin* (1918) painted by Picasso a few months later, is an outstanding example.

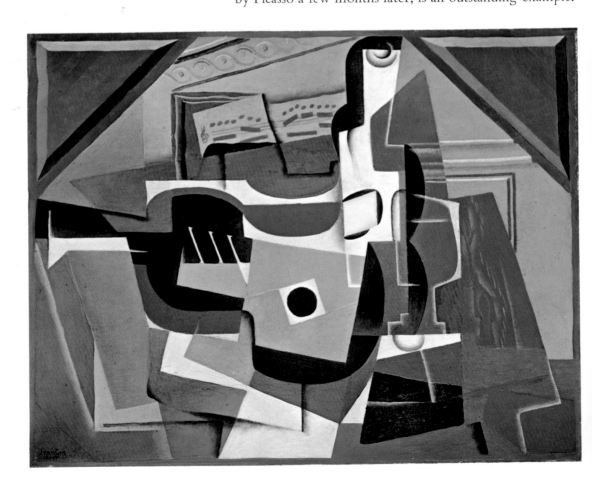

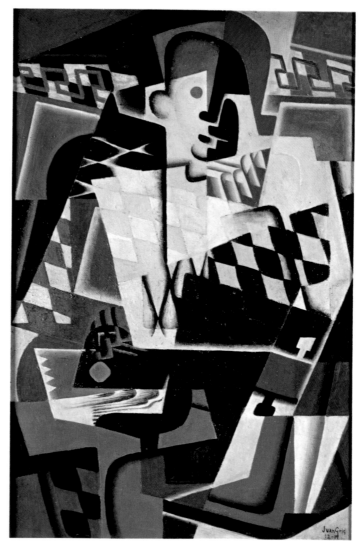

Plate 280

Juan Gris
Harlequin with Guitar, 1917
Oil, 39¹/₄ × 25¹/₂ in.

No. 126

Shortly after this, in 1919–20, Gris, who felt that in the past few years he had been concerned with 'a too brutal and descriptive reality' in his paintings (letter of August 1919), abandoned his late synthetic Cubist style for a more fluid, more 'poetic' type of painting which, while it retained something essential of Cubism, became increasingly legible up to the time of his death in 1927.

Gris' work reflects his intellectual lucidity and integrity, as well as his scientifically conditioned mind. For eight years he went on analyzing, defining and extending the pictorial conceptions and possibilities of Cubism in a limited field of his own until he arrived at a logical

◄ Plate 279

Juan Gris
Still Life with Guitar, 1917
Oil, 28¹/₂ × 36 in.

No. 125

conclusion. Where Braque and Picasso had always relied
on intuition and would momentarily sacrifice stylistic
purity to some strong personal emotion or fantasy, Gris
could not be deflected from the straight path, so that
he remained up till 1919 a highly orthodox exponent of
Cubism.

However, no sooner had Braque, Picasso and Gris succeeded
in enriching and humanizing the late Cubist idiom
than the Purists—Ozenfant and Jeanneret (later known
as Le Corbusier)—launched a movement in opposition
to all that Cubism stood for, proclaiming a machine-
conscious aesthetic designed to express a standardized,
impersonal and inhuman vision of reality. The Cubist
artists, they said, had bankrupted representational art and
created disorder by sanctioning the individual's right to
treat forms as he liked. Equally, the Purists attacked the
non-figurative artists for denying the possibilities of painting by rejecting intelligibility and visually perceived evidence in favour of barren geometrical forms and signs. Thus
the launching of the review *L'Esprit Nouveau* in the
fall of 1920, which became the mouthpiece for these
new theories, was an event which announced the end
of The Cubist Epoch, although the spirit of Cubism
lived on for a long while in the painting of those
few truly creative artists who had been deeply involved.

5

Cubist Sculpture

Cubist sculpture must be discussed apart from the painting because it followed other paths, which were sometimes similar but never parallel. Some of the sculptures in question can be related to Cubist paintings of various dates; others belong to the category of constructions, *collages* and *papiers collés*; while still others are works in which elements of Cubism were used to realize new sculptural forms. There is no simple definition of what constitutes a Cubist sculpture: what counts are the artist's will to figuration and his conception of how to handle form and create volume. It is, therefore, fruitless to look for a common stylistic denominator linking all the sculptures included here. Much Cubist sculpture was frankly experimental, much was tentative or banal, and some of it was made for specific personal reasons by painters, though all of it explores different aspects of visual and formal experience. Speaking generally, Cubist sculpture lacks direction because, before 1914, there was no full-time sculptor with as dominating and creative a personality as Braque, Picasso or Gris in painting, while after 1914 the two major Cubist sculptors, Laurens and Lipchitz, took late Cubist painting as their point of departure.

When Cubist sculptures are assembled in mass they form therefore a disharmonious ensemble, from which a few pieces stand out because the artist's sincerity and inventiveness have enabled him to achieve a convincing sculptural reality. Apart from two pieces by Picasso, and Duchamp-Villon's *Seated Girl*, which can only have been seen at the time by a few friends, no significant Cubist sculpture was made in Paris before 1914–15, when Lipchitz and Laurens belatedly began to evolve a genuinely Cubist sculptural idiom. The only other noteworthy Cubist sculptures made before 1914 were either the work of Gutfreund in Prague, who did not exhibit in Paris, or of Boccioni in Milan, whose *Bottle* was exhibited there in the summer of 1913. Sculpture therefore forms an interesting appendage to, rather than an integral part of, the international Cubist achievement.

Picasso, de La Fresnaye, Czaky and Filla

Pl. 281

Pls. 282, 283

The first true Cubist sculpture was Picasso's impressive *Woman's Head*, modeled in 1909–10, a counterpart in three dimensions to many similarly analytical and faceted heads in his paintings of the time. The influence of sculptural conceptions on Picasso's pictorial thinking in the early Cubist years has already been discussed; here he reversed the process and modeled this *Woman's Head* to test, in the light of reality, his pictorial technique of expressing volume through faceting. Picasso respected the mass of the head and set out to investigate, through surface protrusions and hollows, how light strikes, models or transforms such a complex structure. At the same time, he turned the head on its vertical axis so as to induce the eye to feel its way around it. The experience thus gained was of service to him in the immediate development of his painting. Picasso's only other Cubist sculpture, a small but pretty object, is the *Absinthe Glass* of 1914. Once again there is a close tie-up with Picasso's painting because here, as in the *Woman's Head*, he took an object which he had analyzed and re-created in numerous drawings and paintings of 1913–14 and modeled it in three dimensions. Picasso's treatment of the glass's form like his arrangement of its planes is freer than in the paintings, but Picasso used pointillist dotting on this solid surface in the same way as in his paintings to evoke transparency and create a decorative effect. In addition, he opened up one side of the glass to make its internal volume palpable. Over the

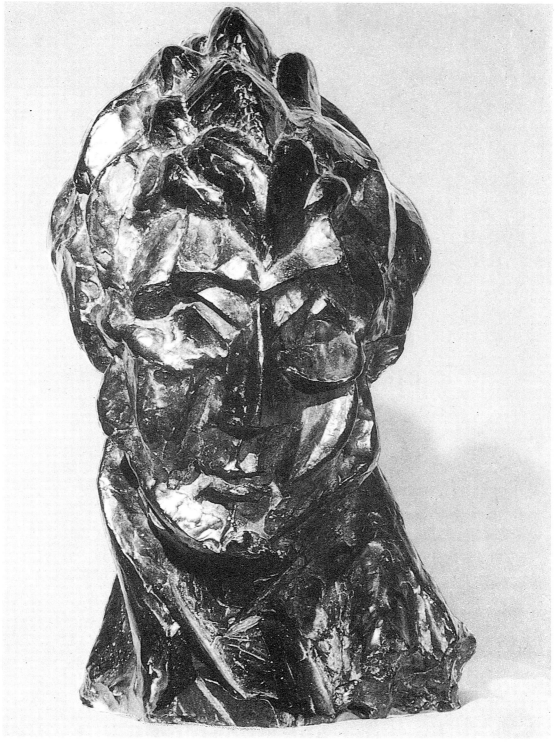

Plate 281

Pablo Picasso, *Woman's Head*, 1909–10
Bronze, $16^{1}/_{4} \times 9^{3}/_{4} \times 10^{1}/_{2}$ in.

234

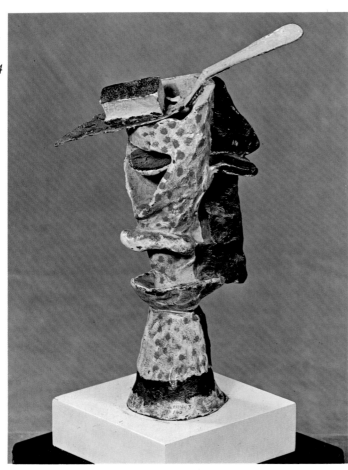

Plate 282

Pablo Picasso
Absinthe Glass, 1914
Painted bronze, $8^1/_2 \times 6^1/_2$ in.

No. 290

rim he placed an actual straining-spoon and a false lump
of sugar, thereby consciously creating, as in his *papiers
collés*, a contradiction between two types of unreal reality.
Yet it is doubtful whether Picasso really thought of this
glass as a sculpture, because he painted each of the six
casts differently, and gave them different textures, thereby
making each into a unique 'object.' Generically, in fact,
the *Absinthe Glass* takes its place among those guitars
and violins which Picasso, like Braque, made of cardboard and string during the summer of 1912 and the
home-carpentered still lifes, made of scraps of wood and
metal, which Picasso constructed in 1914–15. The 1912
musical instruments were primarily investigations of form
and volume, objects existing in paintings transposed for
study in three dimensions. But because of the materials
of which they were made, and their lack of mass, they
became important as fore-runners of *papiers collés* and gave
reality to the idea of the *tableau-objet*. The later and

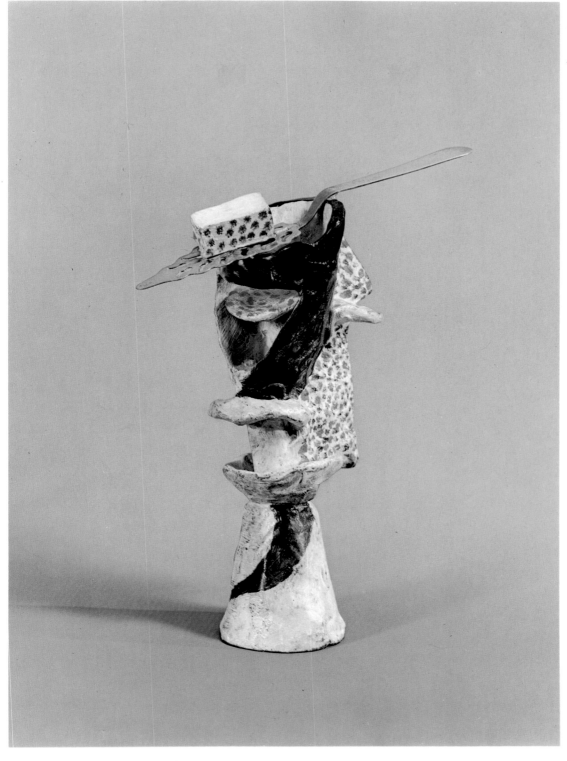

Plate 283   Pablo Picasso, *Absinthe Glass*, 1914   No. 289
Painted bronze, $8^1/_2 \times 6^1/_2$ in.

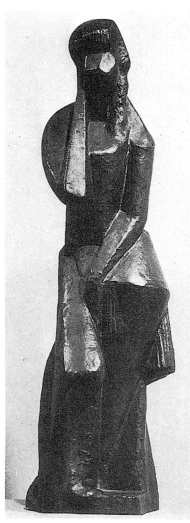

Plate 284

Joseph Czaky
Standing Woman, 1913–14
Bronze, 31¹/₂×8¹/₄×8⁵/₈ in.

No. 60

* See G. Seligman, *Roger de La Fresnaye* (London, 1969), Catalog No. 67, and pp. 20–22.

* See Zervos, *Picasso Catalogue*, Vol. II, Nos. 112, 113; and Vol. VI, Nos. 975, 1064.

more complex still life constructions are still better examples of what was meant by a *tableau-objet*. To make these, Picasso nailed together scraps of wood and metal, much as he composed *papiers collés*, then shaped and painted individual elements to give them a representational significance. Thus Picasso made the humblest materials serve his creative purpose by using them to compose an object which evoked a visual reality, but whose own reality was independent of and additional to the reality evoked.

Early Cubist paintings by Picasso also provided the basic inspiration for de La Fresnaye's *Italian Girl* (1911). De La Fresnaye got to know Duchamp-Villon in the sculpture studio of La Grande Chaumière in Montparnasse in 1910, and Germain Seligman suggests that the small group of sculptures which de La Fresnaye made in 1911 were probably the joint outcome of this friendship and of a desire to master the human figure 'in all its aspects' before attempting 'its abstraction into essential physical and descriptive elements.' At all events, de La Fresnaye's bronze has unmistakable origins in one of his own paintings of 1910, which is not in the least Cubist, *L'Italienne de face*.* But when he came to model the figure, de La Fresnaye clearly tried, in the pose and in the faceting of the body and limbs, to take as a guide certain of Picasso's drawings of 1907,* though he gave the girl a silly simpering facial expression. In short, de La Fresnaye made use of Cubism more as a stylistic mannerism than as a source of formal discovery or invention.

Joseph Czaky, a self-taught Hungarian sculptor living in Paris who was included in the *Section d'Or* show

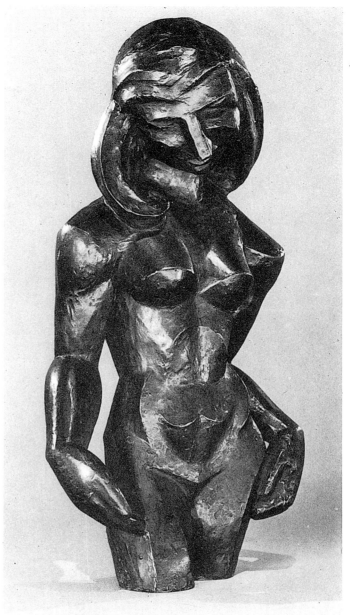

Plate 285

Roger de La Fresnaye
Italian Girl, 1911
Bronze, 24 × 12 in.

No. 155

Pl. 284

in September 1912, is another artist for whom Cubism was a surface discipline. The tentative faceting in Czaky's *Standing Woman* (1913–14) is no more than an aid to evoking volume. On the other hand in his *Head* (1914, Musée Municipal d'Art et d'Industrie, St. Etienne) he used greatly simplified forms and a few broad planes more constructively, though it is easy to find models for this conception in certain 'negroid' heads by Picasso of 1907–08.* In 1919–20 Czaky came briefly under the

★ e.g. Zervos, Vol. II, Nos. 65, 117.

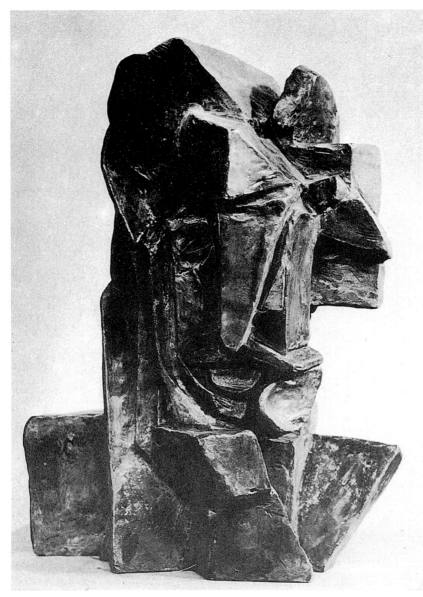

Plate 286

Emil Filla
Man's Head, 1913–14
Bronze, 15³/₈ in. high

No. 94

influence of Laurens and Lipchitz before turning to straightforward figurative sculpture around 1925.

Pl. 286

Another piece of sculpture which can be discussed in this context is Filla's *Head* of 1913–14, his only surviving piece. Here the mass of the head is respected as in Picasso's *Woman's Head* of 1909–10. But Filla treated his head with a severe frontality and tried to create volume not with faceting but with a few block-like forms whose alternately flat and transverse planes are designed to evoke mass. This procedure also reflects the influence of Gutfreund.

Duchamp-Villon and Archipenko

From his beginnings as a self-taught sculptor in 1901–02, until 1912, when he was responsible for carrying out some stylized cubistic ornamentation on the façade of the Cubist House at the Salon d'Automne, Raymond Duchamp-Villon tried his hand at different styles ranging from *art nouveau*, Rodin and Gauguin to Maillol and Matisse. But from the autumn of 1912 on, when he was exposed to the discussions of the Cubist group which met under the aegis of his two brothers at Puteaux,* Duchamp-Villon's sculptural conceptions rapidly changed. This is seen first in *The Lovers* (1913), a classic theme which Duchamp-Villon treated in low relief, the bodies being

* Léger, Gris, Gleizes, and Archipenko were involved.

Pl. 287

Plate 287

Raymond Duchamp-Villon, *The Lovers (Final State)*, No. 75
1913, Bronze relief, 26³/₄ × 39³/₈ in.

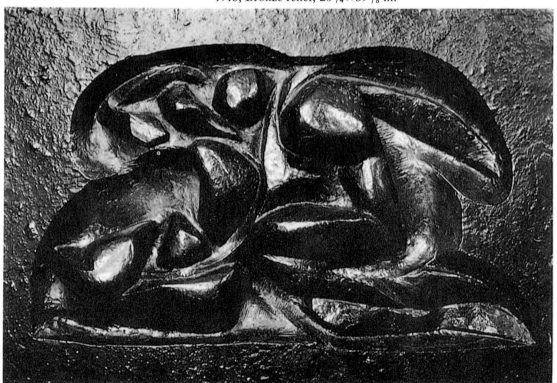

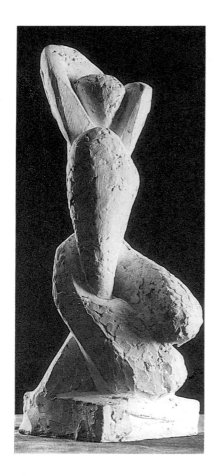

represented with abstract geometricized forms, which are not connected but separated from each other, as in Léger's work of the time, and arranged contrastingly to set up a surface rhythm in a single plane. In his *Seated Girl* (1914) of a year later, Duchamp-Villon carried this procedure fully into three dimensions, re-creating the different parts of the girl's body with a static and unified arrangement of oval or conical forms which are fully rounded and have closed contours. This figure, which is clearly related to paintings by Léger, although without the internal movement evoked by formal and color contrasts, seems to be an expression of Duchamp-Villon's belief that 'The sole purpose of the arts is neither description nor imitation but the creation

Plate 288

Raymond Duchamp-Villon
Seated Girl, 1914
Plaster, $12^1/_2 \times 4 \times 4^1/_2$ in.

No. 76

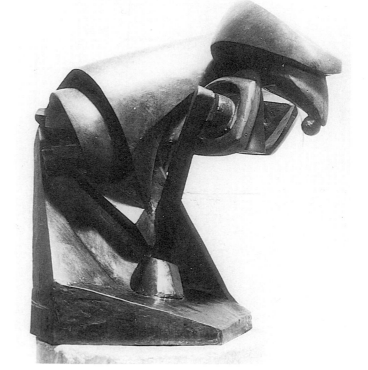

Plate 289

Raymond Duchamp-Villon
Small Horse, 1914
Bronze, $15^3/_8$ in. high

No. 77

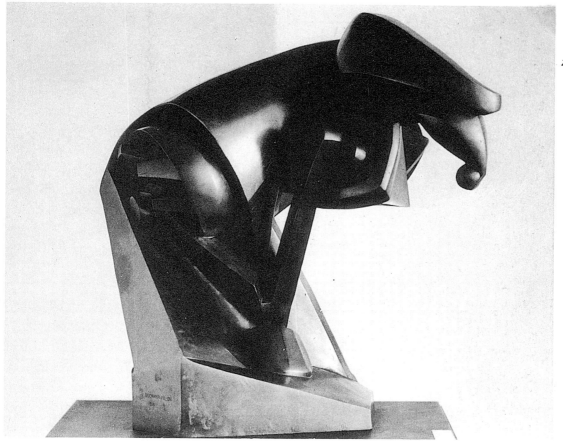

Plate 290

Raymond Duchamp-Villon, *Large Horse*, 1914   No. 78
Bronze, 39³/₈ × 39³/₈ × 20³/₄ in.

Pls. 289, 290

of unknown beings from elements which are always present but not apparent.' Duchamp-Villon's next work, *The Horse* (1914), which was to be his major achievement, represents yet another, although considerably less Cubist, sculptural aesthetic. He began this sculpture in the spring of 1914 as a group with a rider trying to restrain a rearing, almost mechanically impelled, horse. At that time, the representation of the beauty of machines, of speed and of kinetic effects were constant topics of discussion, and Duchamp-Villon had seen how they were expressed in the work of Marcel Duchamp, the Futurists, Picabia and Léger. At all events, when Duchamp-Villon completed the fifth and final version of his *Horse* in August 1914, it was totally transformed and had come to embody a very different sculptural conception. He had dispensed with the rider and extracted from the horse a non-figurative mechanistic symbol of Horse-Power, which was much closer to a Futurist sculptural conception. Thus in the two years between 1912 and 1914, Duchamp-Villon (he was to die in 1918 of typhoid contracted at the front), who had a real understanding of the language of sculpture, looked at the possibilities of making Cubist sculpture and passed on to something else.

The very individual work of Alexander Archipenko, a Russian from the Ukraine who had arrived in Paris in 1908, can also be considered here because he was associated with the *Section d'Or*. In 1912, Archipenko suddenly turned from making conventional figurative sculpture to working in a very modern sculptural idiom of his own invention. His first piece, *Walking Figure* (1912), already displays many of the stylistic elements which from then on were to characterize his work: formal abstraction, the use of forceful rhythms, the replacement of solid volumes by voids, and the reversal of roles between concavities and convexities. The result is an object composed of highly stylized, abstract forms, which have little power to evoke a figurative image, although by the way planes are slanted and rhythms set up the displacement of a mass through space is suggested. There is of course nothing Cubist about such a piece of sculpture. Subsequently (1912–17) Archipenko experimented restlessly with new techniques and new technical means in an attempt to find a sculptural style. But the most he arrived at was a hybrid form which he called 'sculpto-painting.' This entailed the creation, in half-relief, of an illusionistic object made, on the principle of *papiers collés*, of glass, metal, wood, *papier mâché* and other materials affixed to a flat background and painted in garish colors. These works were figurative and constructed along synthetic Cubist lines, but Archipenko half-

Plate 291

Alexander Archipenko
Figure in Movement, 1913
Collage and colored crayon,
$18^{3}/_{4} \times 12^{3}/_{8}$ in.

No. 3

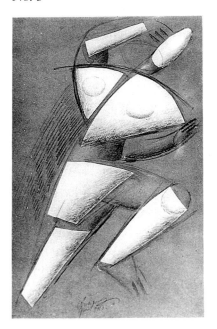

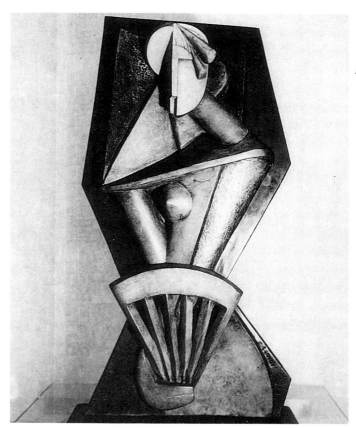

Plate 292

Alexander Archipenko
Woman with a Fan, 1914
Polychrome Bronze, 35¹/₂ in. high

No. 2

Plate 293

Alexander Archipenko
*Head: Construction with Crossing
Planes*, 1913
Bronze, 15 × 7 × 8 in.

No. 1

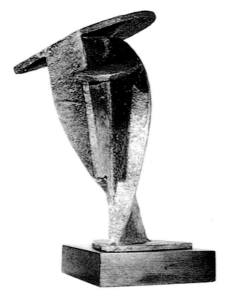

modeled his volumes and composed his figures of rigid geometrical forms—ovoids, cones and cylinders—thereby creating mannered, decorative ensembles rather than sculptures. His *Woman with a Fan* (1914), a painted relief sculpture, shows how soon he substituted decorative stylization for any concern with re-creating reality. Archipenko's most interesting and inventive essay in Cubist sculpture is the *Head: Construction of Crossing Planes* of 1913, which was a serious attempt to transpose the sort of head painted by Braque and Picasso into a simple three-dimensional form. Then in 1917–18 Archipenko made a series of painted still life reliefs, using a planar structure derived from synthetic Cubism, which relate to similar works of that date by Laurens and Lipchitz. At the start, Archipenko seemed to want to create Cubist sculpture, but he soon gave up the struggle and, as George Hamilton has pertinently remarked,★ allowed facile solutions to 'substitute for the content with which his forms might have been endowed.'

★ G. H. Hamilton, *Painting and Sculpture in Europe 1880–1940* (London, 1967), p. 173.

Boccioni and Weber

Boccioni made some twelve sculptures in all between 1911 and 1914: only five have survived, although we know the others from photographs. Most of Boccioni's sculptures were extensions into three dimensions of his pictorial conceptions and hence, as Futurist works, concerned with the continuity of movement in space, with the play of light or with the fusion of a figure and its surroundings. Symbolism, expressionism, simultaneity and Impressionism provide their constituents and there is no evidence in them of Cubist conceptions or techniques. However, *Abstract Voids and Solids of a Head* (late 1912), subsequently destroyed, and *Development of a Bottle in Space* (winter 1912–13), made by Boccioni after his trips to Paris in 1911–12, when he visited Duchamp-Villon and Archipenko in their studios, must both be considered as basically Cubist works. The *Head*★ was executed as a relief in a shallow space and conceived formally in similar terms to certain early Cubist analytical heads in paintings by Braque and Picasso and to Gris' *Portrait of his Mother* (1912). A preliminary drawing, which is more or less naturalistic in conception though slightly formalized, shows a static head flattened and 'attacked' by broad beams of light and space which dig into the cheeks and chin. Boccioni, who, in his Preface to the catalogue of the Exhibition of Futurist Sculpture in Paris in June 1913, wrote of 'the entrance of a void into the solid which is traversed' by a ray of light and claimed to have found a way of representing this by 'uniting *blocks of atmosphere* with more concrete elements of reality,' had literally tested the form-creating possibilities of his theory by transposing this drawing into carved and modeled relief terms. Very soon after this, however, Boccioni set about making a fully three-dimensional sculptural rendering of a bottle and dish standing on a table. Here he cut out

Pls. 294, 295

★ G. Ballo, *Boccioni* (Milan, 1964), pls. 237, 239.

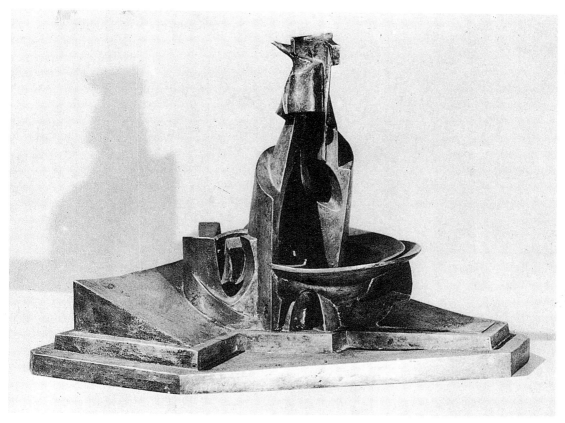

Plate 294

Umberto Boccioni, *Development of a Bottle in Space*, 1912　No. 9
Bronze, 15 × 24 in.

Plate 295

Umberto Boccioni
Bottle, Table and House, 1912
Pencil, 13¹/₈ × 9¹/₂ in.

No. 10

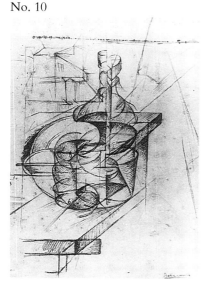

the workings of pictorial light in order to concentrate on
volume, form and the inter–relation of the planes involved.
In other words, he set about reconciling an analytical
Cubist approach with the Futurist concept of active
forces which traverse and radiate from an object existing
in space and time, and thereby create its presence
in relation to its surroundings. 'My sculptural ensemble
develops,' Boccioni wrote in the same Preface, 'in the
space formed by the depth of the volume and shows
the density of every aspect not just a number of immobile
aspects in silhouette.' This statement formulates the
advance that Boccioni considered he had made in his
sculpture over the true Cubist painters. Hence the
way in which Boccioni's *Bottle*, whose form has not
been fragmented, opens up in a continuous spiral
movement to reveal, by an inter-play of convex and
concave surfaces, both its solid form and its interior
volume.

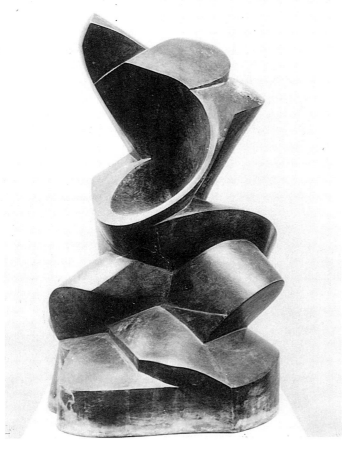

Plate 296

Max Weber
Spiral Rhythm, 1915
Bronze, 24¼ in. high

No. 321

In these two works Boccioni undoubtedly made a remarkable contribution and showed, as had Picasso in
his 1909 *Woman's Head*, as Duchamp-Villon was to do in
his *Seated Girl* (1914), and as Gutfreund was already doing
in Prague, that a sculptural equivalent could be found
for the Cubist conception of representing form, space and
volume in non-imitative plastic terms on the flat surface
of a canvas. However, no-one, it seems, understood or
attempted to follow the different but adventurous leads
of these four artists. Even Boccioni veered away from
Cubist thinking in his subsequent sculptures. Thus these
Cubist sculptures represent a series of interesting beginnings
with no sequels.

This is a convenient point at which to mention also
the unique piece of partially Cubist sculpture by the
American artist Max Weber, *Spiral Rhythm* (1915), which
was inspired by a torso, translated into rounded and
faceted forms, but given an abstract rhythmic evolution.

Pl. 296

Gutfreund

Otto Gutfreund, the Czech sculptor, was in Paris in 1909–10 when he worked under Bourdelle. The first sculptures he made after returning to Prague date from 1911 and show him building up anguished, rather baroque figures through a succession of broadly faceted planes. These build up a sense of mass but also add, by the play of light and shade which they create, to a general dramatic effect. In 1912, however, Gutfreund began to break down his figures into much bolder formal masses, which he assembled as a complex structure of planes —vertical, horizontal and diagonal—whose concavities, convexities, and curves produce a sense of movement and space (*Reclining Woman with a Glass,* 1912–13). This sculptural conception undoubtedly owed a lot to early Cubist paintings, though Gutfreund, like his painter friends of the *Avant-Garde* group, was not interested in producing a calm or monumental effect,

Pls. 297—299

Pl. 302

Plate 297

Otto Gutfreund
Standing Nude, 1911
Charcoal, 17^1/$_2$ × 12 in.

No. 142

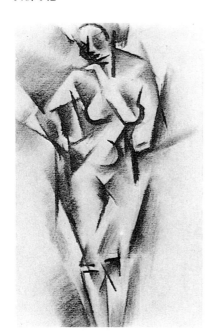

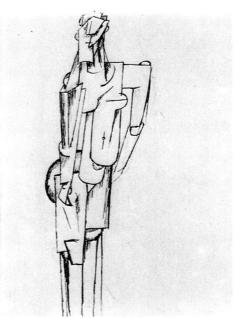

Plate 298

Otto Gutfreund
Study for Sculpture,
1912–13
Ink, 10^7/$_8$ × 8^3/$_4$ in.

No. 143

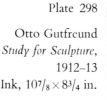

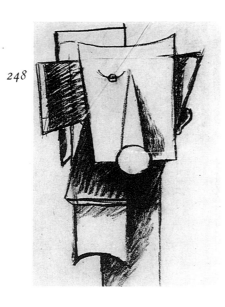

Plate 299

Otto Gutfreund
Man's Head, c. 1914
Charcoal, 18⁷/₈ × 12¹/₄ in.

No. 145

because he wished to infuse his sculpture with a sense of spiritual exaltation (*Female Head; The Cellist; The Embrace* all 1912–13). However, in the last major work he produced before the war, the *Cubist Bust* of 1913, Gutfreund abandoned this conception for a more static, monumental effect. This sculpture, which should be compared with Filla's chunky *Head* of about the same date, is elaborately constructed in synthetic Cubist terms. Planes rising from the base create a pyramidal structure, into which the head is integrated and re-created by a succession of parallel vertical and horizontally transverse planes. The spatial structure is thus established, and volume is then created by a sweeping curve receding from the forehead and by tunneled openings cut into the mass. This *Cubist Bust* is one of the most serious and inventive attempts to transpose the synthetic Cubist technique into

Plate 300

Otto Gutfreund
Woman's Head, 1919
Bronze, 10⁷/₈ in. high

No. 141

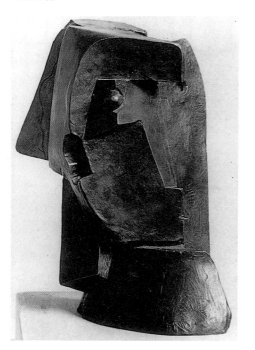

Plate 301

Otto Gutfreund
Cubist Bust, 1912–13
Bronze, 23⁵/₈ in. high

No. 140

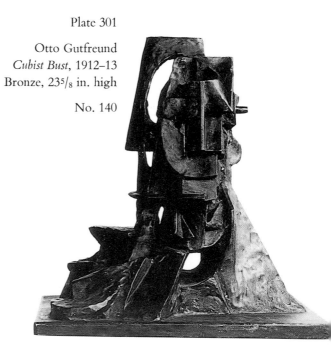

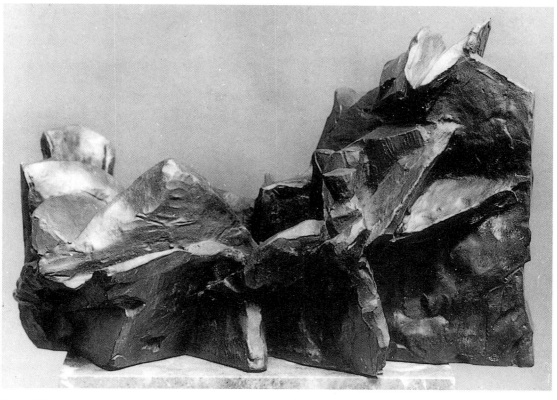

Plate 302

Otto Gutfreund, *Reclining Woman with Glass*, 1912–13　No. 139
Bronze, 7⁷/₈ × 11 in.

sculptural terms. But Gutfreund was not able to pursue his own experiment because he enlisted in the French army and could not work again until 1919. At that time he produced, in Paris, a small *Female Head*, which he again conceived in synthetic Cubist terms, and which seems to owe something to Laurens and Lipchitz,★ as well as some tentative, schematic still life constructions. After that Gutfreund's sculpture ceased to be Cubist, but these few early works represent an interesting personal achievement.

★ He could have seen their works in the gallery of Léonce Rosenberg.

Lipchitz, Gris, Laurens and Braque

In 1914–15 a new conception of Cubist sculpture began to be developed in Paris, under the impact of synthetic Cubism, by Jacques Lipchitz, a Lithuanian who had arrived there in 1909, and Henri Laurens, a native Parisian. These two artists, whose work was not without a reciprocal influence on the painting of Gris, Picasso

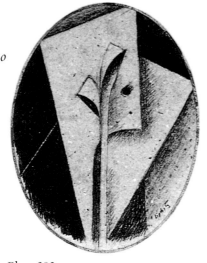

Cubist Sculpture

Plate 303

Jacques Lipchitz
Head (Study for bronze 'Head'), 1915
Pencil, 11 × 9 in. (Oval)

No. 198

Plate 304

Pl. 305

Jacques Lipchitz
Head, 1915
Bronze, 24¹/₂ in. high

No. 191

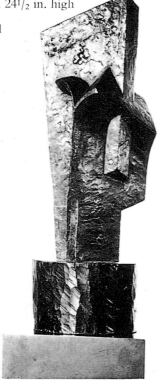

and Braque, were independent spirits who made a remarkable addition to the range of Cubist expression, though in a less experimental and more strictly formal sense than the sculptures discussed hitherto.

During the first four years of his career, Lipchitz produced mannered, *art nouveau*-type decorative figures before taking up Cubist techniques late in 1914. By this time he had already met Picasso, through Diego Rivera, and in 1915 was to become very friendly with Gris. Thus Lipchitz was in contact with two major exponents of true Cubism. His first sculpture which reveals a Cubist influence was *Sailor with a Guitar:* there, a basically naturalistic and roundly modeled figure became stylized through a combination of flat planes, faceted surfaces and disjointed formal elements, which Lipchitz linked in an uncomfortable jaunty rhythm of curves and angles. In 1915–16, however, Lipchitz dispensed with naturalism and the descriptive details which he had used in the *Sailor* to create in *Head*, *Half-Standing Figure* and some similar works, a group of semi-abstract sculptures composed along synthetic Cubist lines. These works (some modeled, others carved in stone) had a figurative significance and remained legible. They were predominantly composed of tall, rectangular planes arranged vertically, but in order to evoke a mass in space Lipchitz set others diagonally or had the verticals traversed at different levels.

This group of works represents the period of greatest concentration and personal discovery in Lipchitz's development of Cubist sculpture. In the years of his friendship with Gris, between 1916 and 1919, Lipchitz's work reflects a different approach to Cubist sculpture.

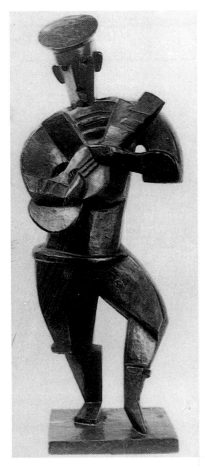

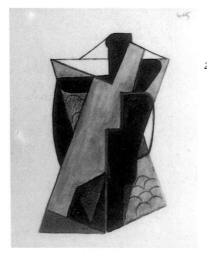

Plate 306

Jacques Lipchitz
Figure, 1915
Gouache, 18$^1/_2 \times$ 14 in.

No. 199

Plate 305

Jacques Lipchitz
Sailor with a Guitar, 1914
Bronze, 30$\times$12 in.

No. 190

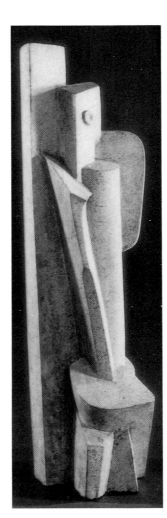

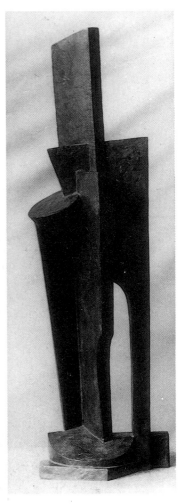

Plate 307

Jacques Lipchitz
Standing Figure, 1916
Stone, 42$^1/_4 \times$9 in.

No. 193

Plate 308

Jacques Lipchitz
Half-Standing Figure, 1916
Bronze, 38$^3/_4$ in. high

No. 192

Pl. 311

Pls. 309, 310

That is to say, he made his subjects—bathers, sailors, a pierrot playing a clarinet, men playing guitars—less abstract and more legible (as Gris was doing), while emphasizing their mass. In these figures, Lipchitz used chunky, geometricized forms, which he articulated, in order to evoke volume, with some analytical faceting, a counter-play of protruding and receding planes, and some curves. These sculptures are thus fuller and more vital than his static works of the preceding phase, but less synthetic Cubist in conception. Between 1920 and 1926, however, Lipchitz was to take up synthetic Cubist methods once more and give them a more plastic sculptural interpretation. But in the meanwhile, under

Plate 309

Jacques Lipchitz
Bather III, 1917
Bronze, 28¹/₂ in. high

No. 194

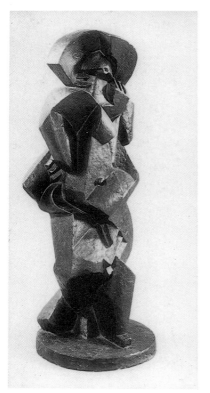

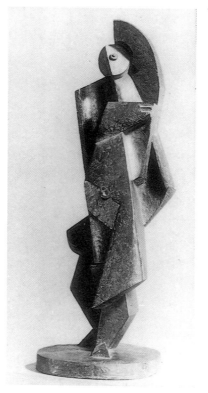

Plate 310

Jacques Lipchitz
Bather, 1919–20
Bronze, 28 × 9 × 9 in.

No. 197

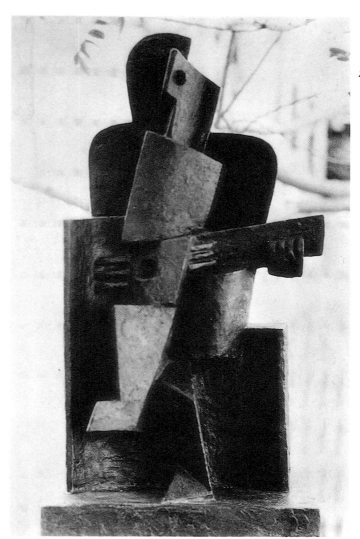

Plate 312

Jacques Lipchitz
Seated Man with Guitar, 1918
Bronze, $30 \times 15^3/_4 \times 13^1/_2$ in.

No. 195

Plate 311

Jacques Lipchitz
Woman with Drapery, 1919
Bronze, 37 in. high

No. 196

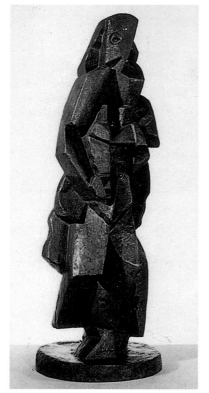

the joint influences of Gris and Laurens, Lipchitz worked (1918–20) on a series of more pictorial low reliefs (some painted) with still lifes as their subject, which were sculptural interpretations of the greatly clarified formal repertoire of late Cubism.

Lipchitz's sculpture before 1914 was banal, just as the late-baroque style he has cultivated since 1928 has led to works which are more vigorous than artistically meaningful. Cubism thus provided Lipchitz with an inspiring formal discipline between 1914 and 1921 and led to his discovering new sculptural methods for evoking form and volume. This was his creative contribution and the fulfilment of his many conversations with Gris. But

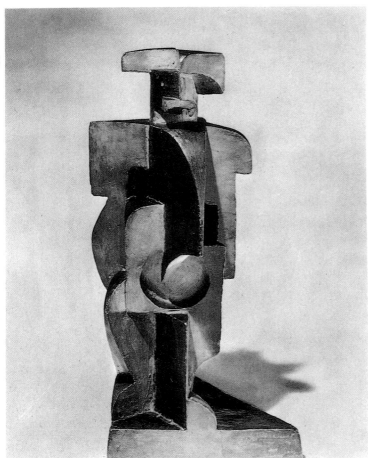

Plate 313

Juan Gris
Harlequin, 1917
Painted plaster, $21^{1}/_{2} \times 13 \times 10$ in.

No. 138

Plate 314 ▶

Georges Braque
Standing Figure, 1920
Bronze, $7^{1}/_{2} \times 2^{3}/_{4}$ in.

No. 48

Pl. 313

in exchange these conversations must also have stimulated Gris to produce his painted plaster *Harlequin* (1918), which was executed under Lipchitz's supervision. The figure is severely frontal and built up with simple, massive, block-like forms, volumes being evoked by planes set at angles (as in Lipchitz's sculptures) and by concavities. The role of color in this sculpture has nothing to do with its decorative role in Archipenko's 'sculpto-painting.' Gris, like Laurens, used color to prevent the planes and volumes of his *Harlequin* being 'distorted' by the play of natural light. This *Harlequin*, which is devoid of decorative motifs or descriptive details (except for the moustache) relates to such figure paintings by Gris as *The Touraine Peasant* (1917–18) and anticipates by its formal clarity and economy the Harlequins he was to paint in 1919–20.

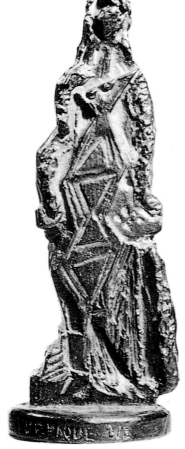

Laurens learned about Cubism directly from Braque, with whom he had a close lifelong friendship from the time of their meeting in 1911. The fruits of this friendship are apparent in the work of both men in different ways and at different times, one of them being Braque's *Standing Figure* of 1920, a decorative figurine which was his first attempt at working in three dimensions. This figurine is not conceived fully in the round and exists more or less on a single plane, the geometric body structure and palette being stamped into the plaster. However, although Braque's handling is more fluid than that of Laurens, one is reminded in the lines of the silhouette, the pose, and the internal structure, of drawings and engravings by Laurens of 1919, as well as of his wooden sculpture *Woman Playing a Guitar* (1919) or his *Standing Nude* of 1921.★

★ See M. Laurens, *Henri Laurens* (Paris, 1955), pp. 75, 92.

Laurens was self-taught and took up sculpture after working with a stone-mason who carved decorative *motifs* on buildings. However, Braque was not Laurens' only close friend among the Cubist painters; by 1915, he was also on very friendly terms with Picasso and Gris, so that throughout the war years (he was unfit for military service) Laurens could remain closely in touch with the development of Cubist painting. Laurens' first Cubist works date from 1915. Those in three dimensions were still life compositions or figures executed in wood or metal, a sort of *tableau-objet* which he was to continue making until 1918.★ These constructions were more carefully made, more elaborated and conceived in more sculptural terms than Picasso's home-carpentered works. Not only did Laurens build up his subject with a clearly articulated structure of planes, to create volume and define a spatial area, but he also distinguished between

★ *ibid.* pp. 22–41. These are unfortunately too fragile to travel.

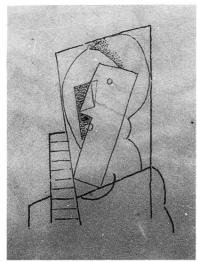

Plate 315

Henri Laurens
Head of a Boxer, 1916
Ink, $5^7/_8 \times 4^1/_2$ in.

No. 167

planes by painting them in different colors. He then completed the reality of his composition by painting in a few descriptive details. These constructed 'objects' are not, properly speaking, sculptures. They are brilliant and inventive interpretations in three dimensions of synthetic Cubist paintings. Laurens represented the same combinations of objects, used the same planar structure, substituted lengths of wire for lines which would have been drawn, and introduced similar decorative passages—pointillistic dotting, checker-board squares. The points of resemblance with paintings by Gris of 1915–17 are unmistakable. But Laurens was also working in two dimensions at the same time (1915–18), treating the same subjects in *papiers collés*. This was a medium which he used most effectively and in his own way, working with bolder simpler forms than either Braque or Picasso had done before 1914 and employing strong chiaroscuro to produce an enhanced relief effect.

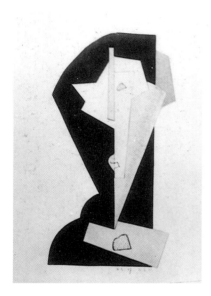

Plate 316

Henri Laurens
Head, 1917
Ink and collage, $21^3/_4 \times 17^1/_4$ in.

No. 164

Plate 317

Henri Laurens
Guitar, 1917–18
Papier collé, $18^7/_8 \times 25^1/_4$ in.

No. 166

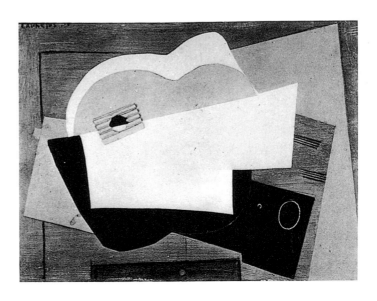

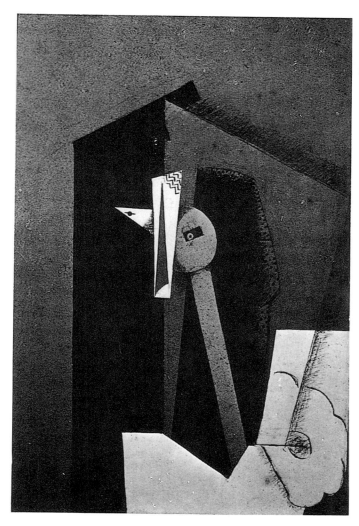

Plate 318

Henri Laurens
Woman with Mantilla, 1917
Papier collé, 23¹/₄ × 15¹/₂ in.

No. 165

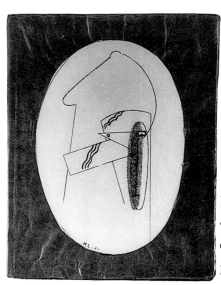

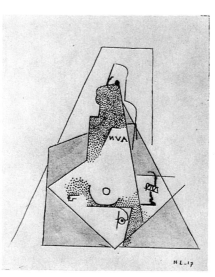

Plates 319, 320

Henri Laurens
Paul DERMÉE: Spirales,
1917
Two etchings
each 12³/₄ × 8⁷/₈ in.

No. 172

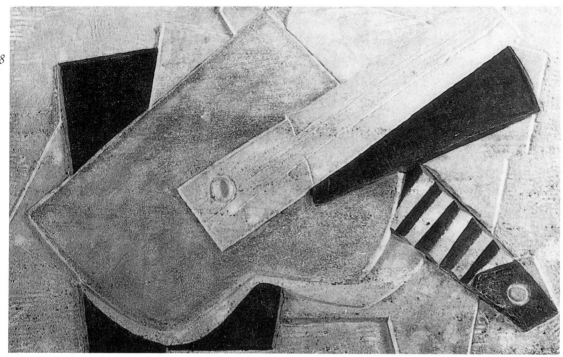

Plate 321   Henri Laurens, *Musical Instruments*, 1919   No. 161
Painted stone relief, $19^1/_2 \times 28^1/_4$ in.

Pl. 321

Pl. 322

Pls. 323, 324

In 1918, Laurens gave up these two methods and took to direct carving in stone or modeling in plaster. This development coincided with an important change in his conception of three-dimensional Cubism. Some of these new works, a series of colored still life reliefs, were surface-modeled transpositions into stone of the sort of compositions he had previously executed in *papiers collés*, and were therefore basically synthetic Cubist in conception (*Musical Instruments*, 1919). But at last Laurens also began to evolve a form of Cubist sculpture existing fully in the round. In the works of this latter type, Laurens worked along synthetic Cubist lines in so far as he relied on frontality and a layer-upon-layer structure of broad parallel planes to evoke volume and establish a progression in space (*Woman with a Guitar*, 1919). However, he complemented this with an invented personal technique of faceting and hollowing-out (*Man with a Pipe*, 1919), derived partly from the analytical Cubist procedure, devised to preserve the frontality and yet, by a system of

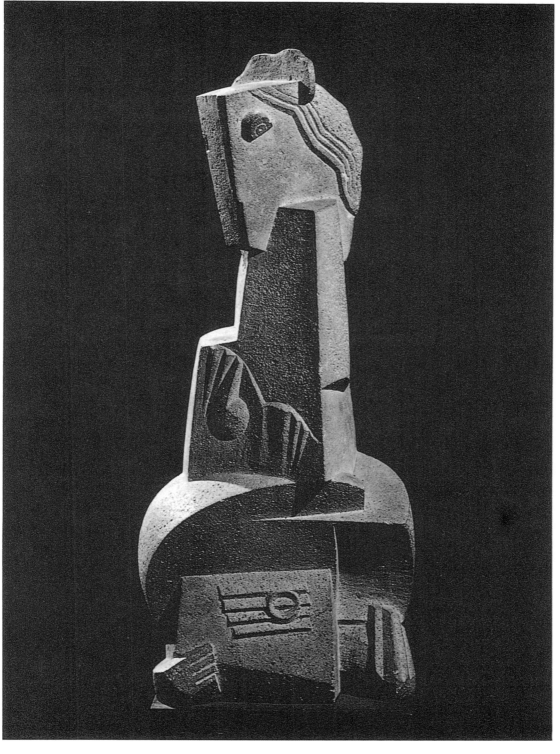

Plate 322

Henri Laurens, *Woman with Guitar*, 1918
Stone, 23^1/$_4$ × 9^7/$_8$ in.

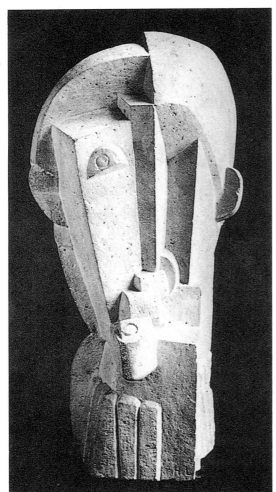

Plate 323

Henri Laurens
Man with a Pipe, 1919
Stone, 14³/₄ in. high

No. 160

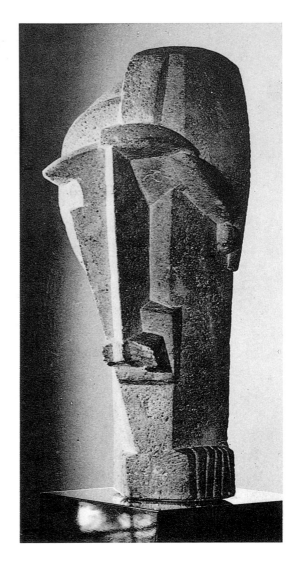

Plate 324

Henri Laurens
Man's Head, 1919
Stone, 17 in. high

No. 159

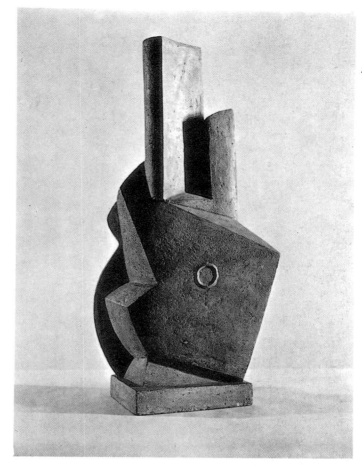

Plate 325

Henri Laurens
Guitar, 1920
Terracotta, 14¹/₄ × 4³/₄ × 3⁵/₈ in.

No. 163

Plate 326

Henri Laurens
Bottle and Glass, 1919
Painted stone,
13³/₈ × 4³/₈ × 4¹/₂ in.

No. 162

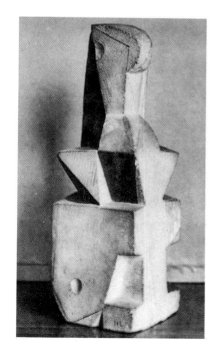

angles, changes of level and penetration, invite the eye to move around and through the mass and feel its solidity. As Laurens himself said: 'In a sculpture it is necessary for the voids to have as much importance as the full volumes. Sculpture is first and foremost a matter of taking possession of space, a space limited by forms' (*Bottle and Glass*, 1919). Laurens' real concern in his Cubist sculptures was with re-creating an image of reality, with preserving a sense of the mass from which it had emerged, and with achieving this through a clear and logical planar structure (*Guitar*, 1920). That is why he feared the distorting effects of 'variations of light' and of cast shadows on stone or terracotta and often painted his sculptures in these media.

Laurens was not the most adventurous of the sculptors who worked in a Cubist idiom. But even with his limited

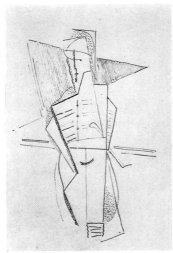

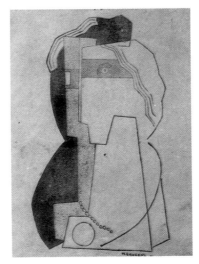

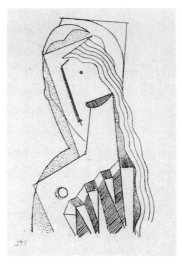

Plate 327

Henri Laurens
Anselme, 1920
Ink, $9^1/_4 \times 6^1/_4$ in.

No. 168

Plate 328

Henri Laurens
Young Woman, 1919
Etching, $7^5/_8 \times 5^3/_4$ in.

No. 169

Plate 329

Henri Laurens
Girl with a Fan, 1921
Etching, $12^5/_8 \times 9^7/_8$ in.

No. 171

aims he achieved results which are impressive, by reason of the artistic sincerity and purely sculptural virtues which his works display. Even Giacometti paid homage to Laurens' unique position among the sculptors of his generation when he wrote: 'Laurens is one of the very rare sculptors who render what I experience in front of living reality, and that is why I find a *likeness* in his sculpture, a likeness which gives me a reason to love and admire it.'

Conclusion

6

After all this we are entitled to ask What is Cubism? There is no easy definition, so we must try to answer the question obliquely. Cubism cannot be defined in terms of style, nor of subject-matter, nor of some particular technique, nor as an aesthetic theory or system. Nor was Cubism inspired by any particular philosophy. It was a combination of vision, of understanding, of veracity, of modernism and of a will to represent a contemporary reality. Cubism was also the outcome of a conviction that the established methods and conventions of art (painting in particular) were outdated and false, and of an intuition that, if they willed it, a new generation of young artists could discover or invent new means of pictorial expression. One major consideration was the determination to express the solid reality of things without having recourse to eye-fooling devices. More than this, Cubism was an attempt to make of each picture a new tangible reality rather than an illusory image either of some imaginary ideal or of some purely visual sensation of reality. This was the essence of the new realism which Cubism enshrined. To quote Braque, its aim was 'not to try and *reconstitute* an anecdotal fact but to *constitute* a pictorial fact.'

In the seven-year period between 1907 and 1914, the true Cubists made all their essential discoveries and innovations and became masters of a new pictorial idiom. From 1914 on, their efforts were directed towards enriching and humanizing a language of which, at that moment, they had done little more than establish the solid foundations. Their conceptions were imitated, misconstrued, travestied, but sometimes interestingly and creatively enlarged upon by their contemporaries.

However, when everything is taken into account, it becomes obvious that the true Cubists and the artists of the various Cubist movements succeeded between them, before 1914, in giving to the twentieth century a new conception of pictorial representation and in changing the course of art throughout the western world.

They had toppled the system of scientific linear perspective which had prevailed in European painting since the Renaissance, and had established the artist's right to look at things from several view-points simultaneously and to incorporate into a work of art knowledge gained from other than purely visual sources. They had separated the pictorial functions of color, form and volume, allowing them to co-exist and function independently. They had established a wholly new relationship between the abstract, formal organization of a work of art and its representational content. They had evolved a more surface-conscious type of painting, and had found a way of expressing volumes and representing space without penetrating into false depth. They had undermined the conception of *belle peinture* and the idea that works of fine art can only be made with fine materials, proving this with the two wholly new techniques of *collage* and *papiers collés* as well as with their scrap constructions. Other artists, in Paris and elsewhere, had taken up these discoveries and applied them to other, often more ambitious, purposes. But there is a vital division between anything Cubist in style or spirit and those supposed extensions of Cubism which turned into non-figuration. Cubism was essentially an art of realism. And the true Cubists felt this so deeply that they turned back each time they found themselves approaching total abstraction

By 1919–20, it was no longer necessary or possible for those who had been involved with Cubism before the war to come together again and continue the movement. The former concentration and sense of communal effort had been dispersed, too many of the artists concerned were asserting their individual personalities, many erstwhile Cubists had abandoned the struggle or were dead, a neoclassical reaction had been launched under the slogan '*Le Rappel à l'Ordre*,' and lastly Purism and Dada had arrived on the scene.

Yet it was at this time that true Cubist art at last came fully into its own in Paris and Braque was accorded the 'great man' status which he had never enjoyed before. Léonce Rosenberg held a series of major one-man shows at his new gallery L'Effort Moderne, including those of Braque, Gris, Léger, Picasso, Gleizes, Laurens and Lipchitz, while a major group of Cubist works was assembled at the Salon des Indépendants of 1920. Also, the dispersal at auction in Paris between 1921 and 1923 of the remaining pre-war stock of Cubist paintings by Braque, Gris, Léger and Picasso, belonging to the Kahnweiler Gallery, brought several hundred examples suddenly before the eyes of an awakening public.

Throughout the 1920s and 1930s the new pictorial conceptions of Cubism continued to influence successive generations of artists, as did the new techniques of *collage* and construction. Cubist methods influenced the art of camouflage during the First World War, and the design of modern architecture afterwards, while for the past forty years the influence of Cubism has penetrated commercial and applied art. Thus it is no exaggeration to say that Cubism initiated one of the greatest artistic revolutions ever, added to which its continuing influence proves that it has been a major force in the development of western art. Fifty years have now passed since the movement as such ended. It is therefore appropriate to survey it as a whole and take stock, as no previous generation has done, of its clarity, strength, inventiveness and ultimate artistic greatness.

APPENDIXES

Bibliography

Very complete Bibliographies, covering history, style criticism, journalism, exhibition catalogs, artists' statements etc., and relating to The Cubist Epoch in France have recently been published in Edward Fry's *Cubism* (London/New York 1966) and in John Golding's *Cubism: A History and an Analysis 1907–14* (2nd edition, London 1968). These two books are easily available for consultation and therefore I shall not duplicate unnecessarily their admirable compilations. Edward Fry's critical and explanatory analysis of true Cubist art, though its range is obviously limited, is the most serious and reliable text on the subject which has yet appeared. In addition, his book contains a useful anthology in English of critical texts of the years 1905–25, particularly noticeable among them being the fascinating statement by Braque (*Architectural Record*, New York, May 1910) which Mr. Fry unearthed and here re-printed for the first time. Unlike any other volume devoted to Cubist art, Mr. Fry's is really *multum in parvo*.

Mr. Fry and Dr. Golding have listed all the early publications on Cubist painting by D. H. Kahnweiler, A. Gleizes and J. Metzinger, G. Janneau etc. No student of Cubism today would forget to look at them, pretentious, confusing and uninspired though for the most part they are. However, no Bibliography will tell the student how essential it is to consult not the daily press of the time but the famous periodicals, and that is why I have decided, in drawing up a short reading list, to mention them more prominently. And here I would also draw attention to the invaluable, annotated collection of all Guillaume Apollinaire's art-writings—G. Apollinaire, *Chroniques d'Art* 1902–18 (Paris 1960)—so brilliantly compiled and edited by Professor L. C. Breunig. If the student will read this one volume he will find that he has saved himself many hours of library research and acquired a vital key to many aspects of Parisian thinking in the period before 1914. But he must not read into Apollinaire's journalistic writings more than they were intended to signify at a particular and brief moment in time.

Artistically, the present exhibition covers a much wider field, especially in terms of the geography of Europe, than either Mr. Fry or Dr. Golding attempted in their books or Bibliographies. So these other aspects require bibliographical implementation. I have therefore listed, under their respective countries, certain publications which are important for the study of national schools. I have also listed any publications which have appeared since 1965 and which seem to me of real value. Similarly, I have listed some little publicized volumes which refer to individual artists included in this exhibition. Lastly I have chosen a few works of a general nature which are informative and reliable.

General

P. CABANNE, *L'Epopée du Cubisme*. Paris, 1963.

H. B. CHIPP, *Theories of Modern Art*. University of California Press, Berkeley and Los Angeles, 1968.

G. H. HAMILTON, *Painting and Sculpture in Europe 1880–1940*. London, 1967.

Jean LAUDE, *La Peinture Française (1905–14) et 'l'Art Nègre.'* Paris, 1968.

France

G. H. HAMILTON and W. C. AGEE, *Duchamp-Villon*. New York, 1967.

A. M. HAMMACHER, *Lipchitz*. London, 1961.

M. LAURENS, *Henri Laurens, Sculpteur*. Paris, 1955.

R. LEBEL, *Sur Marcel Duchamp* (with Catalog). Paris, 1959.

F. MEYER, *Chagall*. Paris, 1964.

G. SELIGMAN, *Roger de La Fresnaye* (with Catalog). London, 1969.

CATALOGS

Apollinaire et le Cubisme, Musée des Beaux Arts, Lille, April 1965.

Guillaume Apollinaire, Bibliothèque Nationale, Paris, November 1969.

La Peinture sous le Signe de Blaise Cendrars, Galerie Louis Carré, Paris, June 1965.

A la Rencontre de Paul Reverdy, Fondation Maeght, St. Paul de Vence, 1970.

PERIODICALS
L'Esprit Nouveau, Paris, 1920–25.
Montjoie!, Paris, 1913–14.
Nord-Sud, Paris, 1917–18.
Les Soirées de Paris, Paris, 1912–14.

Germany
L. G. BUCHHEIM, *Der Blaue Reiter*. Feldafing, 1959.
L. SCHREYER, *Erinnerungen an Sturm und Bauhaus*. Munich, 1956.
N. WALDEN, *Herwarth Walden*. Berlin, 1963.
N. WALDEN and L. SCHREYER, *Der Sturm, Ein Erinnerungsbuch*. Baden-Baden, 1954.

PERIODICAL
Der Sturm, Berlin, 1910–15.

Italy
G. BALLO, *Boccioni* (with Catalog). Milan, 1964.
M. CARRA, *Carlo Carrà* (Catalog), 2 vols. Milan, 1967.
R. CARRIERI, *Il Futurismo*. Milan, 1961.
D. GAMBILLA and T. FIORI, *Archivi del Futurismo*, 2 vols. Milan, 1958–62.
M. W. MARTIN, *Futurist Art and Theory*. London, 1968.

PERIODICAL
Lacerba, Florence, 1913–15.

Czechoslovakia
CATALOGS
Le Cubisme à Prague et la Collection Kramár, Exhibition at Museum Boymans-van Beuningen, Rotterdam, January 1968.

Gutfreund, Exhibition at Museum des 20sten Jahrhunderts, Vienna, April 1969.

PERIODICAL
Umelécky Mesičník, Prague, 1911–14.

Russia

C. GRAY, *The Great Experiment: Russian Art, 1863–1922*. London, 1962.

America

A. ARCHIPENKO, *Archipenko: Fifty Creative Years, 1908–58*. New York, 1960.
M. W. BROWN, *The Story of the Armory Show*, New York, 1963.
L. GOODRICH and J. I. H. BAUR, *American Art of Our Century*, New York, 1961.
H. HESS, *Feininger*, New York, 1959.
B. ROSE, *American Art Since 1900*, New York, 1967.

CATALOGS
Archipenko, Visionnaire International, Smithsonian Institution, Washington D.C., 1969.
The Armory Show: 50th Anniversary Exhibition, Munson-Williams-Proctor Institute, Utica, 1963.

In addition to the publications listed above, students should consult the often highly documented catalogs of important retrospective exhibitions of the following artists held both in Europe and America since 1955: Braque, Gris, Léger, Picasso, Gleizes, Le Fauconnier, Delaunay, Duchamp, Feininger, Mondrian, Severini, Villon, Marc, Malevich, Weber, Laurens, Lipchitz, Herbin and Hayden.

Artists and Their Dates

Artist	Nationality	Dates
ARCHIPENKO, Alexander	Russian-American	1887–1964
BALLA, Giacomo	Italian	1871–1958
BENES, Vincenc	Czech	1883–
BOCCIONI, Umberto	Italian	1882–1916
BRAQUE, Georges	French	1882–1963
BRUCE, Patrick	American	1880–1937
CAMPENDONK, Heinrich	German	1889–1957
CAPEK, Joseph	Czech	1887–1945
CARRA, Carlo	Italian	1881–1966
CÉZANNE, Paul	French	1839–1906
CHAGALL, Marc	Russian-French	1887–
CZAKY, Joseph	Hungarian-French	1888–
DELAUNAY, Robert	French	1885–1941
DERAIN, André	French	1880–1954
DUCHAMP, Marcel	French	1887–1969
DUCHAMP-VILLON, Raymond	French	1876–1918
DUFY, Raoul	French	1887–1953
DUNOYER DE SEGONZAC, André	French	1884–
FEININGER, Lyonel	American-German	1871–1956
FERAT, Serge	Russian	1881–1958
FILLA, Emil	Czech	1882–1953
GLEIZES, Albert	French	1881–1953
GONTCHAROVA, Nathalie	Russian	1881–1962
GRIS, Juan	Spanish	1887–1927
GUTFREUND, Otto	Czech	1889–1927
HAYDEN, Henri	Polish-French	1883–1970
HERBIN, Auguste	French	1882–1960
KLEE, Paul	Swiss-German	1879–1940
KUBISTA, Bohumil	Czech	1884–1918
LA FRESNAYE, Roger de	French	1885–1925
LARIONOV, Michel	Russian	1881–1964
LAURENS, Henri	French	1885–1954

LE FAUCONNIER, Henri	French	1881–1946
LÉGER, Fernand	French	1881–1955
LEWIS, Wyndham	English	1884–1957
LHOTE, André	French	1885–1962
LIPCHITZ, Jacques	Russian-American	1891–
MACDONALD-WRIGHT, Stanton	American-Dutch	1890–
MACKE, August	German	1887–1914
MALEVICH, Kasimir	Russian	1878–1935
MARC, Franz	German	1880–1916
MARCOUSSIS, Louis	Polish-French	1883–1941
MARCHAND, Jean	French	1883–1941
MARIN, John	American	1870–1953
METZINGER, Jean	French	1883–1957
MONDRIAN, Piet	Dutch	1872–1944
MOREAU, Luc-Albert	French	1882–1948
PICABIA, Francis	Cuban-French	1879–1953
PICASSO, Pablo	Spanish	1881–
POPOVA, Liubov	Russian	1889–1924
PROCHAZKA, Antonín	Czech	1882–1945
RIVERA, Diego	Mexican	1886–1957
RUSSELL, Morgan	American	1886–1953
SEVERINI, Gino	Italian	1883–1966
SIRONI, Mario	Italian	1885–1961
SOFFICI, Ardengo	Italian	1879–1964
STELLA, Joseph	Italian-American	1877–1946
UDALTSOVA, Nadezhda	Russian	1886–1961
VILLON, Jacques	French	1875–1963
WEBER, Max	Russian-American	1881–1961

Check List

In measurements, height precedes width and depth.

ARCHIPENKO, Alexander

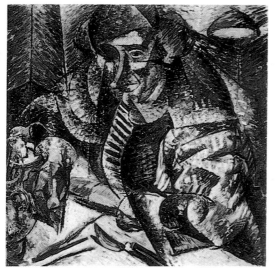

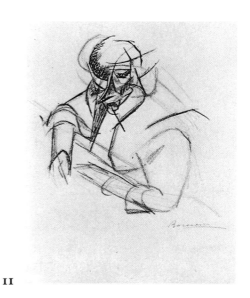

8   **11**

DRAWINGS

[Plate 295]   **10 Bottle, Table and House,**
              1912

              Pencil on paper, 13$^1/_8$ × 9$^1/_2$ in.
              Signed bottom right: *Boccioni*

              Raccolta Civica Bertarelli,
              Milan.

              **11 Study for 'The
              Ungraceful,'** 1912–13

              Ink and charcoal on paper,
              11$^3/_4$ × 9 in.
              Signed bottom right: *Boccioni*

              Raccolta Civica Bertarelli,
              Milan.

[Plate 176]   **12 Study for 'Horizontal
              Volumes,'** 1912

              Pencil and ink on paper,
              17$^3/_4$ × 23$^7/_8$ in.
              Signed bottom right: *Boccioni*

              Raccolta Civica Bertarelli,
              Milan.

[Plate 175]   **13 Figure Study,** 1913

              Pencil, ink and wash on paper,
              11$^1/_2$ × 9 in.
              Signed bottom right: *Boccioni*

              Raccolta Civica Bertarelli,
              Milan.

BRAQUE, Georges

PAINTINGS

[Plate 5]   **14 Nude,** 1907–08

              Oil on canvas, 55$^3/_4$ × 40 in.
              Signed bottom right:
              G. Braque

              Galerie Alex Maguy, Paris.

[Plate 7]   **15 Trees at L'Estaque,** 1908

              Oil on canvas, 31 × 23$^5/_8$ in.
              Formerly signed on back
              (relined)

              Private collection, France.

[Plate 17]   **16 Harbor in Normandy,** 1909

              Oil on canvas, 32 × 32 in.

              The Art Institute of Chicago,
              Chicago, Ill., Samuel A. Marx
              Purchase Fund.

[Plate 18]   **17 Fishing Boats,** 1909

              Oil on canvas, 36 × 28$^3/_4$ in.
              Signed bottom right:
              G. Braque

              coll. Mr. and Mrs. John
              A. Beck, Houston, Texas.

[Plate 23] **18 Piano and Mandola,** 1909–10

Oil on canvas, 36^1/$_8$ × 16^7/$_8$ in.
Signed on back

The Solomon R. Guggenheim
Museum, New York.

[Plate 24] **19 Violin and Palette,** 1909–10

Oil on canvas, 36^1/$_4$ × 16^7/$_8$ in.
Signed on back

The Solomon R. Guggenheim
Museum, New York.

[Plate 16] **20 Rio Tinto Factories,** 1910

Oil on canvas, 25^5/$_8$ × 21^1/$_4$ in.
Signed on back

Musée National d'Art
Moderne, Paris.

[Plate 29] **21 The Table,** 1910

Oil on canvas, 15 × 21^1/$_2$ in.
Signed on back: *Braque*

coll. Mr. and Mrs. Ralph
F. Colin, New York.

[Plate 30] **22 Female Figure,** 1910–11

Oil on canvas, 36 × 24 in.
Signed bottom right:
G. Braque

The Carey Walker Foundation,
New York.

[Plate 42] **23 Violin and Candlestick,** 1910

Oil on canvas, 24 × 19^3/$_4$ in.
Signed on back: *G. Braque*

coll. Rita and Taft Schreiber,
Beverly Hills, Cal.

[Plate 34] **24 Still Life with Dice and
Pipe,** 1911

Oil on canvas, 31^1/$_2$ × 23 in.
(Oval)
Signed on back

coll. Mr. and Mrs. Robert
Eichholz, Washington, D.C.

[Plate 26] **25 Guitar,** 1910–11

Oil on canvas, 9^1/$_2$ × 13^3/$_4$ in.
(Oval)
Signed on back: *G. Braque*

coll. Mr. and Mrs. Norton
Simon, Los Angeles.

[Plate 47] **26 Homage to Bach,** 1912

Oil on canvas, 21^1/$_4$ × 28^3/$_4$ in.
Signed bottom left:
G. Braque

Sidney Janis Gallery, New York.

[Plate 50] **27 The Guéridon,** 1912

Oil on canvas, 45^5/$_8$ × 31^7/$_8$ in.
Signed on back

Musée National d'Art
Moderne, Paris.

[Plate 51] **28 Still Life with Pipe,** 1912

Oil on canvas, 13^3/$_8$ × 16^3/$_8$ in.

Norton Simon Foundation,
Los Angeles, Cal.

[Plate 46] **29 Guitar,** 1912

Oil on canvas, 29 × 24 in. (Oval)
Signed on back: *G. Braque*

The Carey Walker Foundation,
New York.

[Plate 209]   **30**   **Still Life with Clarinet and Violin,** 1912–13

Oil on canvas, $21^5/_8 \times 16^7/_8$ in.
Signed on back: *G. Braque*

Národní Galerie, Prague,
(Kramář Collection).

[Plate 215]   **31**   **The Guitar Player,** 1913–14

Oil on canvas, $51^1/_4 \times 28^3/_4$ in.
Signed on back

coll. Heinz Berggruen, Paris.

[Plate 210]   **32**   **Violin** *(Valse)*, 1913

Oil on canvas, $28^3/_8 \times 21^1/_4$ in.
Signed on back: *G. Braque*

Private Collection, Rome.

[Plate 216]   **33**   **Still Life with Ace of Clubs,** 1914

Oil on wood panel,
$14^1/_2 \times 21$ in. (Oval)

Mrs. Barnett Malbin, Birmingham, Mich. (The Lydia and Harry Lewis Winston Collection).

[Plate 264]   **34**   **Guitar,** 1918

Oil on canvas, $35^3/_4 \times 21^3/_4$ in.
(Oval)
Signed bottom right:
G. Braque

Private Collection, France.

[Plate 263]   **35**   **Still Life with Musical Instruments,** 1918

Oil on canvas, 35×25 in.

Signed bottom center:
G. Braque

Norton Simon Foundation,
Los Angeles, Cal.

PAPIERS COLLÉS

[Plate 199]   **36**   **Glass and Playing Card,** 1912

Papier collé and charcoal on paper, $11^5/_8 \times 18^1/_8$ in.
Signed bottom left:
G. Braque

Los Angeles County Museum of Art, Los Angeles, Cal.

[Plate 198]   **37**   **Man with a Pipe,** 1912

Papier collé and charcoal on paper, $24^3/_8 \times 19^1/_4$ in.
Signed on back: *G. Braque*

Kunstmuseum, Basel, Gift of Raoul La Roche.

[Plate 206]   **38**   **Glass, Carafe and Newspaper,** 1913

Papier collé on paper,
$24^5/_8 \times 11^1/_4$ in.

Private Collection, Basel.

[Plate 200]   **39**   **Still Life on a Table,** 1913

Papier collé on paper,
$18^1/_2 \times 24^3/_4$ in.

coll. Monsieur and Madame Claude Laurens, Paris.

[Plate 201]   **40**   **The Program,** 1913

Papier collé on paper,
$28^3/_4 \times 36^3/_8$ in.

coll. Mrs. Barbara Reis Poe,
Los Angeles, Cal.

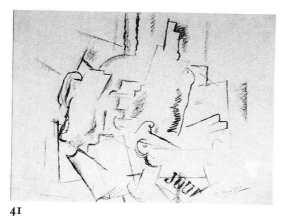

4I

DRAWING

4I **Still Life,** 1912

Charcoal
$18^3/_4 \times 24^7/_8$ in.
Signed bottom right:
G. Braque

Estate of
Lester F. Avnet,
New York.

PRINTS

[*Plate 54*] **42** **Guitar on a Table,** 1909

Etching, numbered bottom
left 11/25; edition of 25
published 1954
$5^1/_2 \times 7^7/_8$ in. on full sheet
$12^1/_2 \times 13^3/_4$ in.
Signed bottom right below
print: *G. Braque*

Private Collection, France.

[*Plate 53*] **43** **Job,** 1911

Drypoint; edition of 100
published 1912

$5^7/_8 \times 7^7/_8$ in. on full sheet
$8^1/_4 \times 12^1/_2$ in.
Signed bottom right below
print: *G. Braque*

The Museum of Modern Art,
New York, Gift of Victor
S. Riesenfeld.

44 **Pale Ale,** 1911

Etching; edition of 50
published 1954
$18^1/_2 \times 13$ in. on full sheet
$22^7/_{16} \times 17^3/_4$ in.
Signed bottom right:
G. Braque

coll. Dr. and Mrs. Abraham
Melamed, Milwaukee, Wisc.

44

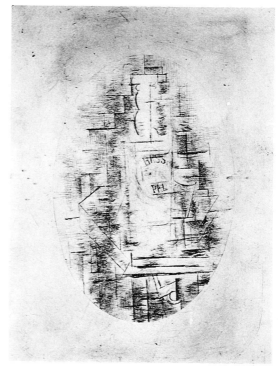

[Plate 38] **45 Fox,** 1911–12

Etching; edition of 100
published 1912
21¹/₂ × 15 in. on full sheet
25¹/₄ × 19⁵/₈ in.
Signed bottom right below
print: *G. Braque*

The Museum of Modern Art,
New York, Abby Aldrich
Rockefeller Fund.

[Plate 55] **46 Bass,** 1911–12

Drypoint and etching; edition
of 50 published 1950
18 × 12¹⁵/₁₆ in. on full sheet
25³/₄ × 19⁵/₈ in.
Signed bottom right below
print: *G. Braque*

The Museum of Modern Art,
New York, Purchase.

[Plate 56] **47 Cubist Still Life II,** 1912

Drypoint and etching; edition
of 50 published 1953
12¹⁵/₁₆ × 17⁷/₈ in. on full sheet
19⁵/₈ × 25¹/₄ in.
Signed bottom right below
print: *G. Braque*

The Museum of Modern Art,
New York, Purchase.

SCULPTURE

[Plate 314] **48 Standing Figure,** 1920

Bronze; one of 3 specially cast
for the artist in 1954. (Exists

also in an edition of 6 in white
plaster made in 1920)
7¹/₂ × 2³/₄ in.
Signed on base: *G. Braque*
Numbered 1/3

coll. Monsieur and Madame
Claude Laurens, Paris.

CAMPENDONK, Heinrich

PAINTING

[Plate 145] **49 Harlequin and Columbine,**
1913

Oil on canvas, 64¹/₂ × 78 in.

coll. Morton D. May,
St. Louis, Mo.

CAPEK, Joseph

PRINT

[Plate 156] **50 Cubist Figure,** 1913

Hand colored linoleum cut on
paper
8³/₁₆ × 4 in.
Signed and dated bottom right:
Joseph Capek/1913

The Museum of Modern Art,
New York, Gift of John Torson.

CARRA, Carlo

PAINTINGS

[Plate 179] **51 Woman with Glass of
Absinthe,** 1911

Oil on canvas, 26⁵/₈ × 20⁵/₈ in.

coll. Dott. Constantino Marino,
Milan.

[*Plate 177*]   **52 Woman at Window (Simultaneity),** 1912

Oil on canvas, 57⁷/₈ × 52³/₈ in.
Signed and dated top left:
C. Carrà 912

coll. Dott. Ricardo Jucker, Milan.

PAPIER COLLÉ

[*Plate 190*]   **53 Bottle of Wine,** 1914

Papier collé on board, 16 × 13¹/₂ in.
Signed and dated bottom right:
Carrà 914

coll. Mr. and Mrs. Sidney E. Cohn, New York.

DRAWINGS

54 Carriage at Night, 1912
(Study for painting of same name)
Pencil on paper, 21⁵/₈ × 29¹/₂ in.

coll. Dott. Massimo Carrà, Milan.

54

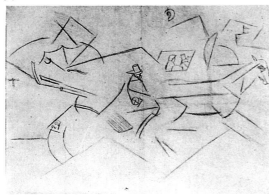

[*Plate 181*]   **55 Boxer,** 1913

Ink on paper, 17¹/₂ × 11 in.
Signed bottom right:
C. Carrà 913

coll. Eric Estorick, London.

[*Plate 182*]   **56 Portrait of Soffici,** 1914

Ink, collage and watercolor on paper, 8¹/₄ × 5⁷/₈ in.
Signed, dated and inscribed bottom right: *C. Carrà 914 ritratto di Soffici.*

coll. Dott. Massimo Carrà, Milan.

[*Plate 184*]   **57 Standing Figure (Idol),** 1914
(First study for painting *Penelope,* 1917)

Pencil on paper, 44⁷/₈ × 18¹/₂ in.

coll. Dott. Massimo Carrà, Milan.

CHAGALL, Marc

PAINTINGS

[*Plate 116*]   **58 Still Life,** 1912

Oil on canvas, 25 × 30³/₄ in.
Signed on back: *Chagall, Paris*

coll. Eric Estorick, London.

[*Plate 117*]   **59 Adam and Eve,** 1912

Oil on canvas, 63³/₁₆ × 44⁷/₈ in.
Signed bottom left

City Art Museum of St. Louis, St. Louis, Mo., Gift of Morton D. May.

CZAKY, Joseph

SCULPTURE

[Plate 284]　　**60 Standing Woman,** 1913–14

Bronze, $31^{1}/_{2} \times 8^{1}/_{4} \times 8^{5}/_{8}$ in.
Signed and dated on base at
left

Musée National d'Art Moderne,
Paris.

DELAUNAY, Robert

PAINTINGS

[Plate 79]　　**61 The Eiffel Tower,** 1911(?)

Oil on canvas, $79^{1}/_{2} \times 54^{1}/_{2}$ in.
Signed and dated bottom right:
r. delaunay 1910
Inscribed bottom left:
La Tour 1910

The Solomon R. Guggenheim
Museum, New York.

[Plate 83]　　**62 The City Seen from an
Open Window,** 1911

Oil on canvas, $57^{1}/_{2} \times 44^{1}/_{8}$ in.
Signed, dated and inscribed
bottom left:　*la ville 1911
r. delaunay*

The Solomon R. Guggenheim
Museum, New York.

[Plate 80]　　**63 The Towers of Laon,** 1912

Oil on canvas, $63^{3}/_{4} \times 51^{1}/_{8}$ in.
Signed bottom left

Musée National d'Art
Moderne, Paris.

[Plate 81]　　**64 Window on the City II,** 1912

Oil on canvas, $15^{3}/_{8} \times 11^{3}/_{8}$ in.
Signed and dated on back

coll. Madame Sonia Delaunay,
Paris.

DRAWINGS

[Plate 76]　　**65 Tower with Ferris Wheel,**
1910 (or 1911?)
(Study for *The Red Tower*,
1913–14; coll. The Solomon
Guggenheim Museum,
New York)

Ink on paper, $25^{1}/_{2} \times 19^{1}/_{2}$ in.
Signed bottom left: *Delaunay,
Paris, 1909–10*; dated again
top left: *1910.*

The Museum of Modern Art,
New York, Abby Aldrich
Rockefeller Fund.

[Plate 77]　　**66 The Eiffel Tower** 1910(?)
(Study for *The Eiffel Tower*,
1911(?); No. 61)

Ink on cardboard,
$21^{1}/_{4} \times 19^{1}/_{4}$ in.
Signed and dated bottom left:
r. delaunay, 1910

The Museum of Modern Art,
New York, Abby Aldrich
Rockefeller Fund.

[Plate 78]　　**67 The Eiffel Tower, Paris,**
1926

Transfer lithograph after
No. 61

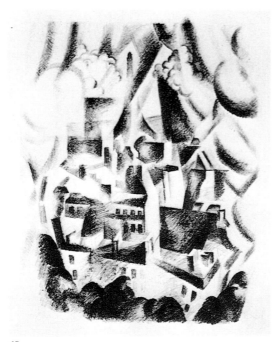

68

24¹/₄ × 17³/₄ in.
Signed bottom left below
print: *r. delaunay*
Inscribed bottom right:
La Tour 1910, dated on back

The Museum of Modern Art,
New York, Abby Aldrich
Rockefeller Fund.

**68 The City Seen From an
Open Window,** 1926

Transfer lithograph after a
painting of 1911,
22³/₁₆ × 16³/₁₆ in.

The Museum of Modern Art,
New York, Lent by The
International Arts Foundation.

DERAIN, Andre

PAINTINGS

[Plate 60] **69 Still Life on a Table,** 1910

Oil on canvas, 36¹/₄ × 28¹/₈ in.
Signed bottom right

Musée d'Art Moderne de la
Ville de Paris, Paris.

[Plate 59] **70 Cadaqués,** 1910

Oil on canvas, 23⁵/₈ × 28³/₄ in.
Signed on back

Národní Galerie, Prague,
(Kramář Collection).

DUCHAMP, Marcel

PAINTINGS

[Plate 107] **71 Portrait,** 1911

Oil on canvas, 57⁵/₈ × 44⁷/₈ in.
Signed bottom left and on
back: *Marcel Duchamp 11*

(L. A. only)   Philadelphia Museum of Art,
Louise and Walter Arensberg
Collection, Philadelphia, Pa.

[Plate 108] **72 Portrait of Chess-Players,**
1911

Oil on canvas, 39⁵/₈ × 39³/₄ in.
Signed bottom left: *Marcel
Duchamp 11*

(N. Y. only)   Philadelphia Museum of Art,
Louise and Walter Arensberg
Collection, Philadelphia, Pa.

[Plate 109] **73 Nude Descending a Staircase No. 1,** 1911–12

Oil on cardboard,
37³/₄ × 23¹/₂ in.
Signed and inscribed bottom
left: *Marcel Duchamp 11*
Nu descendant un escalier

(N. Y. only)   Philadelphia Museum of Art,
Louise and Walter Arensberg
Collection, Philadelphia, Pa.

[Plate 110]   **74 Nude Descending a Stair-case No. 2** (Definitive version), 1912

Oil on canvas, 58 × 35 in.
Signed and inscribed across bottom: *Marcel Duchamp 12 Nu descendant un escalier*
Signed on back: *Marcel Duchamp 12*

(L. A. only)   Philadelphia Museum of Art, Louise and Walter Arensberg Collection, Philadelphia, Pa.

DUCHAMP-VILLON, Raymond

SCULPTURE

[Plate 287]   **75 The Lovers** (Final State), 1913

Bronze relief, 26³/₄ × 39³/₈ in.
Signed bottom right

coll. Mr. and Mrs. A. J. Latner and family, Toronto, Canada.

[Plate 288]   **76 Seated Girl,** 1914

Plaster, 12¹/₂ × 4 × 4¹/₂ in.

coll. Vincent Tovell, Toronto, Canada.

[Plate 289]   **77 Small Horse,** 1914

Bronze, 15³/₈ in. high

coll. Edgar Kaufmann, Jr., New York.

[Plate 290]   **78 Large Horse,** 1914

Bronze, 39³/₈ × 39³/₈ × 20³/₄ in.
Signed and dated on base: *R Duchamp-Villon/1914*

Numbered 4/6

A. (L. A. only)   Walker Art Center, Minneapolis, Minn., T. B. Walker Foundation Aquisition.

Numbered 5/6

B. (N. Y. only)   Munson-Williams-Proctor Institute, Utica, N.Y.

DUFY, Raoul

PAINTINGS

[Plate 8]   **79 Green Trees at L'Estaque,** 1908

Oil on canvas, 28¹/₂ × 23¹/₂ in.
Signed bottom right

coll. Henri Gaffić, Beaulieu s/Mer.

[Plate 15]   **80 Factory,** 1908

Oil on canvas, 36 × 28¹/₂ in.
Signed bottom right

coll. Henri Gaffić, Beaulieu s/Mer.

FEININGER, Lyonel

PAINTINGS

[Plate 137]   **81 Bicycle Race,** 1912

Oil on canvas, 31¹/₂ × 39³/₄ in.
Signed and dated bottom left

coll. Mr. and Mrs. Leonard Hutton, New York.

[Plate 139]   **82 The Bridge I,** 1913

Oil on canvas, 31¹/₂ × 39¹/₂ in.
Signed and dated top left

Washington University Gallery of Art, St. Louis, Mo.

[*Plate 138*]   **83 Gelmeroda IV,** 1915

Oil on canvas, 39^1/$_8$ × 31^1/$_4$ in.
Signed and dated bottom right: *Feininger, 15*

The Solomon R. Guggenheim Museum, New York.

[*Plate 141*]   **84 Avenue of Trees,** 1915

Oil on canvas, 31^3/$_4$ × 39^1/$_2$ in.
Signed bottom right: *Feininger*

Private Collection, New York.

[*Plate 142*]   **85 Markwippach,** 1917

Oil on canvas, 31^3/$_4$ × 39^3/$_4$ in.
Signed and dated top left

Cleveland Museum of Art, Cleveland, Ohio.

DRAWING

[*Plate 140*]   **86 Vollersroda,** 1918

Ink and wash, 7^7/$_8$ × 9^7/$_8$ in.
Signed bottom left: *Feininger*
Inscribed lower center: *Vollersroda*

Los Angeles County Museum of Art, Los Angeles, Cal., Purchased with Graphic Arts Council Funds.

PRINT

[*Plate 136*]   **87 The Gate,** 1912

Drypoint and etching, 10^5/$_8$ × 7^3/$_4$ in.

Signed and dated in plate bottom left: *Lyonel Feininger Sept. 4, 1912*

The Museum of Modern Art, New York, Gift of Mrs. Donald B. Straus.

FERAT, Serge

PAINTING

[*Plate 235*]   **88 Still Life with Violin,** 1913

Oil with collage on canvas, 21^1/$_4$ × 25^5/$_8$ in.
Signed bottom right

coll. Madame Roger Roussot, Paris.

FILLA, Emil

PAINTINGS

[*Plate 149*]   **89 Salome,** 1912

Oil on canvas, 54 × 31^1/$_4$ in.
Signed bottom right

Národní Galerie, Prague.

[*Plate 155*]   **90 Man's Head with Hat,** 1916

Oil on canvas, 28^3/$_8$ × 20^1/$_4$ in.
Signed and dated top right

Národní Galerie, Prague.

DRAWINGS

[*Plate 158*]   **91 Still Life with Pears,** 1915

Watercolor and ink on paper, 10^5/$_8$ × 23^5/$_8$ in.
Signed and dated bottom right

Národní Galerie, Prague.

[Plate 157] **92 Figure,** 1921

Ink on paper, 24⁷/₈ × 18¹/₂ in.
Signed and dated top right

Národní Galerie, Prague.

PRINT

[Plate 150] **93 Female Figure,** 1913

Drypoint, 17¹/₈ × 14 in.
Signed and dated bottom right

Národní Galerie, Prague.

SCULPTURE

[Plate 286] **94 Man's Head,** 1913–14

Bronze, 15³/₈ in. high
Národní Galerie, Prague.

GLEIZES, Albert

PAINTINGS

[Plate 62] **95 Women in a Kitchen,** 1911
Oil on canvas, 46⁵/₈ × 37¹/₄ in.
Signed and dated bottom right:
Alb Gleizes 11

Marlborough Galleries Inc.,
New York.

[Plate 65] **96 Harvest Threshing,** 1912

Oil on canvas, 106 × 138⁷/₈ in.
Signed and dated bottom right:
Albert Gleizes 1912

The Solomon R. Guggenheim
Museum, New York.

[Plate 64] **97 Landscape at Toul,** 1913

Oil on canvas, 35³/₄ × 28¹/₂ in.
Signed and dated bottom left
and on back: *Alb Gleizes 13*

The Columbus Gallery of Fine
Arts, Columbus, Ohio, Gift of
Ferdinand Howald.

[Plate 63] **98 The Football Players,**
1912–13

Oil on canvas, 89 × 72 in.
Signed and dated bottom left:
Albert Gleizes, 1912–13

Lent by the National Gallery
of Art, Washington, D.C.,
Ailsa Mellon Bruce Fund 1970.

[Plate 67] **99 Portrait of Igor Stravinsky,**
1914

Oil on canvas, 51 × 45 in.
Signed, dated and inscribed
bottom right: *Igor Stravinsky
1914 Albert Gleizes*

coll. Richard S. Zeisler,
New York.

[Plate 239] **100 Broadway,** 1915

Oil on canvas, 38³/₄ × 30 in.
Signed, dated and inscribed
bottom left: *Broadway
Alb Gleizes 15.*

coll. Mr. and Mrs. Arthur
G. Altschul, New York.

[Plate 68] **101 Dancer,** 1917

Oil on canvas, 39¹/₂ × 30 in.
Signed

coll. Mr. and Mrs. Sidney
E. Cohn, New York.

DRAWINGS

[Plate 69] **102 Study No. 1 for 'Portrait of an Army Doctor,'** 1915

Ink on paper, 11³/₄ × 9 in. Signed, dated and inscribed bottom right: *Alb Gleizes Toul 1915 pour le portrait du Prof. Lambert.*

The Solomon R. Guggenheim Museum, New York.

[Plate 70] **103 Study No. 2 for 'Portrait of an Army Doctor,'** 1915

Ink on paper, 7 × 5¹/₂ in. Signed bottom right: *Alb Gleizes Toul*

The Solomon R. Guggenheim Museum, New York.

[Plate 71] **104 Study No. 5 for 'Portrait of an Army Doctor,'** 1915

Ink on paper, 9⁵/₈ × 7³/₈ in. Signed bottom right: *Alb Gleizes Toul 1915*

The Solomon R. Guggenheim Museum, New York.

GONTCHAROVA, Nathalie

PAINTINGS

[Plate 163] **105 Cats,** 1911–12 (?)

Oil on canvas, 33¹/₂ × 33³/₄ in. Signed bottom right: *N Gontcharova*

The Solomon R. Guggenheim Museum, New York.

[Plate 162] **106 The Looking Glass,** 1912

Oil on canvas, 35 × 26³/₈ in. Signed on back: *N Gontcharova*

Galleria del Levante, Milan–Munich.

GRIS, Juan

PAINTINGS

[Plate 220] **107 Bottle of Wine and Water Jar,** 1911

Oil on canvas, 21³/₄ × 13 in. Signed bottom left: *Juan Gris*

Rijksmuseum Kröller-Müller, Otterlo.

[Plate 225] **108 Portrait of Picasso,** 1912

Oil on canvas, 36⁷/₈ × 29¹/₄ in. Signed and inscribed bottom left: *Hommage à Pablo Picasso, Juan Gris*

The Art Institute of Chicago, Chicago, Ill., Gift of Mr. Leigh B. Block.

[Plate 221] **109 The Artist's Mother,** 1912

Oil on canvas, 21³/₄ × 18 in. Signed top left: *Juan Gris*

Private Collection, France.

[Plate 223] **110 Guitar and Flowers,** 1912

Oil on canvas, 44¹/₈ × 27⁵/₈ in. Signed bottom right: *Juan Gris*

The Museum of Modern Art, New York, Bequest of Anna

Erickson Levene in memory of
her husband, Dr. Phoebus
Aaron Theodor Levene.

[Plate 224] **III Still Life with Bottle and
Watch,** 1912

(Not in exhibition) Oil and collage on canvas,
25³/₄ × 36¹/₄ in.
Signed bottom left: *Juan Gris*

coll. Herr Hans Grether, Basel.

[Plate 226] **II2 Playing Cards and Glass of
Beer,** 1913

Oil and collage on canvas,
20⁵/₈ × 14³/₈ in.
Signed and dated on back:
Juan Gris 4-13

The Columbus Gallery of Fine
Arts, Columbus, Ohio, Gift
of Ferdinand Howald.

[Plate 227] **II3 Landscape at Céret,** 1913

Oil on canvas, 36¹/₄ × 23⁵/₈ in.
Signed and dated on back:
Juan Gris 9-13

Moderna Museet, Stockholm.

[Plate 229] **II4 Guitar on a Chair,** 1913

Oil and collage on canvas,
39³/₈ × 25⁵/₈ in.
Formerly signed and dated on
back: *Juan Gris 9-13*
(relined)

Private Collection, France.

[Plate 230] **II5 Figure Seated in a Cafe,** 1914

Oil and collage on canvas,
39 × 28¹/₄ in.

coll. Mr. and Mrs. Leigh
B. Block, Chicago, Ill.

[Plate 267] **II6 Still Life in Front of an
Open Window : Place
Ravignan,** 1915

Oil on canvas, 45⁷/₈ × 35¹/₈ in.
Signed and dated bottom left:
Juan Gris 6-1915

(L. A. only) Philadelphia Museum of Art,
Philadelphia, Pa., Louise and
Walter Arensberg Collection.

[Plate 266] **II7 Coffee-Grinder and Glass,**
1915

Oil on canvas, 15 × 11³/₄ in.
Signed and dated top left:
Juan Gris 7-15

Private Collection, California.

[Plate 268] **II8 Breakfast,** 1915

Oil on canvas, 36¹/₄ × 28³/₄ in.
Signed and dated bottom left:
Juan Gris 10-1915

Musée National d'Art
Moderne, Paris.

[Plate 269] **II9 Still Life with Poem,** 1915

Oil on canvas, 31³/₄ × 25¹/₂ in.
Signed and dated bottom left:
Juan Gris 11-15

Norton Simon, Inc., Museum
of Art, Los Angeles, Cal.

[Plate 273] **I20 Fruit-Dish on a Table,** 1916

Oil on wood panel,
19³/₄ × 24 in.
Signed and dated on back:
Juan Gris 3-1916

coll. Gérard Bonnier, Stockholm.

[Plate 271] 121 **Grapes,** 1916

Oil on wood panel, 21³/₄ × 18¹/₂ in. Signed and dated top right: *Juan Gris 6-16*

coll. Mr. and Mrs. Paul Tishman, New York.

[Plate 278] 122 **Portrait of Josette,** 1916

Oil on wood panel, 45¹/₂ × 28¹/₂ in. Signed and dated top left: *Juan Gris 9-16*

Private Collection, France.

[Plate 274] 123 **Still Life,** 1917

Oil on wood panel, 29 × 36 in. Signed and dated bottom left: *Juan Gris 2-1917*

The Minneapolis Institute of Arts, Minneapolis, Minn.

[Plate 270] 124 **Open Window,** 1917

Oil on wood panel, 39³/₈ × 28⁵/₈ in. Signed and dated bottom right: *Juan Gris 2-1917*

(N. Y. only) Philadelphia Museum of Art, Louise and Walter Arensberg Collection, Philadelphia, Pa.

[Plate 279] 125 **Still Life With Guitar,** 1917

Oil on canvas, 28¹/₂ × 36 in. Signed and dated bottom left: *Juan Gris 11-17*

Private Collection, New York.

[Plate 280] 126 **Harlequin with Guitar,** 1917

Oil on wood panel, 39¹/₄ × 25¹/₂ in. Signed and dated bottom right: *Juan Gris 12-17*

The Alex Hillman Family Foundation, New York.

[Plate 277] 127 **Madame Cézanne,** 1918 (After a painting by Cézanne)

Oil on wood panel, 35⁷/₈ × 28³/₈ in.

coll. La Haye Jousselin-Perrone, Paris.

PAPIERS COLLÉS

[Plate 208] 128 **Guitar, Glasses and Bottle,** 1914

Papier collé on canvas, 23⁵/₈ × 31⁷/₈ in. Signed on back: *Juan Gris*

National Gallery of Ireland, Dublin.

[Plate 233] 129 **Fruit-Dish and Carafe,** 1914

Papier collé on canvas, with oil paint and colored chalks, 36¹/₄ × 25¹/₂ in. Signed on back: *Juan Gris*

Rijksmuseum Kröller-Müller, Otterlo.

[Plate 232] 130 **Still Life With a Bunch of Grapes,** 1914

Papier collé on canvas with gouache and pencil, 31⁷/₈ × 23⁵/₈ in.

Signed and dated bottom left:
Juan Gris, 1914

Galerie Beyeler, Basel.

[Plate 265]. **131 Still Life with Grapes,** 1915

Oil, papier collé and watercolor
on board, 10×13 in.
Signed bottom left: *Juan Gris*
Private collection.

DRAWINGS

[Plate 219] **132 Place Ravignan,** 1911

Pencil on paper, $17^1/_8 \times 12$ in.

Estate of
Lester F. Avnet,
New York.

[Plate 222] **133 Flowers in a Vase,** 1911–12
(related to No. 110)

Charcoal on paper, $17^1/_2 \times 12$ in.
Signed bottom left: *Juan Gris*

coll. James W. Alsdorf,
Winnetka, Ill.

[Plate 228] **134 Still Life with a Guitar,** 1913

Watercolor and charcoal on
paper, $25^5/_8 \times 18^1/_4$ in.
Signed and inscribed bottom
right: *A mon cher ami
Kahnweiler, Bien affectueusement
Juan Gris.*

(N. Y. only) Private collection, New York.

[Plate 272] **135 Siphon and Glass,** 1916

Gouache and pencil on paper,
$17^3/_4 \times 13^3/_4$ in.

Contemporary Art Establish-
ment, Zürich.

[Plate 275] **136 Still Life,** 1917

Pencil on paper, $24^3/_8 \times 18^7/_8$ in.

Kunstmuseum, Basel, Gift of
the Karl-August-Burckhardt-
Koechlin Fund.

[Plate 276] **137 Siphon, Checker-board and
Glass,** 1917

Charcoal on paper,
$18^1/_2 \times 12^1/_4$ in.
Signed, dated and inscribed top
right: *à Madame Marcillac,
amicalement, Juan Gris, Paris 1917*

The Art Institute of Chicago,
Ill., Gift of Mr. and Mrs. Leigh
B. Block.

SCULPTURE

[Plate 313] **138 Harlequin,** 1917

Plaster, carved and painted,
$21^1/_4 \times 13 \times 10$ in.

(N. Y. only) Philadelphia Museum of Art,
Philadelphia, Pa., A. E. Gallatin
Collection.

GUTFREUND, Otto

SCULPTURE

[Plate 302] **139 Reclining Woman with
Glass,** 1912–13

Bronze, $7^7/_8 \times 11$ in.

Národní Galerie, Prague.

[Plate 301]   **140 Cubist Bust,** 1912–13
Bronze, 23⁵/₈ in. high
Národní Galerie, Prague.

[Plate 300]   **141 Woman's Head,** 1919
Bronze, 10⁷/₈ in. high
Národní Galerie, Prague.

DRAWINGS
[Plate 297]   **142 Standing Nude,** 1911
Charcoal on paper, 17¹/₂ × 12 in.
Grosvenor Gallery, London.

[Plate 298]   **143 Study for Sculpture,** 1912–13
Ink, colored chalk and pencil
on paper, 10⁷/₈ × 8³/₄ in.
Grosvenor Gallery, London.

144

144 Figure, 1913
Ink and pencil on paper,
17¹/₂ × 12 in.
Grosvenor Gallery, London.

[Plate 299]   **145 Man's Head,** *c.* 1914
Charcoal on paper,
18⁷/₈ × 12¹/₄ in.
Národní Galerie, Prague.

HAYDEN, Henri

PAINTING

[Plate 236]   **146 Still Life with a Bottle of Milk,** 1917
Oil on canvas, 18 × 24¹/₂ in.
Signed and dated bottom right:
Hayden 1917
Private collection, Harrogate,
England.

HERBIN, Auguste

PAINTING

[Plate 114]   **147 The Village,** 1911
Oil on canvas, 32 × 25¹/₂ in.
Signed bottom center: *herbin*
Rijksmuseum Kröller-Müller,
Otterlo.

KLEE, Paul

PAINTINGS

[Plate 147]   **148 Homage to Picasso,** 1914
Oil on board,
13³/₄ × 11¹/₂ in. (Irregular oval)
Signed and dated top left:
Klee 1914-192
coll. Peter A. Rübel, Cos Cob,
Conn.

[Plate 146] **149 Red and White Domes,** 1914

Watercolor on paper on board,
5³/₄ × 5³/₈ in.
Signed top left: *Klee*
Inscribed along base: *Rote u. weisse Kuppeln 1914-45*

Kunstsammlung Nordrhein-Westfalen, Düsseldorf.

KUBISTA, Bohumil

PAINTINGS

[Plate 151] **150 Portrait,** 1911

Oil on canvas, 26 × 20¹/₂ in.
Signed top right:
B Kubista 1911

Národní Galerie, Prague.

[Plate 152] **151 Landscape (The Village),** 1911

Oil on canvas, 18¹/₈ × 21¹/₄ in.
Signed top right:
B Kubista 1911

Národní Galerie, Prague.

LA FRESNAYE, Roger de

PAINTINGS

[Plate 126] **152 Bathers,** 1912

Oil on canvas, 63¹/₂ × 50¹/₂ in.
Signed bottom right:
R de La Fresnaye
coll. Nathan Cummings,
New York.

[Plate 127] **153 Marie Ressort,** 1912–13

Oil on canvas, 58¹/₈ × 38 in.

Albright-Knox Art Gallery,
Buffalo, N.Y.

DRAWING

[Plate 128] **154 Three Figures,** 1913

Charcoal on paper, 19³/₄ × 25 in.
Signed and dated bottom right:
R de La Fresnaye 1913

Los Angeles County Museum
of Art, Los Angeles, Cal.,
Mr. and Mrs. William Preston
Harrison Collection.

SCULPTURE

[Plate 285] **155 Italian Girl,** 1911

Bronze, 24 × 12 in.
Incised at base on right:
R de La Fresnaye 2/6

The Joseph H. Hirshhorn
Collection, New York.

LARIONOV, Michel

PAINTINGS

[Plate 160] **156 Glasses,** 1911–12 (?)

Oil on canvas, 41 × 38¹/₄ in.
Signed bottom right:
M Larionov

The Solomon R. Guggenheim
Museum, New York.

[Plate 161] **157 Woman Walking on the Boulevard,** 1912

Oil on canvas, 45³/₄ × 33⁷/₈ in.
Signed on back: *M Larionov*

coll. Madame Michel Larionov,
Paris.

LAURENS, Henri

SCULPTURE

[Plate 322]   **158 Woman with Guitar,** 1918

Stone, $23^1/_4 \times 9^7/_8$ in.

coll. Madame Claude Laurens, Paris.

[Plate 324]   **159 Man's Head,** 1919

Stone, 17 in. high

Incised near base: *H. L.*

Mrs. Barnett Malbin, Birmingham, Mich. (The Lydia and Harry Lewis Winston Collection).

[Plate 323]   **160 Man with a Pipe,** 1919

Stone, $14^3/_4$ in. high

(N. Y. only)   coll. Mr. and Mrs. Irving W. Rabb, Newton, Mass.

[Plate 321]   **161 Musical Instruments,** 1919

Painted stone relief, $19^1/_2 \times 28^1/_4$ in.

coll. Mrs. A. Sharpe Maremont, Scottsdale, Ariz.

[Plate 326]   **162 Bottle and Glass,** 1919

Stone, painted and carved, $13^3/_8 \times 4^3/_8 \times 4^1/_2$ in.

Incised at base: *H L*

coll. Monsieur and Madame Alfred Richet, Paris.

[Plate 325]   **163 Guitar,** 1920

Terracotta, $14^1/_4 \times 4^3/_4 \times 3^5/_8$ in.

Incised inside base: *H L*

The Museum of Modern Art, New York, Gift of Curt Valentin.

PAPIERS COLLÉS

[Plate 316]   **164 Head,** 1917

Ink and collage on paper, $21^3/_4 \times 17^1/_4$ in.

Signed and dated bottom right: *H L 1917*

coll. Mr. and Mrs. Irving W. Rabb, Newton, Mass.

[Plate 318]   **165 Woman with Mantilla,** 1917

Papier collé on board, $23^1/_4 \times 15^1/_2$ in.

coll. Monsieur and Madame Claude Laurens, Paris.

[Plate 317]   **166 Guitar,** 1917–18

Papier collé on board, $18^7/_8 \times 25^1/_4$ in.

Signed and dated top left: *Laurens 18*

coll. Monsieur and Madame Claude Laurens, Paris.

DRAWINGS

[Plate 315]   **167 Head of a Boxer,** 1916

Ink on tracing paper, $5^7/_8 \times 4^1/_2$ in.

coll. Monsieur and Madame Claude Laurens, Paris.

[Plate 327]   **168 Anselme,** 1920

Ink on tracing paper, $9^1/_4 \times 6^1/_4$ in.

coll. Monsieur and Madame
Claude Laurens, Paris.

[Plate 328]   **169   Young Woman,** 1919

Etching heightened with
watercolor, $7^5/_8 \times 5^3/_4$ in.
Signed bottom right:
H. Laurens, 19

coll. Monsieur and Madame
Claude Laurens, Paris.

PRINTS

170   The Table, 1921

Etching: artist's proof,
$13 \times 19^3/_4$ in.
Galerie Louise Leiris, Paris.

[Plate 329]   **171   Girl with a Fan,** 1921

Etching: artist's proof,
$12^5/_8 \times 9^7/_8$ in.
Galerie Louise Leiris, Paris.

170

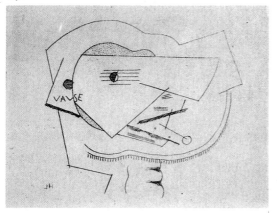

ILLUSTRATED BOOKS

[Plates 319, 320] **172   Paul DERMÉE : Spirales**

Illustrated with two etchings
by H. Laurens ·
Published by Paul Albert Birot,
1917, in an edition of 225
copies, of which 20 signed and
numbered by artist and author.
Each etching $12^3/_4 \times 8^7/_8$ in.
signed and dated on plate:
H L 17

Kunstmuseum, Bern.

**173   Raymond RADIGUET :
Les Pélican**

Illustrated with six etchings by
H. Laurens, one additional
etching on cover
Published by Kahnweiler, 1921,
in an edition of 112 copies
signed and numbered by artist
and author
Cover Etching, $3^{15}/_{16} \times 4$ in.
Plate 1, $3^3/_8 \times 6^5/_8$ in.
Plate 2, $2^9/_{16} \times 1^{11}/_{16}$ in.
Plate 3, $9^7/_8 \times 4^3/_4$ in.
Plate 4, $1^{11}/_{16} \times 2^3/_8$ in.
Plate 5, $2^1/_8 \times 1^{11}/_{16}$ in.
Plate 6, $9^{13}/_{16} \times 6^1/_4$ in.
Full page measures $12^7/_8 \times 9$ in.
Each illustration is signed on
plate: *H L*

The Museum of Modern Art,
New York, Gift of
Mrs. Stanley Resor.

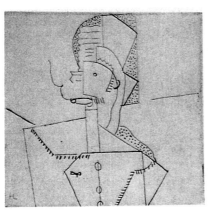

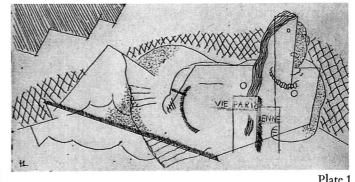

295

Plate 1

Cover

Plate 3

173

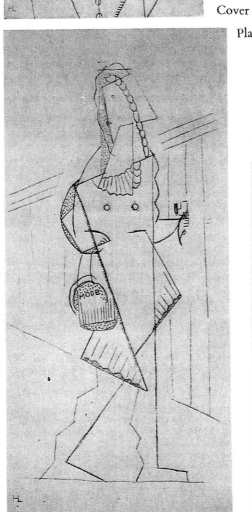

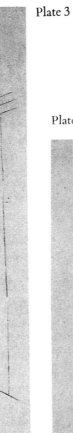

Plate 6

Plate 2

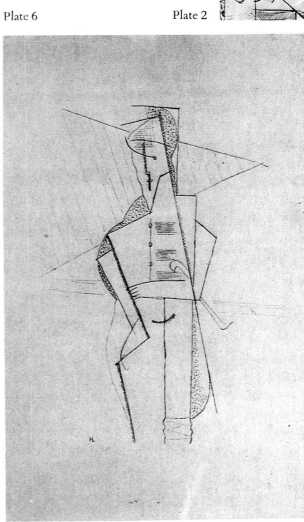

Plate 4

Plate 5

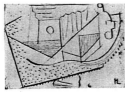

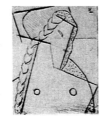

LE FAUCONNIER, Henri

PAINTING

[Plate 61]   **174 Abundance,** 1910–11

Oil on canvas, 75¹/₄ × 48¹/₂ in.
Signed bottom left:
Le Fauconnier
Haags Gemeentemuseum, The
Hague.

LÉGER, Fernand

PAINTINGS

[Plate 84]   **175 Woman Sewing (Portrait of
the Artist's Mother),** 1909

Oil on canvas, 28³/₈ × 21¹/₄ in.
Private Collection, Paris.

[Plate 85]   **176 Table and Fruit,** 1909

Oil on canvas, 33 × 39 in.
Signed bottom right: *F Léger*
The Minneapolis Institute of
Arts, Minneapolis, Minn.

[Plate 86]   **177 Nudes in a Landscape,**
1909–10

Oil on canvas, 47¹/₄ × 67 in.
Signed bottom left: *F Léger*
Rijksmuseum Kröller-Müller,
Otterlo.

[Plate 87]   **178 Smokers,** 1911

Oil on canvas, 51 × 37⁷/₈ in.
The Solomon R. Guggenheim
Museum, New York.

[Plate 88]   **179 Study for 'Woman in Blue,'**
1912

Oil on canvas, 51¹/₂ × 39 in.
Signed bottom right:
F Léger 12
Musée Fernand Léger, Biot.

[Plate 92]   **180 Contrast of Forms,** 1913

Oil on canvas, 39¹/₂ × 32 in.
Signed and dated on back:
F Léger/1913
The Museum of Modern Art,
New York, The Philip
L. Goodwin Collection.

[Plate 89]   **181 The Stairway,** 1913

Oil on canvas, 56³/₄ × 46¹/₂ in.
Signed and dated bottom right
Kunsthaus, Zürich.

[Plate 97]   **182 Houses Among Trees,** 1914

Oil on canvas, 51¹/₄ × 38¹/₄ in.
Signed on back: *Paysage
No. 3 F Léger*
Kunstmuseum, Basel, Gift of
Raoul La Roche.

[Plate 95]   **183 Two Figures,** 1914

Oil on canvas, 31⁷/₈ × 25⁵/₈ in.
Signed and dated on back:
F Léger 14
coll. Mrs. Anne Burnett Tandy,
Fort Worth, Tex.

[Plate 94]   **184 Still Life on a Table,** 1914

Oil on canvas, 35³/₄ × 28 in.
Formerly signed and dated on

back: *Nature Morte F Léger 14*
(relined)

Private Collection, France.

DRAWINGS

[*Plate 91*]   **185 House Among Trees,** 1912

Gouache on paper, 17¹/₂ × 13 in.
Signed and dated bottom right:
F L 12

coll. Mr. and Mrs. James
H. Clark, Dallas, Tex.

[*Plate 93*]   **186 Drawing for 'Contrast of
Forms No. 2,'** 1913

Wash drawing on paper,
19 × 25 in.
Signed bottom left: *F L*

Saidenberg Gallery, New York.

[*Plate 90*]   **187 Two Reclining Women,**
1913

Gouache on paper,
19³/₄ × 25¹/₈ in.
Signed and inscribed bottom
center: *Deux Femmes
Couchées F L 13*

Mr. Stephen Hahn,
New York.

[*Plate 96*]   **188 Woman and Still Life,** 1914

Gouache on paper,
15¹/₄ × 12¹/₂ in.
Signed and dated bottom right:
F L 14

coll. Mr. and Mrs. James
H. Clark, Dallas, Tex.

LHOTE, Andre

PAINTING

[*Plate 113*]   **189 Portrait of Marguerite,** 1913

Oil on canvas, 63³/₄ × 33¹/₂ in.
Signed and dated bottom right:
A. Lhote 1913

Private Collection, Paris.

LIPCHITZ, Jacques

SCULPTURE

[*Plate 305*]   **190 Sailor with a Guitar,** 1914

Bronze, 30 × 12 in.
Incised on back edge of base:
J Lipchitz 14, 3/7

Albright-Knox Art Gallery,
Buffalo, N.Y.

[*Plate 304*]   **191 Head,** 1915

Bronze, 24¹/₂ in. high
coll. Mr. and Mrs. Bernard
J. Reis, New York.

[*Plate 308*]   **192 Half-Standing Figure,** 1916

Bronze, 38³/₄ in. high
Marlborough Galleries, Inc.,
New York.

[*Plate 307*]   **193 Standing Figure,** 1916

Stone, 42¹/₄ × 9 in.

(L. A. only)   Norton Simon, Inc., Museum
of Art, Los Angeles, Cal.

[*Plate 309*]   **194 Bather III,** 1917

Bronze, 28¹/₂ in. high

Incised on base: *6/7 Lipchitz*

Norton Simon, Inc., Museum
of Art, Los Angeles, Cal.

[Plate 312]   **195 Seated Man with Guitar,**
1918

Bronze, $30 \times 15^3/_4 \times 13^1/_2$ in.
Incised on back of base:
Lipchitz

coll. Rita and Taft Schreiber,
Beverly Hills, Cal.

[Plate 311]   **196 Woman with Drapery,** 1919

Bronze, 37 in. high

coll. Mr. and Mrs. Ted Weiner,
Fort Worth, Tex.

[Plate 310]   **197 Bather,** 1919–20

Bronze, $28 \times 9 \times 9$ in.
Incised on base: *Lipchitz*

coll. Jane Wade Lombard and
Leigh R. Lombard, New York.

DRAWINGS

[Plate 303]   **198 Head,** 1915
(Study for No. 191)

Pencil on paper,
11×9 in. (Oval)
Signed bottom right: *Lipchitz*

coll. Mr. and Mrs. Bernard
J. Reis, New York.

[Plate 306]   **199 Figure,** 1915
(Study for Sculpture)

Gouache and crayon on paper,
$18^1/_2 \times 14$ in.
Signed top right: *Lipchitz*

Estate of
Lester F. Avnet,
New York.

MACDONALD-WRIGHT, Stanton

PAINTING

[Plate 196]   **200 Synchromy in Purple,** 1917

Oil on canvas, 36×28 in.
Signed on back:
S MacDonald-Wright

Los Angeles County Museum
of Art, Los Angeles, Cal.,
Purchase with County Funds.

MALEVICH, Kasimir

PAINTINGS

[Plate 165]   **201 Scissors Grinder,** 1912

Oil on canvas, $31^3/_8 \times 31^3/_8$ in.
Signed bottom left: *K M*

Yale University Art Gallery,
New Haven, Conn., Gift of
Collection Société Anonyme.

[Plate 164]   **202 Portrait of Matiushin,** 1913

Oil on canvas, $41^3/_4 \times 42^3/_8$ in.
Signed on back, top left

coll. George Costakis, Moscow.

[Plate 166]   **203 Musical Instruments,** 1913

Oil on canvas, $32^7/_8 \times 27^3/_8$ in.
Formerly signed top right;
illegible after restoration

Stedelijk Museum, Amsterdam.

MARC, Franz

PAINTING

[Plate 144] 204 **Stables,** 1913–14
Oil on canvas, 29$^1/_8$×62$^1/_4$ in.
Signed bottom right: *M*
The Solomon R. Guggenheim
Museum, New York.

MARCOUSSIS, Louis

PAINTING

[Plate 124] 205 **Bar du Port,** 1913
Oil on wood panel,
31$^7/_8$×20$^1/_8$ in.
Signed and dated bottom right:
Marcoussis 1913
coll. Madame Marcoussis, Paris.

DRAWINGS

[Plate 118] 206 **Portrait of Gazanion,** 1912
India ink and pencil
on paper, 25×19$^1/_4$ in.
Signed top left: *M*
coll. Bernard Walker,
Bloomfield Hills, Mich.

[Plate 237] 207 **Still Life on a Table,** 1921
Gouache on paper, 20×12 in.
Signed and dated bottom left:
Louis Marcoussis 1921
coll. Mr. and Mrs. Arthur
G. Altschul, New York.

PRINTS

[Plate 122] 208 **The Beautiful
Martiniquaise,** 1912
Drypoint (Unique print of

second state), 15$^3/_4$×11$^7/_8$ in.
Signed and dated bottom right:
Marcoussis 1912
coll. Madame Marcoussis, Paris.

[Plate 119] 209 **Portrait of Guillaume
Apollinaire,** 1912
Drypoint (First version),
19$^1/_2$×11 in.
Signed bottom right

(N. Y. only) Philadelphia Museum of Art,
Philadelphia, Pa., Louise and
Walter Arensberg Collection.

[Plate 120] 210 **Portrait of Guillaume
Apollinaire,** 1912–20
Etching and drypoint (Second
version) numbered bottom
left X/X (30), 19$^3/_8$×10$^{15}/_{16}$ in.
Signed and dated bottom right:
Marcoussis 1912—1920
The Art Institute of Chicago,
Chicago, Ill., Gift of Mr. and
Mrs. Morton Neumann in
memory of Carl O. Schniewind.

[Plate 123] 211 **Head of a Woman,** 1912
(Study for No. 208)
Drypoint, 11$^1/_4$×8$^5/_8$ in.
Signed and dated bottom right,
covered by mat:
19 L M 12
The Art Institute of Chicago,
Chicago, Ill.

METZINGER, Jean

PAINTINGS

[Plate 73] 212 **Cubist Landscape,** 1911
Oil on canvas, 32×39 in.

Signed bottom right:
J Metzinger

Sidney Janis Gallery, New York.

[Plate 72]   **213 Portrait of Gleizes,** 1912

Oil on canvas, 25¹/₂ × 21¹/₄ in.
Signed bottom right:
Metzinger

Museum of Art, Rhode Island
School of Design, Providence,
R. I.

[Plate 75]   **214 Dancer in a Cafe,** 1912

Oil on canvas, 57¹/₂ × 45 in.
Signed bottom left:
Metzinger

Albright-Knox Art Gallery,
Buffalo, N.Y.

[Plate 238]   **215 Still Life,** 1917

Oil on canvas, 32 × 25⁵/₈ in.
Signed and dated bottom right

The Metropolitan Museum of
Art, New York, Acquired by
M. L. Annenberg Foundation,
Joseph Hazen Foundation and
Joseph Hazen.

DRAWING

[Plate 74]   **216 Head of Woman in a Hat,**
1912

Charcoal on paper,
21¹/₄ × 18¹/₂ in.
Signed bottom right:
J Metzinger

Estate of
Lester F. Avnet,
New York.

MONDRIAN, Piet

PAINTINGS

[Plate 129]   **217 Horizontal Tree,** 1911

Oil on canvas, 29⁵/₈ × 43⁷/₈ in.
Signed bottom left: *Mondrian*

Munson-Williams-Proctor
Institute, Utica, N.Y.

[Plate 133]   **218 Tree,** 1912

Oil on canvas, 37 × 27¹/₂ in.

Museum of Art, Carnegie
Institute, Pittsburgh, Pa.

[Plate 131]   **219 Female Figure,** *c.* 1912

Oil on canvas, 45¹/₄ × 34⁵/₈ in.
Signed bottom left: *Mondrian*

coll. S. B. Slijper, on loan to
Haags Gemeentemuseum, The
Hague.

[Plate 135]   **220 Color Planes in Oval,** 1914 (?)

Oil on canvas, 42³/₈ × 31 in.
(Oval)
Signed at bottom: *Mondrian*

The Museum of Modern Art,
New York, Purchase.

DRAWINGS

[Plate 130]   **221 Self-Portrait,** *c.* 1911

Charcoal and ink on paper,
25 × 19 in. (probably inked
much later)

coll. Mr. and Mrs. James
H. Clark, Dallas, Texas.

[Plate 134] **222 Church Façade,** 1912

Charcoal on paper mounted on board, $39 \times 24^3/_4$ in.
Signed and dated bottom right: *P M 12*

Estate of
Lester F. Avnet,
New York.

[Plate 132] **223 Reclining Nude,** *c.* 1912

Charcoal on paper mounted on board, 37×63 in.
Signed bottom left: *P M*

Sidney Janis Gallery, New York.

PICABIA, Francis

PAINTING

[Plate 111] **224 Procession in Seville,** 1912

Oil on canvas, 48×48 in.
Signed bottom right: *Picabia*
Inscribed top right:
La Procession Seville

coll. Herbert and Nannette Rothschild, New York.

DRAWING

[Plate 112] **225 Star Dancer and Her School of Dancing,** 1913

Watercolor on paper,
$2\overset{.}{1}^7/_8 \times 29^7/_8$ in.
Signed and dated bottom right: *Picabia 1913*

The Metropolitan Museum of Art, New York, The Alfred Stieglitz Collection.

PICASSO, Pablo

PAINTINGS

[Plate 2] **226 Les Demoiselles d'Avignon,** 1907

Oil on canvas, 96×92 in.

(N. Y. only) The Museum of Modern Art, Aquired through the Lillie P. Bliss Bequest.

[Plate 4] **227 Still Life with a Skull,** 1907

Oil on canvas, $45^1/_4 \times 34^5/_8$ in.
Signed on back

Hermitage Museum, Leningrad.

[Plate 9] **228 Nude with Draperies,** 1907

Oil on canvas, $59^7/_8 \times 39^3/_4$ in.
Signed on back

Hermitage Museum, Leningrad.

[Plate 11] **229 Three Women,** 1908

Oil on canvas, $78^3/_4 \times 70^1/_2$ in.
Signed on back

Hermitage Museum, Leningrad.

[Plate 13] **230 Horta de San Juan: Factory,** 1909

Oil on canvas, $20^7/_8 \times 23^5/_8$ in.
Signed on back

Hermitage Museum, Leningrad.

[Plate 14] **231 Seated Woman,** 1909

Oil on canvas, $36^1/_4 \times 29^1/_2$ in.
Private Collection, France.

232 Landscape with a Bridge, 1909

Oil on canvas, 31⁷/₈ × 39³/₈ in.
Signed bottom right: *Picasso*

Národní Galerie, Prague.

233 Nude, 1910

Oil on canvas, 38¹/₂ × 30 in.

Albright-Knox Art Gallery,
Buffalo, N.Y.

**234 Portrait of D. H. Kahn-
weiler,** 1910

Oil on canvas, 39⁵/₈ × 28⁵/₈ in.

The Art Institute of Chicago,
Chicago, Ill., Gift of
Mrs. Gilbert W. Chapman
in memory of Charles
B. Goodspeed.

235 Woman, 1910

Oil on canvas, 39¹/₂ × 32¹/₄ in.
Signed on back: *Picasso*

coll. Mrs. Gilbert W. Chapman,
New York.

**236 Absinthe Glass, Bottle, Pipe
and Musical Instruments on
a Piano,** 1910–11

Oil on canvas, 19³/₄ × 51¹/₄ in.
Signed on back: *Picasso*

coll. Heinz Berggruen, Paris.

237 Man Smoking a Pipe, 1911

Oil on canvas, 36 × 28¹/₄ in.
(Oval)
Signed top right: *Picasso*

The Kimbell Art Foundation,
Fort Worth, Tex.

238 Still Life with Clarinet, 1911

Oil on canvas, 24 × 19³/₄ in.
Signed on back: *Picasso*

Národní Galerie, Prague.

**239 La Pointe de la Cité (The
Point of the Ile de la Cité,
Paris),** 1911

Oil on canvas, 35¹/₂ × 28 in.
(Oval)

Norton Simon, Inc., Museum
of Art, Los Angeles, Cal.

240 Clarinet Player, 1911

Oil on canvas, 41³/₈ × 27¹/₈ in.
Formerly signed on back
(relined)

Private Collection, France.

**241 Violin, Glass and Pipe on
Table,** 1912

Oil on canvas, 31⁷/₈ × 21¹/₄ in.
(Oval)
Signed on back: *Picasso*

Národní Galerie, Prague.

242 Seated Woman with Guitar,
1913

Oil on canvas, 39³/₈ × 32 in.
Signed bottom right:
Picasso 13

The Pasadena Art Museum,
Pasadena, Cal., Gift of Galka
E. Scheyer.

[Plate 211] **243 Musical Instruments,** 1913

Oil on canvas 39³/₈ × 31⁷/₈ in.
(Oval)
Signed on back

Hermitage Museum, Leningrad.

[Plate 214] **244 Playing Cards, Bottle and
Glass,** 1914

Oil on canvas, 14¹/₂ × 19³/₄ in.
Signed and dated top right:
Picasso 1914

coll. Dr. J. B. Hanson, Monaco.

[Plate 218] **245 Fruit-Dish, Bottle and
Guitar,** 1914

Oil on canvas, 36¹/₄ × 28³/₄ in.
Signed bottom right: *Picasso*

Private Collection, Rome.

[Plate 217] **246 Ma Jolie,** 1914

Oil on canvas, 18¹/₂ × 21⁵/₈ in.
Signed on back: *Picasso*

coll. Mr. and Mrs. Harry
W. Anderson, Atherton, Cal.

[Plate 243] **247 Vive la France,** 1914

Oil on canvas, 20¹/₂ × 25 in.
Signed on back

coll. Mr. and Mrs. Leigh
B. Block, Chicago, Ill.

[Plate 242] **248 Still Life with Fruit,** 1915

Oil on canvas, 25 × 31¹/₂ in.
Signed and dated bottom right:
Picasso 15

The Columbus Gallery of Fine

Arts, Columbus, Ohio, Gift of
Ferdinand Howald.

[Plate 244] **249 Guitar, Bottle and Flute on
a Table,** 1915

Oil on canvas, 42 × 28 in.
Signed and dated top right:
Picasso 15

coll. Wright Ludington, Santa
Barbara, Cal.

[Plate 246] **250 Woman with Guitar,** 1915

Oil on canvas, 72³/₄ × 29¹/₂ in.
Signed center right: *Picasso*

coll. Mr. and Mrs. Norton
Simon, Los Angeles, Cal.

[Plate 245] **251 Harlequin,** 1915

Oil on canvas, 72¹/₄ × 41³/₈ in.
Signed and dated bottom right:
Picasso 1915

The Museum of Modern Art,
New York, Acquired through
the Lillie P. Bliss Bequest.

[Plate 258] **252 Harlequin,** 1918

Oil on canvas, 58 × 26¹/₂ in.
Signed bottom right: *Picasso*

coll. Joseph Pulitzer, St. Louis,
Mo.

[Plate 257] **253 Bottle, Playing Card and
Pipe on Table,** 1919

Oil on canvas, 19³/₄ × 24 in.
Signed and dated bottom left:
Picasso 1919

Norton Simon, Inc., Museum
of Art, Los Angeles, Cal.

[Plate 248]   **254 Girl with a Hoop,** 1919

Oil on canvas, 31¹/₈ × 16³/₄ in.
Signed and dated top right:
Picasso 1919

Musée National d'Art
Moderne, Paris.

[Plate 1]   **255 Still Life on a Table in
Front of an Open Window,**
1920

Oil on canvas, 64¹/₂ × 43 in.
Signed and dated bottom right:
Picasso 1920

Norton Simon, Inc., Museum
of Art, Los Angeles, Cal.

[Plate 262]   **256 Three Masked Musicians,**
1921

Oil on canvas, 80 × 74 in.
Signed bottom left: *Picasso,*
dated on back; inscribed bottom
center: *Fontainebleau 1921*

(L. A. only)   Philadelphia Museum of Art,
Philadelphia, Pa., Gallatin
Collection.

Papiers collés

[Plate 204]   **257 Bottle and Glass,** 1912

Papier collé, charcoal and oil
on paper on canvas,
24³/₈ × 18⁷/₈ in.
Signed on back: *Picasso*

(N. Y. only)   Kunstsammlung Nordrhein-
Westfalen, Düsseldorf.

[Plate 205]   **258 Bottle and Glass on Table,**
1912–13

Charcoal, ink and collage on

paper, 24⁵/₈ × 18⁵/₈ in.
Signed on back

The Metropolitan Museum of
Art, New York, The Alfred
Stieglitz Collection.

[Plate 212]   **259 Glass and Bottle of Bass,**
1913

Papier collé, pencil, wash and
wood shavings on paper,
22⁷/₁₆ × 17³/₄ in.

(N. Y. only)   Private Collection, New York.

[Plate 203]   **260 Guitar and Glass,** 1913

Papier collé on paper,
18⁷/₈ × 14³/₈ in.
Signed on back: *Picasso*

Marion Koogler McNay Art
Institute, San Antonio, Tex.

[Plate 202]   **261 Still Life with Newspaper,**
1914

Papier collé and pencil on
paper, 25⁵/₈ × 19³/₄ in.
Signed and dated bottom right:
Picasso 9/1914

coll. Dr. Jean Dalsace, Paris.

[Plate 207]   **262 Glass, Pipe and Lemon,** 1914

Papier collé on paper,
19³/₄ × 25¹/₂ in.
Signed and dated top right:
Picasso 1914

Swiss Private Collection.

Drawings

[Plate 10]   **263 Nude with Drapery,** 1907

Watercolor and pencil on

paper on canvas, $12 \times 9^1/_4$ in.
Signed bottom left: *Picasso*

Mrs. Robert E. Simon, Los
Angeles, Cal.

[Plate 12] **264 Standing Figure,** 1907–08
(Study for *Three Women*)

Watercolor on paper,
$24^3/_{16} \times 16$ in.
Signed bottom right: *Picasso*

The Metropolitan Museum of
Art, New York, Gift of Miss
Leah Barnett in memory of
Dr. Avrom Barnett.

[Plate 21] **265 Woman's Head,** 1909

Ink and wash on paper,
$25 \times 19^3/_8$ in.
Signed and dated on back

The Metropolitan Museum of
Art, New York, The Alfred
Stieglitz Collection.

[Plate 22] **266 Woman's Head,** 1909

Ink and wash on paper,
$24^3/_4 \times 18^7/_8$ in.
Signed and dated on back

The Metropolitan Museum of
Art, New York, The Alfred
Stieglitz Collection.

267 Female Nude, 1910–11

Charcoal on paper,
$19^1/_{16} \times 12^5/_{16}$ in.
Signed on back

The Metropolitan Museum of
Art, New York, The Alfred
Stieglitz Collection.

[Plate 40] **268 Standing Woman,** 1911

Ink on paper, $12^1/_2 \times 7^1/_2$ in.
Signed bottom right and on
back: *Picasso*

coll. Mrs. Bertram Smith,
New York.

[Plate 39] **269 Man's Head,** 1911–12

Charcoal on paper,
$24^1/_2 \times 19$ in.
Signed on back

The Metropolitan Museum of
Art, New York, The Alfred
Stieglitz Collection.

267

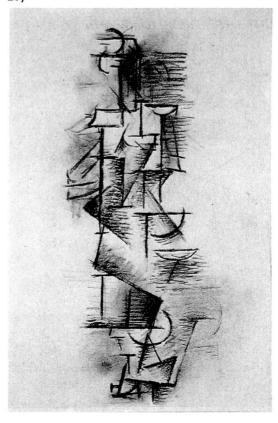

[Plate 57]   270 **Seated Man,** 1912
                     Ink on paper, $12^1/_8 \times 7^3/_4$ in.
                     The Metropolitan Museum of
                     Art, New York, The Alfred
                     Stieglitz Collection.

[Plate 247]   271 **Woman with Guitar,** 1914
                     Pencil on paper, $25 \times 18^3/_4$ in.
                     The Solomon R. Guggenheim
                     Museum, New York.

[Plate 250]   272 **Still Life with Guitar,** 1915
                     Pencil and watercolor on
                     paper, $5^3/_4 \times 4^3/_4$ in.
                     Signed and dated bottom right:
                     Picasso 15

                     coll. Mr. and Mrs. Norton
                     Simon, Los Angeles, Cal.

[Plate 249]   273 **Still Life with Clarinet and
                     Guitar,** 1915
                     Pencil and watercolor on
                     paper, $7^1/_2 \times 6$ in.
                     Signed bottom right: *Picasso*

                     coll. Mr. and Mrs. Norton
                     Simon, Los Angeles, Cal.

[Plate 251]   274 **Man Seated at Table,** 1916
                     Gouache on paper,
                     $10^3/_4 \times 8^3/_4$ in.
                     Signed and dated top right:
                     Picasso 1916

                     coll. Heinz Berggruen, Paris.

[Plate 256]   275 **Man with Pipe Seated in
                     Armchair,** 1916
                     Gouache, watercolor and pencil
                     on paper on canvas,

$13 \times 10^3/_{16}$ in.
Signed bottom right: *Picasso*
coll. Rita and Taft Schreiber,
Beverly Hills, Cal.

[Plate 260]   276 **Open Window at
                     St-Raphael,** 1919
                     Gouache on paper,
                     $13^3/_4 \times 9^3/_4$ in.
                     Signed and dated bottom left:
                     Picasso 19

                     Private Collection, New York.

[Plate 259]   277 **Pierrot and Harlequin,** 1920
                     Gouache on paper,
                     $10^1/_2 \times 8^1/_4$ in.
                     Signed bottom left: *Picasso*
                     Private Collection, New York.

[Plate 261]   278 **Guitar and Music Score on
                     a Table,** 1920
                     Gouache on paper, $10^1/_2 \times 8$ in.
                     Signed bottom left:
                     Picasso, 20

                     Private Collection, New York.

PRINTS

                279 **Two Nude Figures,** 1909
                     Drypoint; edition of 100
                     printed in 1909,
                     $5^1/_8 \times 4^5/_{16}$ in.
                     Signed bottom right: *Picasso*
                     The Museum of Modern Art,
                     New York, Purchase.

[Plate 20]   280 **The Fruit Dish,** 1909
                     Drypoint; edition of 100

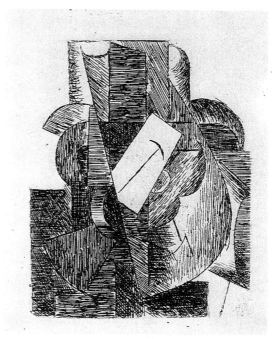

printed in 1909,
$5^1/_8 \times 4^3/_8$ in.
Signed and numbered bottom
right: *Picasso 81/100*

Los Angeles County Museum
of Art, Los Angeles, Cal.,
Purchase with Junior Art
Council Funds.

[Plate 37] **281 Bottle of Marc,** 1911–12

284

Drypoint; edition of 100
printed in 1912,
$19^{11}/_{16} \times 12$ in.
Signed bottom right: *Picasso*

The Museum of Modern Art,
New York, The Lillie
P. Bliss Bequest.

279

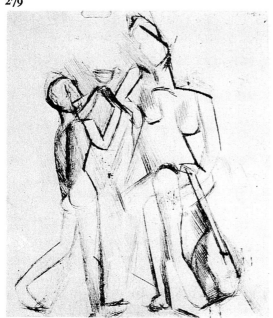

[Plate 52] **282 Man's Head,** 1912

Etching; edition of 100 printed
in 1912,
$5^1/_8 \times 4^5/_{16}$ in.
Signed bottom right: *Picasso*

The Museum of Modern Art,
New York, Gift of Abby
Aldrich Rockefeller.

[Plate 252] **283 Man with a Dog,** 1914

Etching; edition of 50 printed
in 1930,
$10^7/_8 \times 8^5/_8$ in.

The Museum of Modern Art,
New York, Larry Aldrich Fund.

284 Man with a Hat, 1914–15

Etching; printed in 1947 as an
illustration to a new edition of
A. Gleizes and J. Metzinger
Du Cubisme (Paris 1947)
$2^3/_4 \times 2^1/_8$ in.

coll. Edward Albee, New York.

[Plate 253] **285 Man with a Guitar,** 1915

Engraving; edition of 100
printed in 1929,
$6^1/_{16} \times 4^9/_{16}$ in.
Signed bottom right: *Picasso*

A. (N. Y. only)   The Museum of Modern Art,
New York, Gift of Mr. and
Mrs. Walter Bareiss.

B. (L. A. only)   Los Angeles County Museum
of Art, Los Angeles, Cal.,
Purchased with Graphic Arts
Council Funds in memory of
Sigbert Marcy.

ILLUSTRATED BOOKS

[Plates 48, 49] **286 Max JACOB : Saint Matorel**

Illustrated with 4 etchings by
Picasso executed at Cadaqués
in the summer of 1910
Published by D. H. Kahnweiler,
Paris, in February 1911 in an
edition of 106 copies signed by
author and artist

(Plates I and III   Plates I and IV, $7^3/_4 \times 5^9/_{16}$ in.
not illustrated)   on full page $10^1/_2 \times 8^7/_8$ in.
Plates II and III, $7^3/_4 \times 5^1/_2$ in.

The Museum of Modern Art,
New York, Purchase.

[Plates 254,   **287 Max JACOB : Le Siège de**
255]   **Jérusalem**

Illustrated with 3 drypoints by
Picasso executed in 1913
Published by D. H. Kahnweiler,
Paris, in January 1914 in an
edition of 106 copies signed by
author and artist

Plate I, $6^3/_{16} \times 4^9/_{16}$ in.
(Not illustrated) Plate II, $6^1/_8 \times 4^1/_2$ in.
Plate III, $6^5/_{16} \times 4^5/_{16}$ in.

The Museum of Modern Art,
New York, Gift of Frank
Crowninshield.

SCULPTURE

[Plate 281] **288 Woman's Head,** 1909–10

Bronze, $16^1/_4 \times 9^3/_4 \times 10^1/_2$ in.
Incised on left side of neck:
Picasso

A. (N. Y. only)   Fort Worth Art Center
Museum, Fort Worth, Tex.,
Gift of Mr. and Mrs. J. Lee
Johnson III.

B. (L. A. only)   Same sculpture but numbered
on neck 3/9 (re-cast of 1959),
Norton Simon, Inc.,
Museum of Art, Los Angeles,
Cal.

[Plate 283] **289 Absinthe Glass,** 1914

Painted bronze with silver
spoon
One of 6 identical but
differently painted casts,
$8^1/_2 \times 6^1/_2$ in.
Signed near base with letter
'*P*' raised in bronze

The Museum of Modern Art,
New York, Gift of
Mrs. Bertram Smith.

[Plate 282] **290 Same sculpture differently
painted**

Philadelphia Museum of Art,
Philadelphia, Pa., Gallatin
Collection.

POPOVA, Liubov

PAINTINGS

[Plate 168]   **291 Two Figures,** 1913
Oil on canvas, $63 \times 48^7/_8$ in.
coll. George Costakis, Moscow.

[Plate 167]   **292 The Traveller,** 1915
Oil on canvas, $56 \times 41^1/_2$ in.
Norton Simon, Inc., Museum
of Art, Los Angeles, Cal.

PROCHAZKA, Antonin

PAINTING

[Plate 154]   **293 Girl with a Peach,** 1911
Oil on canvas, $13^3/_4 \times 11^7/_8$ in.
Signed bottom right:
Ant. Procházka
Národní Galerie, Prague.

RIVERA, Diego

PAINTINGS

[Plate 115]   **294 Portrait of Jacques Lipchitz,**
1914
Oil on canvas, $25^5/_8 \times 21^5/_8$ in.
Signed and dated bottom right:
D M Rivera 14
The Museum of Modern Art,
New York, Gift of T. Catesby
Jones.

[Plate 240]   **295 The Café Terrace,** 1915
Oil on canvas, $23^7/_8 \times 19^1/_2$ in.
Signed bottom left: *D M R*

The Metropolitan Museum of
Art, New York, The Alfred
Stieglitz Collection.

SEVERINI, Gino

PAINTINGS

[Plate 193]   **296 Armored Train in Action,**
1915
Oil on canvas, $46 \times 34^1/_2$ in.
Signed bottom right:
G Severini
coll. Richard S. Zeisler,
New York.

[Plate 191]   **297 Seated Woman,** 1916
Oil on canvas, $39^3/_8 \times 31^7/_8$ in.
(Oval)
Signed bottom center:
G. Severini
(N. Y. only)   coll. of Mr. and Mrs. Eugene
J. Keogh, New York.

[Plate 192]   **298 Still Life with Pumpkin,**
1917
Oil and collage on wood,
$36^1/_4 \times 25^5/_8$ in.
Signed bottom right:
Severini: dated on back
coll. Dott. Emilio Jesi, Milan.

PAPIER COLLÉ

[Plate 173]   **299 Still Life with 'Lacerba,'**
1913
Papier collé, gouache, ink and
charcoal, $19^5/_8 \times 23^5/_8$ in.
Signed and dated bottom
center: *G. Severini, 1913*

Musée d'Art et d'Industrie,
St. Etienne, France.

DRAWINGS

[Plate 174]   **300 Self-Portrait in Straw Hat,**
1912

Charcoal on paper,
21¹/₂ × 21⁹/₁₆

The Art Institute of Chicago,
Chicago, Ill., Gift of Margaret
Bay Blake.

[Plate 178]   **301 Dancer,** 1912–13

Crayon on paper, 26 × 18⁷/₈ in.
Signed bottom right:
G. Severini

The Museum of Modern Art,
New York. Anonymous gift.

[Plate 183]   **302 The Train in the City,** 1914

Charcoal on paper,
19⁵/₈ × 25¹/₂ in.
Signed bottom right:
G. Severini

The Metropolitan Museum of
Art, New York, The Alfred
Stieglitz Collection.

[Plate 187]   **303 Bottle, Vase and Newspaper
on Table,** 1914

Charcoal and collage on paper,
22¹/₈ × 18⁵/₈ in.

The Metropolitan Museum of
Art, New York, The Alfred
Stieglitz Collection.

[Plate 188]   **304 Seated Woman,** 1914

Watercolor on paper,

16 × 13¹/₂ in.
Signed bottom right:
G. Severini

coll. Mr. and Mrs. Sidney
E. Cohn, New York.

SIRONI, Mario

PAINTING

[Plate 185]   **305 Self Portrait,** 1913

Oil on canvas, 20¹/₄ × 19¹/₄ in.
Signed and dated bottom left:
Sironi 1913

Galleria Civica d'Arte
Moderna, Milan.

SOFFICI, Ardengo

PAINTINGS

[Plate 186]   **306 Lines and Volumes of a
Figure,** 1912

Oil on canvas, 13³/₄ × 11³/₄ in.

Galleria Civica d'Arte
Moderna, Milan.

[Plate 171]   **307 Decomposition of the
Planes of a Lamp,** 1912

Oil on board, 13³/₄ × 11³/₄ in.

coll. Eric Estorick, London.

UDALTSOVA, Nadezhda

PAINTINGS

[Plate 169]   **308 At the Piano,** 1914

Oil on canvas, 42 × 35 in.

Yale University Art Gallery,
New Haven, Conn., Gift of
Collection Société Anonyme.

[Plate 170] **309 Violin,** 1914

Oil on canvas, $20^7/_8 \times 16^{15}/_{16}$ in.
Signed on back (by artist's son
A. Drevin)

coll. George Costakis, Moscow.

VILLON, Jacques

PAINTINGS

[Plate 100] **310 Little Girl at Piano,** 1912

Oil on canvas, 51×38 in. (Oval)
Signed on left: *J. Villon*
Dated on back

coll. Mrs. George Acheson,
New York.

[Plate 98] **311 The Dinner-Table,** 1912

Oil on canvas, $25^3/_4 \times 32$ in.
Signed and dated top right:
J. Villon 1912

coll. Mr. and Mrs. Francis
Steegmuller, New York.

[Plate 104] **312 Portrait of Mlle Y. D.,** 1913

Oil on canvas, $50^3/_4 \times 35$ in.
Signed bottom right:
Jacques Villon

Los Angeles County Museum
of Art, Los Angeles, Cal., Gift
of Anna Bing Arnold.

PRINTS

[Plate 106] **313 Portrait of an Actor
(Felix Barré),** 1913

Drypoint; edition of 32,
$15^3/_4 \times 12^3/_8$ in.
Signed bottom right

The Art Institute of Chicago,
Chicago, Ill., Gift of Frank
B. Hubachek.

[Plate 105] **314 Tightrope Walker,** 1913

Drypoint; edition of 28,
$15^3/_4 \times 11^7/_8$ in.
Signed bottom right

The Art Institute of Chicago,
Chicago, Ill.

[Plate 101] **315 Mlle Y. D., Full Face,** 1913

Drypoint; edition of 28,
$21^5/_8 \times 16^3/_8$ in.
Signed and numbered bottom
left: *17 J Villon*

coll. Mr. and Mrs. Louis
Kaufman, Los Angeles, Cal.

[Plate 99] **316 The Dinner-Table,** 1913

Drypoint; edition of 30,
$11^1/_8 \times 15^1/_8$ in.
Signed bottom right:
Jacques Villon

The Museum of Modern Art,
New York, Purchase.

[Plate 102] **317 Portrait of a Young
Woman,** 1913

Drypoint; edition of 25,
$21^1/_2 \times 16^1/_4$ in.
Signed in plate bottom right

Los Angeles County Museum
of Art, Los Angeles, Cal.,
Purchase with County Funds.

[Plate 103] **318 Yvonne in Profile,** 1913

Drypoint; edition of 23,

21¹/₂ × 16¹/₄ in.
Signed in plate bottom right

Los Angeles County Museum
of Art, Los Angeles, Cal.,
Purchase with County Funds.

WEBER, Max

PAINTINGS

[Plate 195]   **319 Athletic Contest,** 1915

Oil on canvas, 40 × 60 in.
Signed bottom right:
Max Weber 1915

The Metropolitan Museum of
Art, New York, George
A. Hearn Fund.

[Plate 197]   **320 Rush Hour, New York,** 1915

Oil on canvas, 36 × 30 in.
Signed and dated bottom right:
Max Weber 1915

The National Gallery of Art,
Washington, D.C., Gift of the
Avalon Foundation 1970.

SCULPTURE

[Plate 296]   **321 Spiral Rhythm,** 1915

Bronze, Cast No. 3/3,
24¹/₄ in. high
Signed on base

coll. Hale R. Allen, New York.

Index

Photo Credits

The Author and the Publishers wish to thank the Museums, Galleries and Private Collectors who kindly supplied photographs for this book and acknowledge the work of the following photographers:

Bacci, Milan; S.P.R.L. Bauters, Brussels; Barney Burstein, Boston; Geoffrey Clements, Staten Island, New York; François Daulte, Paris; Editions Cercle d'Art, Paris; Hans J. Flodquist, Stockholm; John R. Freeman and Co., London; Giacomelli, Venice; Gilbert Studios Ltd., Toronto; Sherwin Greenberg, Buffalo; Hence Griffith, Dallas; Peter Heman, Basel; G. Howald, Berne; Etienne Hubert, Paris; Walter Klein, Düsseldorf; Joseph Klima, Jr., Detroit; Paulus Leeser, New York; Robert E. Mates, New York; J. Mer, Biot; O. E. Nelson, New York; Richard Nickel, Park Ridge, Ill.; Giorgio Nimatallah, Milan; Irving J. Newman, Greenwich, Conn.; Karl Obert, Santa Barbara, Cal.; Phaidon Press, London; Photothèque Européenne, Paris; Eric Pollitzer, Garden City Park, New York; Gordon Roberton, London; Walter Rosenblum, New York; Savage Studio, St. Louis, Mo.; John D. Schiff, New York; Robert S. Scurlock, New York; Service de Documentation des Musées Nationaux, Versailles; Elton Schnellbacher, Pittsburgh, Pa.; Adolph Studly, New York; Soichi Sunami, New York; Eric Sutherland, Walker Art Center, Minneapolis; Charles Swedlund, Chicago; Taylor and Dull, New York; Thames and Hudson, London; F. J. Thomas, Hollywood; Charles Uht, New York; Malcolm Varon, New York; Marc Vaux, Paris; Ron Vickers, Toronto; and Alfred J. Wyatt, Philadelphia.